Djuna Barnes

Interviews

Djuna Barnes

Interviews

Edited by Alyce Barry
Foreword and Commentary by
Douglas Messerli

 SUN & MOON PRESS
Washington, D.C.

© Sun & Moon Press, 1985

"James Joyce; A Portrait of the Man Who Is, at Present, One
of the More Significant Figures in Literature," © 1921 by The Vanity
Fair Publishing Company, Inc.; © 1949 by Condé Nast Publications, Inc.

The interviews in this collection appeared originally in the *New York
Press, Bruno's Weekly,* the *New York Morning Telegraph Sunday Magazine,*
the *New York Sun Magazine, Vanity Fair, Charm, McCalls, Theatre Guild
Magazine, Physical Culture,* and *Unmuzzled Ox.*

Cover drawing: *Sitting Over There in the Wide Chair Like a Throne* [Lillian
Russell], by Djuna Barnes
Cover design: Katie Messborn

Library of Congress Cataloguing in Publication Data

Barnes, Djuna, 1892-1982
  Interviews

  I. Title

ISBN: 0-940650-36-3 (cloth)
        0-940650-37-1 (paper)

Publication of this book was made possible, in part, through a matching
grant from the National Endowment for the Arts and through contributions to The Contemporary Arts Educational Project, Inc.

Sun & Moon Press
4330 Hartwick Road
College Park, Maryland 20740

Foreword

When I first encountered the interviews of Djuna Barnes in 1973, I perceived them as entertaining journalistic pieces with little of the genius and complexity of her serious fiction. After all, by Barnes's own admission these were lighter endeavors—almost hack work, the way she spoke of them—done to pay the rent.

Upon the publication of *Smoke and Other Early Stories* in 1982, however, I began to reread the interviews, with the idea of possibly collecting some of them in a book which might demonstrate Barnes's journalistic talents. Almost immediately I began to see these seemingly light entertainments as something different from what I had remembered; and by the time I had reread all of the interviews, I had utterly revised my opinion. Here, in the words of actors, playwrights, artists, stage and film directors, novelists, boxers, dancers, singers, a union organizer, and a religious zealot, were nearly all of Barnes's major literary themes; here were the roots of the voices of her fictional characters—Julie and Sophia Ryder, Dr. O'Connor, Felix Volkbein, Nora Vote, and others. The more I worked with them, in fact, the more I came to understand these pieces less as standard journalism than as fascinating experiments in the impressionistic characterization that Barnes would perfect in her short stories, *Ryder, Nightwood,* and *The Antiphon*.

Later still, after I had read further about each of the

figures Barnes interviewed, I grew to see these works as a distorted but highly revealing record of the period the interviews covered, 1914-1931—one of the greatest eras of American arts. And increasingly in the past few months, working with Alyce Barry on the final details of this collection, I have come through these writings to understand Djuna Barnes more clearly, to hear in her voice and the voices of those she interviews some of the vitality, frustration, and despair she must have experienced throughout these early years of her career.

The longer one invests time in any undertaking, of course, the more one finds value in the activity or object; and one would have to be a martyr to research and scholarship to admit that one had invested several years in an endeavor which had no serious intent. However, I have not recounted my transformation regarding these interviews in order to draw attention to my own particular relationship with them, but rather to suggest that the general reader of these works may have to overcome certain presuppositions and will have to invest more than a superficial reading of the interviews in order to discern their literary worth. The casual reader of Barnes's *Interviews*, while enjoying their patter of gossip and wit, will have to be alert to Barnes's style and structures if he or she wishes to perceive them as anything more than trivial musings of celebrities of the period.

Fortunately, as in her early stories which appeared in the same mass media, Barnes provides her readers with several clues that direct them away from the superficial to the social, political, and—ultimately—metaphysical implications of what her celebrities do and say.

One need only pick up the style section of any local newspaper and read an interview therein to discern some of the differences of which I am speaking. The vast majority of newspaper interviews, for example, recount the celebrity's biography at some point in the piece; it is important, after all, to know why the person is being interviewed and why the newspaper reader should pay attention to what the interviewee is saying. But in the majority of Barnes's interviews—most strikingly in her earlier newspaper works—there is little attempt to place the celebrity in the context of his or her own history. Mimi Aguglia, for example, seemingly has little to commend herself to the reader other than the fact that she has "entered into America as spice and pepper into a good pot roast." Irvin Cobb is brought face to face with the interviewer simply by a "generous catcall of destiny." The reader previously unacquainted with Arthur Voegtlin would discover little of his credentials through Barnes's interview other than the fact that he works at the Hippodrome. Doubtlessly, as Alyce Barry points out in her Preface, the audience of the day knew a great deal more of these figures than we now do. Perhaps the figures Barnes interviewed did not need extended introductions; certainly no interviewer today would feel compelled to recount the accomplishments of Paul Newman or Billy Graham.

Barnes's celebrities, however, were not always the "superstars" of the day. Moreover, Barnes seems to go out of her way to obfuscate just that material which journalists generally employ to establish who, where, what and when—in short, the facts. "Back behind scenes, where the blue of Herod's court lay chilly upon wilted palms that clung to dingy netting, the tropics just out of mothballs," writes Barnes of the *Salome* setting where she interviews Mimi Aguglia. "SCENE. A vaultlike cellar, cold, dark, clean, resembling the better class of, let us say, Parliamental minds," begins her description of the location of her interview with Lou Tellegen. Examples are numerous in this volume.

Such writing, quite obviously, differs from standard journalism in its literary qualities; the radical metaphors, the philosophical asides, the scriptlike format, and numerous other rhetorical devices all draw the reader away from the everyday world and place him in a fabricated space, where nearly any kind of statement or behavior is possible. Accordingly, Barnes is freed to have these real-life figures speak as if they were all Oscar Wilde on one of the wittiest days of his life. Many of the people Barnes interviewed were truly quick-witted and glib; but one does wonder about the authenticity of Barnes's conversations with figures such as the popular comedienne May Vokes, for example, who begins her interview by saying:

> Dearie, please don't interview me just for a few minutes. It is as bad to plunge into publicity as it is into a cold bath.... While you're thinking I'll tell you something that will help you to forget me. I'll make myself insignificant; I'll dwindle, I'll become illiterate. The illiterate are never chronicled.

One cannot help but wonder whether the otherwise inarticulate Jess Willard really reacted to Barnes's needling question about whether he wasn't "hazy about every other individuality" than his own, by answering, "One doesn't feel any different than a successful businessman. It's an art, that's all." Did Flo Ziegfeld really describe a vampire as "a woman who eats lightly of uncooked things; who walks out between tall avenues of spears to die, and doesn't, and finally spends the evening in an orgy of virtuous dreams"? One devoutly wishes it were so, but one has doubts.

The avid reader of Djuna Barnes immediately recognizes in the greater number of the witticisms mouthed by these celebrities the voice of Barnes herself. As Alyce Barry has noted, however, it matters little; for Barnes is at the center of these interviews in other ways as well. What impressions we get of these figures—and what remarkable impressions they are!—emanate from Barnes's personal, always intelligent and often disturbing vision. Closer in tradition to the British anecdotist John Aubrey than to the American newspaper, Barnes's portraits are forged from the interchange of the writer and her subject. Unlike the objectivist products of our contemporary columnists, Barnes's interviews were written from her mind and heart and contain as much information about the interviewer as they do about the celebrities. Placing herself in the most vulnerable of positions, Barnes records in these interviews a history different from that of the journalist or biographer: her writing focuses rather on the history of the relationship between the author and the figure of whom she writes. Through these interviews, it is clear, Barnes was affected. Whether they were truly as she conceived them or not, these figures evoked from her admiration (Frank Harris, Helen Westley, and James Joyce, for example), laughter (Flo Ziegfeld, Irvin Cobb, and Wilson Mizner), harsh judgment (Billy Sunday), and even envy (Donald Ogden Stewart). These were her literary mentors, the figures through whom she learned her craft and with whom she would identify throughout her life.

In the context of the relationships she chronicles, it is disconcerting to realize that Barnes outlived everyone in this volume. It is no wonder that the Djuna Barnes I met in November 1973 could only bemoan that "it's terrible to outlive your own generation. I wish I could be dead." For as early as 1930—when she admitted to Donald Ogden Stewart that she wouldn't really mind dying—she must have already felt something close to that. Many of the older generation—Vernon Castle, Gaby Deslys, Lillian Russell, Diamond Jim Brady, Raymond Hitchcock, Mother Jones, and John Bunny—had already died; and others such as Frank Harris, Flo Ziegfeld, and Wilson Mizner would follow in the next couple of years. By 1973 Djuna Barnes, living a hermitlike existence, was alone with her memories.

This volume, one hopes, will bring back some of those memories for all of us.

—Douglas Messerli

Editor's Preface

THE reader experiencing Djuna Barnes for the first time will find her use of punctuation and grammar, particularly in this volume, rather unorthodox. We have attempted to retain the original wherever possible, changing and modernizing only where readability otherwise appeared to suffer. Although structure seemed archaic in many cases, we decided that to alter it would do violence to Barnes's style, and in all such instances style was given precedence over grammatical standardization.

Barnes held a number of unorthodox political and social views as well, some ahead of her time, others regrettably typical of her day. It is neither our role nor our intention to make apology for her views, or to censor them from our current perspective. Accordingly, we have left her language and the words of those she interviewed as they originally appeared, knowing that some readers may find particular words and attitudes objectionable. But in these cases, we considered the integrity of the work as literature to be our first and rightful priority.

Lastly, it is our hope that this volume will not only entertain as a literary work of art, but that it will prove useful as an historical resource, reintroducing several personalities now almost forgotten. A researcher using these interviews should remember, however, that in the hands of Djuna Barnes the celebrity interview, unlike an interview in today's news magazine or newspaper, is a form of art which does not depend entirely for its immediacy or value upon the actual words of the person interviewed. Certainly many of Barnes's contemporaries were already familiar with the celebrities she encountered, a familiarity which lent a presence to their reading experience which today's reader lacks; for these original readers, there may have been more "fact" than there is for us today. But "fact" is of secondary importance in these pieces. Whether Barnes extracts the fantastical statements and musings which abound in these interviews from the person speaking, or entirely creates them, is essentially irrelevant so long as they resound so strikingly off the ear and, so often, off the soul as well.

As is the case with any undertaking of this sort, the generous support in time and ideas from several individuals and institutions made our work possible. Dr. Donald Farren and Jesse Hinkle of the Special Collections of the University of Maryland Library gave advice and provided materials for this volume, as did Geraldine Duclow at the Theatre Collection of the Free Library of Philadelphia, Billy Klüver and Julie Martin, and the staffs of the Periodical and Newspaper Room of the Library of Congress and The Billy Rose Theatre Collection of The New York Public Library's Performing Arts Research Center at Lincoln Center.

Barbara Shaw lent her editorial eye to her remarkably accurate and speedy typesetting, as did Susan Bee to her meticulous proofreading; Wendy Melechen was available day and night to photograph the numerous drawings which punctuate this book. Joseph and Debra Ross and Joanne Gelles spent long hours in researching and proof-reading; and Alan Swift and Howard N. Fox saw to it that we received good food and entertaining company for the many months of work on this publication.

Finally, we would like to give special thanks to Philip Langner and The Theatre Guild and to Condé Nast Publications, Inc. for allowing us to reprint some of the interviews contained herein.

—Alyce Barry

Contents

The Wild Aguglia
and Her Monkeys

Sicilian by birth, Mimi Aguglia was discovered by American producer Charles Frohman, who brought her to the United States in 1908. Returning to America five years later, Aguglia performed in Italian versions of Electra *and Oscar Wilde's* Salome, *which made her an overnight sensation. Her voluptuous dance of the seven veils, perceived as scandalous in its day, typed her as a "torrential" siren for the rest of her life. The* New York Times *reviewer asserted that her performance "outsalome[d] all Salomes," as she "writhed" over the head of John the Baptist "as no other Salome has ever writhed." Her interview with Djuna Barnes took place a week after the opening, and Aguglia clearly had an impact on Barnes, who wrote of her two years later in her tale, "What Do You See, Madam?"*

Still beautiful at forty-eight, Aguglia appeared as Salome again in a San Francisco revival of the play in 1933. She found a second career in films, appearing in minor roles with Jane Russell in Howard Hughes's The Outlaw, *with Shelley Winters in* The Cry of the City, *with Kathryn Grayson and Mario Lanza in* That Midnight Kiss, *and with Anna Magnani and Burt Lancaster in* The Rose Tattoo. *Aguglia died in 1970.*

MIMI Aguglia has entered into America as spice and pepper into a good pot roast. Into the world of cutlery has come a sharper knife. Into the well-ordered life of our society a human has catapulted some hundred pounds of passionate flesh. The devil is inadequate in his absolute grandeur when Mimi sleeps.

Back behind scenes, where the blue of Herod's court lay chilly upon wilted palms that clung to dingy netting, the tropics just out of mothballs, Mimi Aguglia spoke of a temperamental world. "You have such beautiful, calm women in America; yes, and so simply gowned, and they do not have to marry because the family says so, and they do not have to stay in the house all day and wish they were born men that they might enter politics. The suffragist, ah!" The shoulders go up in a violent shrug. "The suffrage is not good for the woman; it is less good for the artist. Let the men do something, eh?" This very naively. "I have children. Off the stage I'm a good mother; on, I am, I hope, a good actress. Always I love the animals, and oh! the lion Diaz gave me—I hug him so.

"I do not want the American to think I like only tragedy. I like the comedy; but the comedy depends upon the word, and I cannot make you understand. I'm going to begin with the less subtle emotions, so!"

The long, dark eyes, with their sudden flashes of white, glinted like the sun between two sullen borderlands. With the same inscrutable calm she watched the monkeys, the company's monkeys, the company with six Aguglias on the program; the company which was entirely married and bids fair to become a Hippodrome

Metallic Impressions

production if multiplication continues at the present rate of speed.

In a quarter of an hour she was due as Salome, and yet she gathered handsful, armsful, of monkeys to her, and cried over them in Italian and spoke of the good spaghetti.

Then she stood before the public, palpitating in fine, small shivers, elemental emotions and spangled net.

Slowly, with feet that curled, she came, browned and spangled, and shaking with tinsel, blue in the blue light of the court, swaying prophetically.

She took her balance on the brink of the well and offered John her soul in all the shapes that a heroically tragic woman could offer it, and was scorned. From every staccato scream, from every sudden-reached crescendo of misery, from every backward head shake and every troubled posture, in every lunge and the spasms of her dancing, she was getting her pride back. This was the epic of undulating spaghetti, turmoil of tragic chiffon, damp spurning feet. The back-thrust head, the lure and the scorn and the contempt and the desire of scarlet lips. And, then, the fight on the mat.

There wasn't much left of John to gurgle over, only the matted, tousled hair that maddened her fingers into hazy shakings, and sudden darts and halts of the greedy palm. Then the cry and the tightening of the already taut body, with head and arms and passion in the platter. The very climax of Mimi Aguglia's art of expression.

Silence, as she lies there, a figure before a head, contemplating the unresistance of resisting lips, and then the obeyed command, as twenty arms crash down upon her frail omnipotence. The overturned victory, the scream of death realized;

The Blue Light and Mimi

woman-churned ether, and two straight, clutching hands dragging down sheer set jaws. The end of the oblique eyes, the soft sound of a woman's body threshing the inevitable, and—back to the monkeys again.

Yes, the Vernon Castles Have a Home and They Occasionally Tango Past It

Vernon Castle and Irene Foote met in 1910, when he was working as straight man for comedian Lew Fields and she was auditioning for theatrical parts. Dissatisfied with his vaudeville act and with her attempts to become an actress, the newly married couple traveled to Paris to appear together in a revue, only to see it postponed for several months. In financial straits, the Castles were rescued by their servant, Walter Ash, who won enough in gambling to feed the three of them until the show finally opened. Their performance caught the eye of Papa Louis of the famous Café de Paris, and their dancing career had begun.

News of the death of Irene's father brought them back to the United States a month after the sinking of The Titanic. *Their Paris fame won them an engagement at the Café de l'Opera on Broadway, and they quickly became America's favorite dance team. The dances they made famous—the Castle Walk, the Grizzly Bear, the Maxixe, the Lame Duck, and the Half-in-Half—inspired a national dance craze and turned Irene into an international trendsetter for fashion. When entering the hospital for a minor operation, for example, Irene bobbed her hair, and American women followed suit; when Irene wore a ribbonlike band of pearls to keep her hair in place, women everywhere donned the "Castle Band," which we still associate with the flappers of the 1920s.*

During the height of their dancing careers, the Castles were in constant demand both as performers and teachers, often appearing in simultaneous productions—which resulted in the hectic schedule of which Barnes writes. Vernon was the better dancer of the two, leading Irene effortlessly through their fluid and graceful dances at the Palace, the Victoria, and their own nightclub, Sans Souci.

By 1915 they were appearing in Broadway musicals such as Irving Berlin's Watch Your Step *and in motion pictures such as* The Whirl of Life. *But the English involvement in World War I increasingly distracted British-born Vernon and ultimately led him to enlist in the Royal Canadian Flying Corps. He was killed in 1918 while training flyers for the Corps in Houston.*

Irene continued to make films until 1924 and wrote their memoirs, Castles in the Air, *which became the source for the Fred Astaire and Ginger Rogers movie,* The Story of Vernon and Irene Castle.

WHAT do the Vernon Castles do between two o'clock at night and eleven in the morning? We all know what they are doing from 11:01 A.M. to 1:59 A.M. The schedule runs something like this: Pupils from 11:00 to 3:00; due at the Palace Theater, 3:10; Hammerstein's Victoria, 3:50; Castle House, 4:00 to 6:30; a private lesson somewhere along Fifth Avenue; then Hammerstein's at 9:10, the Palace 9:50; due at Sans Souci, 11:30.

They clasp hands and unite steps and give the public

the perfection of their teamwork. Society stops, with tea-
cup raised, and lets its heart beat to the measure of
heels; they have mastered the airy with airy souls; they
have captured smiles.

Seemingly they are content—content to take life on the
jump, to keep on going and never stop. One would say
that there was no home life, and yet—

The Vernon Castles have a home. He bought it and she
gave it up to a population of pups. That's the only reason
they have a house. The apartment owners dislike animals
and so the Castles have a home. Do they ever go to it?
Do they ever eat? Do they ever sleep? Do they ever taste
domestic life?

Oh yes—Vernon can cook; he makes immaculate egg
sandwiches.

In the chill of a disheveled evening he feeds them to
her and asks, "Are you content?"

"Yes."

"Are we—living?"

"I think so."

"And what shall we do—in the end?"

"Keep more dogs."

"And after that?"

"Keep—still."

How many hours do they devote to sleep? Something
like eight or nine. As much as anybody gets, you say.
Yes, as much sleep as anyone gets. But when do they ride,
drive, walk, talk, think, dream, hope, relax, pace, post-
pone, pulsate? When do they ramble, rest, rise, run?
When do they learn the relation of man to his wife and
wife to her man? When do they cooperate over the alu-

minum? When do they bathe?

Entirely unnecessary; they are making money at present. Later, they say, they will live.

"I regret only one thing—that there are not thirty-four hours to a day that I might dance longer, because I have forgotten how to walk," she says. Therefore, at 2:45 she reaches for her cloak, he reaches for his wife, and they go home. They dream in yoke, they are harnessed to the same star, they go to the same tune, they are wound to the same revolutions a minute.

What of it? They are among the stars, and they who have learned the rhythms of the axis and swing to the swinging planets may gather points even to the five of the stars; they can be forgiven the gravel that comes of tread-

They Go to Bed

ing the walks of the unknown.

Therefore, hurry through the day, dance till there's nothing left of you, for there's 2:00 A.M. waiting. She never sews, for that is something that she has never had time for. The clock that stands on the mantelpiece never has been wound, for t.here has never been time. There is no ticking in the home of the Castles. Nothing moves save the ordinary heavy feet or the prowling pups.

A silent house it is, inhabited by silent hopes. Some day they are going to live. They are curled into the dollar sign and the kinks of Irene's frocks are spiral. Sometimes they do not go home, but once in a while they do, and he can cook. He feeds her an egg sandwich. He says:

"Do we regret our family?"

"No; there is not time—it's 11:30."

Presently she says, "I might, if I had time, think of something that would help the world," and he replies, "No time, it's 3:10."

Only at last, the dancing and the day done, and with the cold gray of a new dark upon them, sometimes they whisper, "We are going pretty swiftly; the ball is moving; will anything cling to it when its spinning is—done?"

Charles Rann Kennedy Explains the Meaning of Tangoism

Actor and dramatist Charles Rann Kennedy was born in Derby, England in 1871 and performed in his own and others' plays in both England and the United States. Grandson of the noted Greek scholar for whom he was named, Kennedy was equally at home in classical tragedy, Shakespearean comedies, and the melodramas from his own pen.

His first stage appearance was at Her Majesty's Theatre in April 1897 in The Seats of the Mighty, *and over the next few years he toured in various plays. After meeting actor-director Ben Greet, he joined Greet's company, serving as business manager and later acting in* The Tempest, Twelfth Night, Much Ado About Nothing, As You Like It, *and* Everyman. *He performed as the Doctor in* Everyman *in his first New York appearance at Mendelssohn Hall in 1903. In the years following, Kennedy began writing plays, including* What Men Dare, The Servant in the House, The Winterfeast, The Necessary Evil, The Chastening, The Admiral, The Idol Breaker, *and* Face of God.

In 1913 he resumed acting, appearing in Chicago in his own play, The Necessary Evil, *and he continued to act in the Greek tragedies* Alcestis, Antigone, Hippolytus, Medea, Electra, *and* The Trojan Women *over the next decade. In*

1924 he returned to London temporarily to perform in his
The Chastening, *which was refused a license by the British
Censor. He toured with both* The Chastening *and* The Ad-
miral *in the United States later that year. Kennedy also
played small roles in the original film version of* Little Old
New York *and in* Crime Without Passion, *in which Helen
Hayes and Fanny Brice had cameo roles. He died in California
in 1950 at the age of seventy-nine.*

O UT of all the velvet in the world Charles Rann
Kennedy took two yards for a collar, over which to
circulate new problems, keyed up with just a dash of
mustard.

Out of all the human architecture in the world he took
to himself the stature of a man who should walk in No. 8
Romeos. Instead he succumbed to fate, which gave him
the eyes of a dreamer, the hair of a cave man, the smile
of a humorist, and the hands and feet of a woman.

Like some elastic cherub, gone old for want of better
understanding, Kennedy's large face looks out at you from
a haven of hair as the heron from the sedge of the marsh.
I told him that I was thinking of him as "Cherub
Kennedy," and he laughed a little and seemed amused.

It is the usual and natural thing, the cornering of a
man: the pelting with impertinent questions, of going
away and telling the world that he raises his feet and
rests them easily upon the fender of fame; that he reaches
over and plucks rose leaves for the filling of his pipe.
To say that when he smiles he lays bare a white, quivering

ultrapersonality. And easy, too, it is to say, that he is an all-around good-tempered, good-looking fellow—which same no one on this earth is wholly—and gets away with it.

Printer's ink was made to run the rim of the halo, and printer's lead was made to hold down Venus. In spite of this, for once let me take a nice man, a genius, and tell that which is true as well as charming.

"Cherub Kennedy" is not all cherub. Dream Kennedy is not all dream. Genius Kennedy is not all—well, perhaps he is.

Yet when I went down out of the heavy strength of inch-deep carpets and stood in the chill of the green outer hall, through the panels of the door that had closed upon me I heard Chopin stealing softly. It was a fine situation, and Chopin had lent himself to it.

Kennedy is human, even terribly human. Sometimes reaching for an epigram he plucks a plum; sometimes reaching for a plum his wide, sweeping hands grow amazed at their emptiness. And yet Kennedy says things.

Speaking for a moment of his seven plays of seven characters each, he said, "The easiest thing in the world is the most difficult. If you want to produce a masterpiece, make the task difficult enough and your striving will make it a little greater than it might ordinarily have been. Everyone asks me if this plan of seven characters does not limit me. I answer, was *The Servant in the House* good? Was *The Winterfeast* good? Is *The Idol Breaker* better? And always the answer comes in capitals—YES.

"You know," he said, dropping the topic abruptly and waving a glowing pipe, "America has a tendency to build cities. We have no city here yet, but we're going to have.

And here I want to say something about the country wherein I gained my freedom.

"Take for a start your newspapers. To read them one would think that we were going to hell. We aren't, you know. You judge by that little society of grocers that think they are the upper class—the side-stepping, vice-clutching, devil-mimicking lunatics.

"I don't know the tango, but I do know tangoism, and I know that it is a mere barbaric steaming up of flaccid souls. It's decadent America, that's all. The most of us, the best of us, are the ones who may go to a cabaret for a while, but who can come away and not be one of the crazed.

"It's always the frayed edge of the shawl that we notice, and it's the frayed edge of sin that catches our attention. The papers take it up because the jaded businessman wants something over which to gulp his coffee, and his wife something over which to raise white, horrified fingers and about which she can say, 'Tch-tch,' between horror-knocking teeth, 'what is this world coming to?'

"It isn't coming to anything, everything is coming to it, and it's coming fast. The little society of grocers think they are the whole circus, whereas they are only a side show. But wait a while and you'll see. Really, you know, we are getting all sorts of decent people in society—or at least well-meaning people, and well-meaning counts, a little.

"Your definitely vile in America are kicking up a rumpus in the garbage, thinking it's confetti, but your heroic, stolid, home-loving people are writing the lines that later America shall speak. When someone writes a universal biography, then we will understand and mend our ways. Animal slaughter is not terrible to most of us, because no one ever wrote a chapter on a cow.

"Put your hearts and your pockets into circulation and all's right with the world. Our mouths take on the shape of a rubber ring over the iniquity of our neighbors. We won't be so likely to do that when we understand that which our neighbor does is of no account. As soon as the curtain goes down in No. 20 we put sin—in our thoughts—behind the dimity; as soon as the curtain is drawn aside we think more of the sins in our own chambers. We Americans are too new to be thoroughly good neighbors. None of us are willing to go zero for God.

Sometimes
I Play Romeo

"I'm strongly for suffrage, too. There's a militant in the family, though we are a little ashamed of our English sisters and their methods. Take, for instance, the slashing of the Rokeby Venus. Why, that's only a little less terrible than the Boer War.

"But don't estimate America's strength by the capacity of her electric chair. Your halos are in the back street, and they are twenty thousand strong."

Slowly, with dreaming fingers, he refilled his pipe. With roving eyes he looked about the room, resting at last upon the balcony, high up, where stood a life-size picture of his wife; and then he said softly, "Sometimes I play Romeo, you know."

Somewhere in a back room I could hear the song of a servant at her work, and Kennedy, too, heard it but went on steadily:

"The greatest thing now going on is machinery. After we developed brick, we built. After all, a city is not mere mortar, stone and brick. There's inspiration in it, and I do believe, soul. Americans are not less than patriots, they are more than patriots."

"And now," I said, "tell me about *The Idol Breaker*— you have hardly spoken of yourself."

"Well, don't you think that, after all, it's a very little thing to speak of when one is dreaming the world?" he asked, smiling over his velvet collar. "I think there will be a greater chance for art when America understands tragedy. You don't understand the meaning of it here. You can't feel it as we of the old countries can. There a man inherits the tragedy of tears and dies to an immortal ancestry. You're so new here. We're so old there, for sin and hope and life and death and the whole of eternity are in the skin, and when we weep it's blood and when we laugh it's knack, handed down to us from ages that have laughed. Tears in America are entirely of the paper; laughter is an experiment. When America shall have wept ten thousand pocket handkerchiefs into oblivion, then and not till then, shall I have full success."

"Then don't you consider that you have full success now?" I questioned, biting the trademark off the pencil.

"No; only one of my plays was a success, *The Servant in the House*, and that the critics ripped up the back, as they have ripped me. Take, for instance, the length of my hair. I wore it short until I found that the people approved of it that way—after that I wore it long. My last play is selling steadily, but it is not making the money it should. The public is going mad over it; it's my best of three good plays. The last act was rewritten seventy-three times, and now it can't be improved upon. The idea, and I suppose that's the main thing in having seven plays of seven characters each, was to give the actors, five men and two women, a repertory of plays, one for each day in the week. And, by the way," he added, a gleam of fun in his eyes, "I smoked seven different pipes over *The Idol Breaker*. Well, we all have to do what comes to us—but success is not all that it seems.

"Some people say that it is not right to put religion on the stage. I say that Christ needs the play. He's made worse things than that His mediums: the ordinary grafter in the pulpit, the street corner orator, the humbler humbugs of every town.

"You get God and His Son clean on the stage, for there

He is preached without hypocrisy. The person speaking the lines is an actor and is there for the art in the lines and not for the heft of the plate.''

And then he told me something which, upon second thought, he decided not to let me print, and I came away.

Gaby's Reputation for Reckless Deviltry Is Shattered

French-born Gabrielle Deslys ran away from a convent at the age of sixteen to become an actress on the stage, for which she knew she had little talent but for which she correctly perceived her beauty and ambitions would be sufficient. Deslys began as a music-hall singer in Paris, where King Manuel of Portugal fell in love with her, brought her home to Portugal, and awarded her with a $70,000 pearl necklace. When the populace heard of the gift, a revolution resulted and Deslys was forced to escape the country in a haycart.

This was but the first of numerous theatrical exploits which surrounded her name with publicity and legend. Back in France, she was linked with Jean Cocteau, who upon witnessing her dance le jazz in the Casino de Paris, wrote a prose poem about her. Sir James M. Barrie, the Scottish creator of Peter Pan, demonstrated his infatuation with this extravagant "queen of glamour" in his entertainment Rosy Rapture. Her true love, however, was rumored to be the gentleman-actor Basil Hallam, matinee idol of the day, noted for his role as "Gilbert the Filbert."

With her partner, Harry Pilcer, Deslys acrobatically danced her way into the hearts of American theatregoers, and she remained in the United States to star in several early Para-

mount films. But her major rôle *was that of an extravagant celebrity, greeting stage-door crowds in plumaged dresses and hats of osprey and paradise feathers.*

After World War I, the French revealed that Deslys had spied for them, using her dark coloring to pose as an Hungarian woman and uncovering numerous German secrets. Deslys died in Paris in 1920 of cancer of the throat, leaving her estate to the poor of Marseilles.

WE are going to take something from Gaby Deslys.
Not her patience, for that has been taken and regained too often to count; not her right to a normal supply of clothes, for that, too, has been taken from her; nor her reputation, for long ago that was taken to make a column on.

I am going to take something away from Gaby that will be a new loss. No more can she be a picturesque little vagabond nor a shallow water siren, for I am going to take away her reputation for reckless deviltry, her alleged heating up of the piper.

Gaby is a child; it is even a little pitiful to see her mimic the step of the woman she could not be. Only a half-grown bit of a thing, who lifts her shoulders in great heavings or world-thrust wonder, regretful that she could not be funny without stepping within the shadow, sorry that laughter was bought at the price bad eggs are a dozen.

Canaries were dearer by a feather when Gaby was born—Gaby, who has been an impostor with her silence. In the time when frauds are disclosed and the Senate and the police force, yea, and the very clerks of state, are all raked into the reckoning, why hasn't anyone exposed Gaby Deslys?

It seems that a devil posing in the livery of an angel can't get away with it long, but a person may, with no chance of discovery, parade in red.

Passing behind the scenery of the last act, where twenty men lower the drop crystals and take them away until the evening; where some maid is talking in high, brittle French; where, struggling over the disheveled finery of a disheveled scene, one comes in upon a parallel bit of stage manager, cursing in poetical, damp English a set of tousle-headed chorus girls. Sitting high upon a box, rocking his body to the refrain of "Prunella," sits that inimitable boy, Harry Pilcer. Still the cadence of some superhusky throat takes up the refrain over and over, and still somewhere in a two-by-nothing dressing room you can hear the loud, resolute, honest crescendo of Mlle. Gaby, coming out of her war paint.

And suddenly the desire to interview is gone, for fear that the frail little output of the Deslys family may be tired.

If someone in front had intended offering Gaby an insult, let him come back and see her, all damp from hard dancing. The intent will end in the offering of a pillow.

The French exclamations and pantings of irritation, of getting out of clothes and into street garments, continue. Still one hears the rolled English *r* as Gaby addresses the American maid, and still the tramping up and down of the chorus that cannot please the energetic Harry Pilcer.

Then the door opens, there is a burst of light, the

Canaries Were Dearer by a Feather When Gaby Was Born

intoxicating, opulent smell of three kinds of face powder and French lilies, and there stands "The Belle of Bond Street," her forehead shirred in a newly cut fringe of golden hair, smiling and wide-eyed with lashes guiltless of paint.

Having chased around the arena with bull-like ferocity, bent upon catching the butterfly in Gaby, panting with the exercise, grabbing a dauntless, daring mouthful of oxygen, breaking into the cockpit with a double-barbed wire stretched across your sense of decency, with electric gloves on you stand at last, steaming with heat and the tide coming in over your shoulder blades, with the prey in the corner looking up with sorrowful, tired, wistful eyes, holding back all the woe in the world. Having set out to catch a butterfly, it is very disconcerting to end up on a piece of lumber opposite the eyes of a young woman who laughs for the dollar and then donates fully half of it to the buying of temperamental crepe.

"Won't you sit down?" she says, and there is nothing to sit down upon save twenty-nine beautiful dresses, and, "Won't you excuse me?" and there is nothing to excuse. Hooking up a velvet dress, she stands beside the mirror. Looking in, you feel that life has been unkind; your own reflection is heavy, of the heaviness of an official stick of office blue, while Gaby is a French red of exceeding sharpness and a fine hair line.

And I asked her about life.

"Life is very terrible," she said quietly. "Very terrible and very sad and very hopeless, and yet I do not want to seem ungrateful. Do you quite understand? I have had such a big success—in a money way. I have been so happy to amuse. I have had such patience with your men, the young, who do not understand, and your old, who do not want to. It sounds ungrateful when I say, through all the mask of the laughter of my reputation, that the world is a very bitter place; it makes the tears in my heart, and I am tired. Nobody reading this will believe it, but I want them to understand that Gaby had hopes of becoming something far different from the woman the public believes her.

"I don't enjoy any part of life but my acting. How can I? I get no time. Wickedness does not bloom behind the footlights, sin has no room to gain momentum in the chorus. Heads and feet are too close and the minds too occupied. Oh, but I love my theatre—" (and we wish we could give it the funny twist she did) "—oh, more than—" (her voice lost its vivid color, and a tinge of that French that comes running in hesitant eagerness came into her tones) "—more than my God."

She slid her hand along her breast until it held the foot of the golden cross hanging beneath her string of far-famed pearls. The real Gaby, perhaps, beneath the Gaby of the poster. "I am the good Catholic, oh, very good Catholic. I love Heem so, and I want to please Heem so very much, but I think my church has given me up because I could not give up dancing. I suppose that I would not be an actress if I loved it enough. Every time I come upon the stage I hide the cross so to fool Heem a little while, for I love to dance.

"In America it is very hard for me. I cannot be the Gaby that they know in Paris. There I can play real comedy, ah, the funny kind of comedy where you laugh until you cry. Here they have no comedy, but they have better drama. In Paris no one adds vegetables to my accomplishments, as they did in New Haven. Your young men do not know how to be funny without being vulgar, isn't that it? When they feel like laughing they misinterpret the feeling and think it goes with violence and garden truck. Ah, well, I do not mind if they are happy. There is only one life in which to be glad, ma'm'selle."

"Then don't you believe in another world? In a heaven and a hell?"

She looked at me for a long time and finally, pinning a lily in her belt, stood shaking her head. "No, there is nothing after this world—for me, anyway. I think that one has all the time here to prove all the best and all the worst in them." And then she shrugged and laughed for the first time, as though amused. "That makes it easier to dance, you know," she finished.

"The world's a very small place, isn't it?" she questioned presently, lifting her gold-crowned head and looking at me sideways. "So very small and full of neighbors—soon you get to know everybody. It's not that way in Paris, that part of the world where a girl marries a big man and has children and grows fat and somebody comes along and imagines them at cafe tables drinking wine and chattering gaily. That's not really the way, see? Only some of us. We sing a little while and then are still. We dance a while and then die. We weep a bit and laugh a bit and someone else takes our place. All the curtain calls cannot be for Gaby. All the attention cannot be for Gaby. All the future cannot be for Gaby."

"Do you think that women can make for themselves

as big a place in the professional world as men?'' I asked, wondering why I stood here holding up to attention the wilted, tired doll-girl while I plied her with questions that she never thought to answer.

"Oh, yes, if you begin soon enough. Begin with the cradle. Teach them one thing right from the beginning, then they can do as great things as the men. Men, you see, want to do a thing, and ten minutes later they are what they want to be. It isn't that way with women. Still, I don't want to vote. I have got enough to do now.''

"And are you all French, Mlle. Deslys?''

"All French, yes—solid.''

She did not laugh at her own joke, because it was the joke of a foreigner unfamiliar with our language. Presently she said between a row of pins, "I remember when I was a child I wanted to do all the things the men did. I wanted to be a soldier. I used to think it would be beautiful to march away some day with the sun on one's head and the earth beneath one's feet. And how nice it would be to blow the plume out of one's eyes and how nice it would be to look back at the faces in the windows and see the tears of all the family. The tears shed for this one that walked beside me, perhaps, and then to come upon the casement with my tears. And I would wake up a girl and think that after all it would not be so nice to die.''

She shook her shoulders and with it departed some of her gloom, and then she sighed, "Oh, ma'm'selle, if you know how hungry I am! I dance so long and so very hard and I want supper so bad. So if you have got all the interview in your mind, I be so pleased to go.''

I Wanted to Be a Soldier

"Perhaps," I ventured, a light illuming the situation, "that is why you feel so dolorous about everything?"

She nodded. "Maybe. Listen, I'll tell you a secret. My mother is coming from Paris soon to see me, and I am so glad this piece is a success so that she will excuse me for dancing."

"Then didn't your parents want you to become an actress?"

"No; just wanted me to marry and have a family. My father especially."

"And where do your father and mother live, and what do they do?"

"They don't do anything. Am I not making money? My mother lives in Paris. My father in the south of France."

"Then—there is a disagreement in the household?"

"No." She did not look at me this time. "Just the temperature of the south of France agrees with my father. That is all."

And then I left her, calling behind her in her high, swift French.

You can gather a good deal in a corridor, and there I met Pilcer carrying a great box. "Isn't she a wonder, so full of life and energy and so misunderstood? Goes home every night, like me," he added, pulling at a piece of excelsior. "I have just furnished a new home for my mother. This is a new silver teapot," he added. Then he smiled in his boyish way and, bowing, followed Gaby through the door.

Still, one may gather a lot on the stairs, and there I met Sam Bernard. "Jove! she's a great little girl, ain't she? Does me proud—well, sufficiency."

Sometimes it will be "we" who go to see her and the friends of the friends, and they will all applaud. And will be, as I was, a trifle mystified at the number of single gentlemen who manage to be minus a family between two and six. Stout men, who glower upon the rest of the audience through heavy-rimmed spectacles, roped down by the weight of opulent satin ribbon; shallow, thin gentlemen in spare morning coats, who go out every intermission and add something to an already very thin substance. Middle-aged and old, all crowding to the front, unsandwiched by the slender shoulders of their womankind. And as the gentlemen come down the aisles, always single—for no man brings his brother—the usher smiles a bit behind her program and the gentleman smiles too, and the three women that are in the audience look the house over to discover the one who has escaped them.

And then there is the silence of the orchestra, the tuning of the orchestra, the crash of the orchestra, and the curtain goes up. And there is the quivering of music and stamping of feet like sudden summer, and then there is Mlle. Deslys again, and everything goes over in the same manner. And you have to turn to the beginning of this article to get the illusion straightened; and once more, face to face with her, she will say, "Won't you sit down?" and there is nothing to sit down upon, and she will say, "Won't you excuse me?" and there is nothing to excuse.

And then you will remember what I said, without going back all over it again, that canaries were dearer by a feather when Gaby was born.

I Could Never Be Lonely Without a Husband, Says Lillian Russell

Lillian Russell was the American woman's ideal and the American male's sex symbol for more than twenty years. Stunning in appearance, vivacious, wholesome, and good-natured in personality, "the American beauty"—as she was nicknamed—made a career on the stage, in film, and in light opera. While her image was more flamboyant and robust than that of her successor, Marilyn Monroe, she suffered similarly from unhappy marriages and personal tragedies.

Born Helen Louise Leonard in 1861, she debuted as a star at Tony Pastor's Theater on November 22, 1880, billed as "the English Ballad Singer." Over the next few years, she performed in Tony Pastor's travesty on The Pirates of Penzance, *titled* The Pie Rats of Penn Yann, *in straight versions of Gilbert and Sullivan's* Patience *and* The Sorcerer, *and in other musicals such as* The Spirit of the Times. *For three years from 1883 to 1885, Russell performed in England in various revues and shows; but she was wooed back to the United States by a $20,000 salary to appear at New York City's Casino. There she acted in her greatest successes,* The Princess Nicotine *and* An American Beauty. *It was in these Gay Nineties that Russell developed a close, platonic friendship as dinner companion to the renowned Diamond Jim Brady.*

When Barnes interviewed her in 1914, Russell was making the shift in her career from light opera to burlesque. A few years earlier she had replaced burlesque singer Fay Templeton at the Weber and Fields Music Hall, and in 1912 Russell had rejoined Templeton in Weber and Field's production of Hokey-Pokey.

By 1915, however, Russell was beginning to have weight problems and, although her critics continued to praise her beauty and grace, her voice had begun to show its age. The same year she starred with Lionel Barrymore in her only feature film, Wildfire, *which was greeted by mixed reactions from the critics and public alike.*

Her later years were devoted to political activities, including an appointment by President Warren Harding to investigate immigration problems. She died the following year, 1922, in Pittsburgh.

I N walks Lillian Russell.

Six bounteous ruffles gird her at the knees, white duchess laces enhance the splendor of her throat, the odor of Eastern incense lies heavy on everything. Grotesque potentates, squatting, smirk over their imprisoned rose leaves and myrrh; the switching tail of a sun god moves restlessly in the corner where long silken, dust-somber draperies shut out the light from Broadway.

I could just make her out in the dim room, sitting over there in the corner upon a wide chair like a throne, just make out the high-piled drift of gold that is her hair, the still beautiful eyes, only half-claimed from youth, the smiling mouth that has expressed all that can live within a black satin gown.

I leaned forward. I did not like to shatter the silence that was unbroken save for the spit-spitting of a chafing dish somewhere in a rear room.

The roses in the vase spilled a purple gloom upon the floor. Even then I could not have spoken, but from somewhere I caught the sound of a clock.

"All this is very mysterious and wonderful," I said, nodding toward the Eastern decorations in the room. "Do you believe, Miss Russell, that surroundings affect us?"

"More than anything," she said softly, "more than inheritance, more than inclination, more than one can really comprehend. If our vacant society would do with less gilt upon their chairs, they might donate more gold to their store of wisdom. These surroundings just tally up to the best that's in me. I am deeply contented when alone, without the sense of the hurry of the present day. I lift up a porcelain Buddha and hold him in my hand; it is peace to me, happiness. I could never be lonely without a husband, but without my trinkets, my golden gods, I could find abysmal gloom."

"What, then, do you think the surroundings of a Huerta should be."

"A comprehensive circle of guns," she replied without a minute's hesitation. She leaned forward and, cupping her hands, drew into them a wilted rose. I was beginning to make more headway in the Eastern twilight that had lodged upon one floor of an apartment house in Manhattan, and I could see what she must have been twenty years ago by what she was now.

The singing of passionate notes had made her chest a

little deep, so that she swayed like a great, languorous harebell. She had a home, and could not be called a house-wife; she had a husband, and could not be called adoring, for more than anything else, Miss Russell has acquired poise.

I asked her about her home life.

"I am as well contented with an apartment as a home. So many times I have read that the real home cannot be found in apartments, and I know better, because I've found mine. You can be just as happy as you like in any sort of apartment, providing you have the apartment spirit. Of course the best and the most agreeable place to double up and become domestic is in a nice large house; but here, all I have to do is reach out my arm, this way, and pass James the butter, and out this way, and close the piano for the night.

"All I have to do to pass on my thoughts to my husband is to think. I don't have to speak. That makes a great difference, I can assure you. So many pleasing episodes of one's life are spoiled by shouting. You never heard of an unhappy marriage unless the neighbors have heard it first."

"But," said I, "haven't you any violent views about anything?"

"Ah, yes—the Panama Canal controversy! When I think of any other country meddling with the thing that we have suffered and worked for, I become furious. It in-censes me; it puts me into a black rage. I could do war; I could fulfill the portent of a six-inch gun; I could make death telling—oh, I am passionate about this, because I know, I have been down there. To some people it is a mere ditch with a network of steel. It is a valley of shadows out of which America has come, and it is interlaced with blood and tears, and I cannot think of it without losing control.

"It has become beautiful, from a vermin-racked town. Now they are proud of their hospitals. Not a patient in them—that's a record."

"But," I inquired, "have you no violent views nearer home?"

"Not that I can recall at present, unless it is my occasional visits to the kitchen. I have to be pretty determined to get there; my cook does not like me to mess about, but I have a particular passion for mushrooms, you know. Wait, I'll give you the recipe, then you poor, deluded persons may really discover what heaven is dished up in onions.

"Put a lump of butter in a chafing dish (or a saucepan) and a slice of Spanish onion and the mushrooms minus the stem; let them simmer until all are deliciously tender and the juice has run from them—about twenty minutes should be enough—then add a cupful of cream; let this boil. After it has come to a boil, squeeze in the juice of a lemon. There you are; that's the only way in the world to cook them, and it's the only way that you will want them after you have had them that way once."

"But fancy," said I, "if you had a date that evening!"

"Oh, you're worrying about the onion. It is no longer an onion when the cream and the lemon have been added; not an onion, but an epic."

At this juncture entered a square of white linen and a ruffle, that reminder of social, as well as domestic

Sitting Over There in the Wide Chair Like a Throne

obligations, accompanied by a freshly framed painting of a dog.

"It's French," Miss Russell commented, turning, about to scrutinize it, a yard-square stretch of canvas supporting a morsel of velvet cushion, and upon this a little irreproachable island, a mere penwiper of a long-haired dog with a plaintive look in the eyes that came of breeding.

It was one of those poodle pups who, after a long bolt upon the road of progress, has selected his mother and father so well that he has been considered a thoroughbred and therefore worthy of a yard square of canvas.

"Take it away," she said presently and returned to the conversation. "That was my only pet; he died a little while ago. I have had no pets since. I cannot bear to have caged birds and I don't care for cats, and I can't keep horses up here and I won't have another dog, so you understand the reason for the lack of other moving bodies other than myself."

"And about suffrage?"

"I was brought up on mother's milk and suffrage. Don't you know that my mother was the famous Cynthia Leonard, who ran for President years ago? Ah, yes, I'm for suffrage and hope that it comes soon in my time, so that I can vote, and I'll vote good and stiffly."

"What about the modern dressing?"

"Wonderful! What more sensible than modern clothes? No binding, no nonsense, nothing extra, just sufficient and an end, just becoming and dignified, just normal and healthy and sane."

"Well, then, what about the modern dances?"

"Splendid! Much prettier and more healthful than the

old-fashioned dances. I believe in them. They will not die; they are here to stay, they should stay, and they will stay. A few variations, perhaps, a few new steps, but otherwise the same, excepting the dip; that will die, it is not graceful, not interesting, not even indecent; it will die.''

"Well, then, don't you think at least something is going to the dogs, Miss Russell—surely some one thing?''

"I can't think of a single thing. Let me see—with women in the world how can things go to the dogs.''

"Then you firmly believe in the women?''

"I never find a single fault with a woman. I can give the men a jolly calling down at times, but my sisters, they are splendid, they have such great ideals, even if they are tied into knots by husbands; they have aspirations even if they have not as yet learned to walk on the outer side of the street.''

"But the thing that's going to the dogs?'' I reminded her.

"But I can't think of anything that is going to the dogs really and truly. I think that America is about all right and the rest of the time I work. When a woman is busy she hasn't time to fasten the straps about the wrists of the infamous. When one is busy cultivating roses she cannot speculate on cactus.''

And then she thanked me.

"What for?'' I inquired.

"For not having asked me a single question about the way I preserve my good looks. Everyone always asks that first. For a few minutes you have let me forget my face, and I want to forget it. I get very tired of it— very, very tired of it. I hate a mirror sometimes.

"What, after all, is there great in being beautiful? To be a great woman, a great person, one must have suffered, even as our women in Panama suffered, as our women have suffered in great crises. What have I done that I should be famous—nothing but powdered a bit gently the cheeks that God gave me and smoothed the hair that I was born with, laughed and proven a faultless set of teeth. Any grinning idol, well painted, can do as well, but the real women, the big women, are those who toil and never write of it, those who labor and never cry of it, those who forfeit all and never seek reward. Begin this article with the name of Lillian Russell, but end it with the name of such as was Cynthia Leonard."

Out of the purple dusk I walked, and the simple-minded porcelain Chinaman smirked at me from the piano, and the wise-mouthed sun god rolled sightless eyes toward the peacock feathers and the array of silver mugs, and the incense rolled on and up about the chair like a throne with its burden like a queen.

Diamond Jim Brady

Born the son of a saloon keeper on Manhattan's West Side in 1856, James Buchanan Brady was (according to his biographer, John Burke) "the most omnipresent eater in the nation's history" and simultaneously (to quote Fortune *magazine) was "the greatest capital goods salesman of them all."*

Brady left home at the age of eleven and worked for a time as a bellhop at the then fashionable St. James Hotel, from whose clientele he learned—in that Flash Age of Tweed Ring corruption—that conspicuous symbols of wealth such as gold chains and diamonds meant power and access to the best rooms in the house. At fifteen he landed a job as a baggage handler at Grand Central Terminal and worked his way up to station agent. Brady became popular with John M. Toucey, the general manager of the New York Central, but a small scandal involving Brady's brother, Dan, resulted in his being fired. Toucey found him another job, however, as a railroad supply salesman, and—after buying his first diamond—Brady went on the road, selling handsaws and, later, railroad undercarriages at such a phenomenal rate that within a few short years his wealth put him in a league with Andrew Carnegie and J. P. Morgan.

Brady spent most of his free time and the money from his unlimited expense account on the theatre and music halls of the day and—with actresses and celebrities such as Lily Langtry, Mary Anderson, and Lotta Crabtree on his arm— at his favorite eating places, Delmonico's and Rector's

Restaurant. His most famous and regular of dining compan-
ions, however, was Lillian Russell, who accompanied him
for years to the lobster-palace feasts which made him famous
and fat. Friend Wilson Mizner described Brady's eating habits
as those of a man "who liked his oysters with clams, and his
steaks smothered with veal cutlets."

As charitable as his girth, Brady, bedecked in diamonds
from his cane to the buttons of his vest, wowed nearly
everyone with whom he came in contact: John L. Sullivan
mistakenly took the teetotaler Brady's gargantuan consump-
tion of root beer as a sign of the man's ability to hold his
liquor; Charlie Chaplin, who joined in one of Brady's lavish
celebrations, awoke in a bathtub; and New Yorkers in the
street did not soon forget witnessing his ride in a horseless
carriage, the first to be driven through the City. His insatiable
appetite for food and pleasure—particularly his fondness for
orangeade—eventually resulted in a serious kidney stone
blockage, and Brady was rushed to The Johns Hopkins Uni-
versity Hospital in Baltimore. The removal of the stone and
a strict diet ordered by his doctors brought down Brady's
weight for a time. But as soon as he had recuperated, he
returned to his bacchanalian activities in New York.

With the new dance crazes at their height in 1916-17,
Diamond Jim hired Irene and Vernon Castle to teach him;
and, by night, he elephantinely turkey-trotted and tangoed
away his last year at the Palais de Dance, at the Jardin de
Dance, and at Flo Ziegfeld's New Amsterdam Theater rooftop.

Knowing he was near death, Brady traveled to Atlantic
City, where he died on the morning of April 13, 1917. He
left most of his fortune to The Johns Hopkins University
Hospital, which built a urological clinic in his name.

I NEVER fully believed in Diamond Jim Brady, until one summer, on a boardwalk evening, I caught sight of his breastwork lights.

Shining out of the dark like a searchlight at sea, he bore down upon me, supreme under the dominance of three headlights, running slowly with the tide of the traffic, smiling out of heavy, condescending depths, which held off fiercely the banked, black eyebrows. So he came abreast. The diamonds upon his breast fell into the sign which is the Brady advertisement, and he was past, gone in the night, a mere moving black shape in broadcloth.

"Have you any love for our ordinary society?" I asked him when I met him later.

"No."

"Do you look to it for your salvation?"

"I need no salvation. I'll go where I'm going with smooth edges."

"Do you regret anything?"

"Yes; the death of Bohemia."

"Nothing else?"

"I regret sometimes that I did not have children."

"Shall you ever marry?"

"Not if I can keep sane a little longer."

"Are you happy?"

"I do not know what you mean by happiness; my car is slowing down."

He laid a great turquoise-plagued hand upon his knee, and leaning forward said, "I'm an old man."

An old man and yet not sixty. What does it matter if senility can dance the tango, if age-warping limbs can bend to the dip? What does it matter if death can be

*Though He Is a Diamond in the Rough You Can't Get Away from
Him Without Taking a Memory You Are Not Likely to Forget*

cheated into a measure?

"At what rate are you running?"

"I should say about ninety miles an hour. I go to bed at half past one in the morning. I find that I'm tired then."

"Oh."

"It's because I have a thousand faucets, but only one on tap—orangeade. I forego the orange blossoms and drink the fruit."

"Shall you ever taste liquor, just to find out what it is like?"

He shut his eyes. "I am not curious," he said softly— then bursting into one of those roars that make him difficult to choose from the lions, said, "What is it in man that makes him desire drink and tobacco? I don't pretend to be a moralist. I'm not. I like to see people loyal to their particular brand of hell, but it amuses me sometimes to see the languid pile they choose. Now, I have nothing to say to a woman that smokes a cigarette. It's not my business, but I don't like it, that's all.

"There's one thing that I particularly dislike and that's being told how a certain play went off. That's why I attend first nights, to forestall the man who says: 'Have you seen so and so?' and if I were to answer no, would take my time, and coat lapel, and tell me about it. Also I like the first nights because there's a crowd that you get on no other night. There are speeches and one's mind is not biased by the opinions of the newspaper critics, and it gives the comedian (I like musical comedy best) a chance to make comments about my jewelry. I don't want to spoil any of his fun, you see. This," he added, throwing out an arm, "is my jeweler."

A thin little man with a high-bridged nose moved in the sparse crescent of the window at the far end of the room and bowed—a mechanical, inward movement at the waist which took into a deep fold of obscurity his belt buckle—and straightened up again, his hands held behind him as though to keep them still from their very desire to order the setting of Diamond Jim's stones into some new and complicated design.

The fact that Diamond Jim's jewelry is not beautiful we feel is not the fault of this particular silent jeweler, but the fault of a man who, desiring the beautiful, thought it out by the block and not by the cut.

A great half-stone like a robin's egg, embellished by an inch mounting of gold, smothered his scarf pin; down the easy slide to his watch chain loped three more half-robin's eggs, ending in a picket fence of turquoise. Under his vest (he showed me) was a band of them.

Still farther underneath (he told me) were yet more.

If you are sharp you can catch glimpses of Brady between his jewelry.

Someone has said that two years or so ago Diamond Jim exchanged an old washer for a new. He lay prone awhile, and when he arose some of his diamonds were doing interior illumination. It was not a noisy thundering of rivets, for Brady is not boiler iron. It was done noiselessly, and without newspaper comment for a while. And then finding that he could dance the tango and get away with it, and that he could stay out at nights and get away with that, too, Brady racked his mind for the thing that would show his gratitude. Finally he gave to Johns Hopkins University a hospital, which will be dedicated on October 7.

It is for the men of the country alone.

This was his gratitude, but not the limit.

"I am going to dedicate my body to them when I die," he said, "so their good work will come back to them."

Sometimes he tells a funny story about himself, but not if he knows it. Sometimes his friends tell funny stories about him, and they know it thoroughly well.

Jack Bates tells one. Last summer Bates was doing honor to a few stripes in a cylindrical bathing suit while his bull pup skirmished around the sand-scuffing toes of Brady. Upon his sea sandals Brady wears diamonds. Presently the pup got suspicious, barked and made a lunge. Out shot the circular toe of that gentleman; a yelp from the dog, and a diamond was missing—one other stone was doing interior service. Brady brought a suit and demanded that the dog be killed.

"Nothing doing," returned the judge. "Can't kill a dog on the first bite. You'll have to invite him to a second combat before the court can give you the option of his life."

Brady considered; so did Bates. The dog which had been, in its heyday, worth only fifty dollars, arose and soared into the market at $500. The dog grew somewhat lopsided, owing to the extreme weight of the diamond, but Bates loved him with a passionate, yearning sort of affection that would not let the dog out of his sight. Brady fumed, cussed and wore a pound of chuck roast about his ankle for a couple of days, but Bates kept the dog fed to the hilt.

The dog may get away from Bates some day—no, I'm not trying to advertise any particular brand of sausage.

Diamond Jim slowly opened his silver and gold glass case and withdrew his glasses. He looked at them a while and returned them again.

"Yes," he said presently, "there are a lot of things said about me and the company I keep. If I care for the society of actresses, why should your conventional people make such a hue and cry? I like that life that is the life that likes me. They care for me in Bohemia, and they don't in the other circles. There's nothing for me excepting in my own crowd.

"If a girl would rather be seen with me and wine than with a wedding ring and a worried look, that is her business and not mine. I am like George Moore. I like all women too well."

"Yes," I interrupted, "but how about the girl?"

"What about the girl? She chooses it; I did not make her. Half of the world believes in one thing, the other half in another; only one half is stronger because it is not free.

"I never married because I did not have those convictions. If I had married, ten to one she would have made me gray before my time and have taken all my money and broken up my home. Husbands are all right for those who like them, and wives, too, but I'm not the marrying brand."

He turned back to his desk and made a memorandum, answered the telephone, and made a last parting remark.

"Say that I like New York. It is the best summer resort in the world—you are within an hour's ride of everywhere, and the sea is fine. Sometimes I regret I was not a Roman. They had such a lot of time and baths."

He pulled down his vest and hid from view a few

hundreds' worth; he buttoned his coat and hid a few thousands' worth; he gloved his hands and hid a few millions' worth; he straightened his tie and smiled.

"Now go away and tell the world that I am a bear, that I drink beer and offer up girls as a sacrifice; go away and tell them that Brady is not Diamond Jim Brady, but damned Brady. Tell them I do not smoke here, perhaps, but hereafter. And tell them that no matter what they may say of me, I have enough of the sport in me to add to it, 'I should worry!' "

Well, watch him on the floor spreading the passion for gems, listen to him groan in man-laboring simplicity, watch one pump go before the other, and then say that he is not a good sport.

I met his secretary in the hall. He leaned toward me and whispered behind his hand:

"Did you notice how stout he seemed to be about the hip pockets?"

I nodded.

"Bunkers," said the lad.

"Bunkers?" I repeated.

"Bunkers, yes. Ten handkerchiefs in each pocket!"

"Has he a cold?" I inquired.

"Naw, not a cold; they are for protection when people bump into him while dancing."

"What do they bump into him for?"

"They try to knock some of his diamonds off."

Also, another bit of information is that he hangs his underwear in his safe.

I got out of the office building, but on my way up Broadway I met a friend who was mutual.

"Been interviewing Jim?" he inquired. "Did he tell you about his belief in New York as a summer resort? Well, once he was out swimming, and presently he got tired and lay over on his back and floated. He has 'em even on his B.V.D.'s.

"Well, he may have been floating a minute, perhaps, when someone set up a hollering. We were all of us taken off our guard. We thought it was Fire Island unmoored."

And once we asked Lillian Russell about him, and she said:

"Brady is the best man in the world. He never drinks or smokes, he never dissipates—only in jewelry. And by the way, diamonds are not his favorite gems; pearls are."

And so he came to my knowledge, as he comes to the knowledge of all who see him—a rumor at first and then a solid fact. Though he is a diamond in the rough, you can't get away from him without taking a memory that you are not likely to forget. He could pass into many stages of life, but never into oblivion, for oblivion is a comfortable place where there is nobody who was ever somebody.

Brady may pass on, but he is too heavy for it to be on and up.

Flo Ziegfeld Is Tired of Buying Hosiery

Chicago-born Florenz Ziegfeld was the son of a German musician who became President of the Chicago Musical College. Spurning the "high" culture of his upbringing, the young Flo found his mentors in Buffalo Bill and Annie Oakley, who performed in Chicago in 1883. At the age of twenty-four, he was sent by his father—recently named Musical Director for the Columbian Exposition—to secure performers for the Exposition. Much to the distress of the elder Ziegfeld, his son returned with a mélange of jugglers, circus bands and acrobats which, with his management of Sandow the Strongman, launched his career as a grandly theatrical producer.

Ziegfeld's first Broadway venture was the reuniting of the comedy team of Charles Evans and William Hoey. Traveling with Evans to London in search of new faces, Ziegfeld found both a new star and a lover in the singer Anna Held. Within a few months' time, Ziegfeld promoted her—through press announcements describing her milk baths and other private activities—to celebrity status. Refused a divorce by her Roman Catholic husband, Held and Ziegfeld lived together unwed until their union was recognized as a common-law marriage in 1904.

It was in Paris two years later that Ziegfeld first beheld the Folies Bergère, which was to serve as the model for his own Follies. But Ziegfeld, shrewdly recognizing the differences in cultures, chose to eschew the risqué burlesque elements of the French production in favor of a sexless glorification of the female form. Opening in 1907, the Ziegfeld Follies, in its idealization of womanhood and its amalgamation of vaudeville, minstrel show and spectacle, found an immediate audience that would demand its annual return until the fall of the stock market in 1929. The stars of the Follies—Marilyn Miller, Bert Williams, Fanny Brice, and Eddie Cantor—and the many other actresses who first performed as Ziegfeld girls —among them, Barbara Stanwyck, Paulette Goddard, and Irene Dunne—secured the Follies' and Ziegfeld's position in the history of American theatre and in the hearts of theatre-goers for decades after the demise of his extravaganzas.

At the time of Barnes's interview, Ziegfeld, having divorced Held in 1912, had just married actress Billie Burke. Burke—known at the time for her roles in serious dramas by Sir Arthur Wing Pinero and Somerset Maugham, and most remembered today for her role as the Good Witch in The Wizard of Oz—married Ziegfeld between the Saturday matinee and evening performances of Jerry, the play in which she was performing.

During the 1920s, Ziegfeld would expand his producing activities to include more unified musical dramas and comedies such as Rio Rita, Show Boat, Rosalie, and Whoopee. The advent of the Great Depression made it increasingly impossible to mount the lavish productions he required, and when his life ended in 1932 Ziegfeld was penniless. Ironically, he died in Hollywood, home to the film musicals that would serve as surrogates over the next two decades for Ziegfeld's live entertainments.

BETWEEN the devil and the deep blue sea there is
an alternative—Flo Ziegfeld.

He's a narrowly built man, slender and somewhat
given to moments of exasperating poise; the last remaining splint to a season's backbone, absolutely under the
dominance of fold on fold of high, white stock, close-
mouthed and satirical-eyed.

Billie Burke, his bride, has him roped to the mast—
there's no getting away from it. Flo Ziegfeld sits down a
minute and tries to forget her, but into the back of his
mind, where he is trying to think up something to get
the play over, creeps the elusive mist of Billie's hair.

Getting at Ziegfeld is a task devoid of principle. You
have to be a good liar, wholly daring and willing to
risk your immortal soul. The doorkeeper upon his perch
looks at you from long years of experience and tells you
that Mr. Ziegfeld is not there and never will be while
you stay, and if you see Ziegfeld for yourself he will
still repeat that he is not there, and say it fearlessly.

I came in upon a dim row of seats draped in gray linen,
the mourning for an audience gone, and down in front,
his arms about the rail, sat Flo.

The stage was a thing in the future, with future possibilities at work upon it. Girls—the thin arabesque of
laughter, pitching white organisms in silk who threw
more than barbarianism into the dance, while Bert Williams sang gutterally from a great bronze throat a song
that the public will never hear.

I didn't see anything terrible about it, nor did I see
anything glamorous or grand or inspiring or even beautiful. All I did see, all that made a new impression upon

me, was the number of limbs that a girl manages to
secrete about her when she has nothing much on and
nothing much to do, and sits down, only to arise at a
shriek from the manager. The only high life about it was
the dash of a vivid gehenna in the sudden gashed red
of a badly painted mouth.

And I sat with Flo Ziegfeld's agent; I hope that he liked
the taste of the top of his cane. I sat there so long and
the rehearsal meant so little that all I recall now was that
a girl with a very large picture hat sang with a rather
too rich voice, while the shadow lay upon her cheek
bones and the bridge of her nose, a song stating that she
desired to be one with the cradle of love.

Incidentally, the cradle did not seem to interest Ziegfeld,
for he shrugged his shoulders or called to his manager,
and once he said something that made it look as though
the singer would have to hunt another vehicle to draw
her into the avenue of the successful.

Dark speculations drifted across the pale footlights.
Ziegfeld moved ever so slightly and grunted. Sometimes
the manager, stepping far forward, remarked that he
thought that such and such a song was going to be ''a
devil of a number,'' while the light-haired man sat well
back upon the piano stool and thumped out of the piano
all the resonance that he knew how to. Chorus girls
dropped listlessly out to the water filter.

Someone has said that the prettiest girls in America
come into Ziegfeld's knowledge as a diamond into a kit.
Looking at the chorus, I knew that there would have to
be some winnowing if an unblemished reputation were
to be kept.

The atmosphere that is Ziegfeld's is so insidious, so mystic a thing, and withal so silent, that I did not know that he sat next to me until I heard him speak.

"My God!" he breathed, "she's wonderful! More wonderful than anything that can be imagined of her—and so new, so new!" It was Billie again.

"Yes," I said. "But why so new?"

"To me," he answered, almost inaudibly. "I used to think dark hair was pretty. Lord, but I was young!"

"But isn't it?" I objected.

"Isn't it what?" he said, and his face had lost all its reminiscent look.

"You know," he went on presently, "I have to pick out all the shoes and stockings and other things that go with a show, and I'm tired to death of hosiery. It's like being another Brigham Young, only he had an incentive, because there the stockings were in the family—" He paused.

"Well," I said, by way of encouragement and keeping him talking, "it gives you a fine chance to exercise your taste."

"What's that?" he queried, and stood up suddenly. "Excuse me." He passed over the set of seats as though that were an ordinary parlor stunt, and returned presently with his shoemaker and a young lady he called by her first name. Then he was entirely lost for a few moments. When he came back he was as far from shoes as the original mermaid.

"Terrible lot of temperament in the chorus," he remarked. "Gets things all tangled up—I say," he called up to the manager once more and canned another song and set still another running in its place.

"That song," he said, "was given to me with the composer's assurance that it had not been published, and now I find that there are professional copies on the market. Composers are all alike: they will say anything, sign anything, and then go away and do as they please. I guess there's something demoralizing in music. They think life goes along in octaves. Well, I'm only one of the million who get stung. That song, 'I Wonder Who Paid Mrs. Rip Van Winkle's Rent' was promised to me, then they handed it over to Bernard. The only way to get the best of a composer is to kill him, and I can't do that."

"What?" I said.

"I can't kill him. It's against the law—I don't see why."

"We sympathize, I'm sure."

"Who's that?" he said again, and was once more off the track. "The public thinks that I like musical comedy, that I admire 'Undine Adrift' and 'Birth of Venus' effects. All delusion and folly! I like to laugh, but I'm not crazy about musical comedy, except as a money-getter; as a money-getter it's a bird!

"I know how to pick out my girls—my God, but she's a wonder!—never stout, slim, well formed, red-haired— say, did I say red-haired? Well, anything in the line of hair, only the temperament must not be sluggish; no go- to-sleep-in-the-middle-of-the-day girls, understand, and most of all, personality."

"How do you get your girls?"

"I get them by the foot." He thrust his chin into his stock. "I look at their feet and at their hands. You can tell a lot about a girl that way. I never listen to their voices, because a good voice never has a beautiful face to back it up.

"I choose good lookers and good dancers. All the cabaret artists that have made good have been at one time or another in my chorus—all excepting the Castles."

"What particular thing about a girl attracts you?"

"Her personality, her brittleness—you get the meaning? —the number of grains of purport that she's able to percolate per second—and then, of course—"

"Yes?"

"Then, of course, there's the coloring. Personally I like it very vivid—red—say, did I say red? This business is all pretty much a gamble, anyhow. The thing that makes the real money is a clever little play with, say, five actors. You have only five salaries to pay, and you take in money.

"In musical comedy you rely upon the strength of the stock in the soup to make it go down, and you have five hundred or more salaries to pay. Then the songs. The only real good hit in this year's *Follies* that I've found yet is a song about the vampire—it's a peach!"

"Which, the vampire or the song?"

He eyed me closely and shut his stubborn mouth and did not smile. I was properly terrified and asked him to give me his definition of a vampire.

"A vampire," he returned, "is a woman who eats lightly of uncooked things; who walks out between tall avenues of spears to die, and doesn't, and finally spends the evening in an orgy of virtuous dreams. That's time wasted. A vampire is a good woman with a bad reputation, or rather a good woman who has had possibilities and wasted them."

"Beautiful!" I said. "And what does she look like?"

"What does what look like?" Ziegfeld asked, and, rising once more, sent a telegram off by a messenger boy who had until then been a part of the gloom. Coming back, he canned a few more songs and groaned.

"I hope you are not feeling ill," I said.

"No," he answered.

"You are not discouraged about this show, are you?"

"No," he said once again.

"Because that would be a foolish thing to do; it's likely to be a success."

"Well," he burst out, "that does not prevent me from suffering the tortures of the damned, does it?" He groaned in a soft monotone and set his head in his hands.

"I'm awfully sorry," I said, and did not know why, and he answered, "Thank you."

I turned to the press agent. "Often like this?"

"Always."

"That so? What's the reason?"

"Nobody knows."

"Isn't he ever cheerful?"

"Oh, always!"

"But this is despair."

"Dear me, no; that's temperament."

"Oh!" I said.

"You see," murmured Ziegfeld, "I am having the deuce of a time. I never know who is going to be the principal when I get through. I never end with the people I start with. I pick a girl from the chorus, often, to take the place of some star who has fallen. It's very depressing."

"Well, it makes people sit up and take notice."

"What does?" and he groaned again softly.

"And now," said I, by way of a final exit, "you should say something nice about your wife. She has said such a lot of nice things about you—you just can't do less."

"Haven't I said all there is to say? Didn't I say she was more wonderful than she looks? Red hair is all I care for —now."

Suddenly he shook himself roughly and put his arms behind his head. "I'm homesick, that's all; homesick for Chicago."

"And your wife, where is she?"

He looked at me again with wide, inhuman, unruffled eyes.

"I said I was homesick, didn't I?" And there was no sense of humor about his tragically calm face—a face that had been set and coldly tempered by the fires of competition.

So he looked at me and presently his face faded away into indistinct murmurings of the press agent; and the substance, the ether, the haze, that goes by the name of Ziegfeld had taken itself off as imperceptibly as it had come.

I stood in the glare of a Broadway day and a cabby swore at me gently for looking his horse between the eyes for fully a minute as I smiled inanely and remembered, and, remembering, smiled again.

Interviewing Arthur Voegtlin Is Something Like Having a Nightmare

Billed as the largest theater in the world, New York City's Hippodrome presented some of the most spectacular theatrical events since the performances in the ancient Roman Hippodrome of charioteers and gladiators. A typical production during the Hippodrome's heyday might include everything from reenactments, with life-size ships, of great naval battles to tableaux of Dutch tulip gardens, from prairie villages threatened by sandstorms and fire to lush and exotic desert oases inhabited by choruses of Bedouins and belly dancers.

Artistic director of the Hippodrome from its opening in 1905, Arthur Voegtlin was variously described by the press and in the Hippodrome's own program as "the brains" and "the genius" behind these productions. From his Pinafore—*performed on a larger than life-size pirate ship—to his annual musical pageants conceived with composer Manuel Klein and lyricist William J. Wilson, Voegtlin served as theatrical alchemist to more than a decade of theatregoers, blending various elements of circus, vaudeville, tableau, opera, and burlesque into unforgettable extravaganzas. Among his many spectacles were* A Society Circus, America, Wars of the World, *and* Under Many Flags.

It was during the last-named of these productions, less than a year after Barnes's interview, that a bitter argument with Lee and J. J. Shubert, owners of the Hippodrome, led to Voegtlin's physical ejection from the theater, and to his being fired. This was the first in a series of causes, least of which was the rise of cinema, that led to the great theater's closing.

Voegtlin continued to produce spectacular shows for several years at the Miami Shores Theater and elsewhere.

I AM still trying to figure out whether Arthur Voegtlin is a very simple man or a very complicated organism. I might, at one stage of the encounter, have said that he was not only ingratiatingly a boy, but that he was a soul that one so seldom finds—a soul, let us say, that would almost rather have been born and brought up among the daisies. But later (for it took me some two weeks to get what I did at last procure) I came to the conclusion that he was perhaps, the biggest fraud in the City.

I don't mean a political, economic, or official fraud—just a nice social fraud, the kind that says, "Chase me, because I'm worth catching." Or no; now I believe that he really is a charming fellow, but that his office corps is rather too careful of him, as though he were likely to give too much of himself to the public.

At least, his secretary calmly announced on my last attempt, "Oh, yes, he's in the building, but I'm not going to let him know you are here; he talked too long to you last time."

This was almost illuminating.

I talked for two superb hours to Arthur Voegtlin in the Hippodrome.

He walks out of a tiled blank—he is terribly tall, terribly thin. Into the same stretch of mathematical construction he returns. Whether he went into the realm of the swaying elephants through a neck-cramping trap door that lets down onto steep, dusty stairs, or if he went up into the dimly lit costume rooms, I never knew.

I had no reverence for him at all, which he said he liked.

I knew that he was a big man, and when a thing is big enough, like the Statue of Liberty or the Woolworth Tower, one does not stoop; on the contrary, before great things the back of one's head knows the shoulder blades.

If he was born up a flight of stairs, he was the first in the family who knew how to come down; if he had been born deep, he would have been king ore and his value heavy in the pan.

And there is no man so generous with his time when he wants to give it. Even if the counselor for Mexico or the Sahib's slave cook is waiting for him with a boat to catch at 1:15, still he will throw his leg over the table end and tell you that he doesn't like your clothes.

And then you will weep. For what he says is terribly bitter or terribly sweet, and you laugh or weep accordingly.

Personally, I do not think there is a more ruthlessly kind man in the world. He is kind until he has got you into a corner, he is kind until he has crowded you up the steps, he is kind until he has you upon the battlements; he is kind until, with slender, symmetrical gentleness of hands he whirls you upon space, a crooked, hysterical human body shattered with the downward plunge he meant should kill you.

And when you have died at last, bathed in the vivid color of the broken flesh, he will tilt his hat back and once more put the flags at half-mast for the requiem. A captain without an army, an army without a weapon, a weapon without a single sense of compassion. And once more he will return to the De Profundis of the Hippodrome.

He is known as the "Silver King" to those who have worked with him for many years, and a soft-voiced, gentle woman who is more than charming will tell you that sometimes he does say something when he talks.

Few people have been permitted a survey of the inner life of the greatest stage in the world.

"Reporters," says Voegtlin, "are rushed through. But you," he added, "are going through on leaden feet."

In July the interior of the Hippodrome is dusk, and if I had been suddenly deprived of his guidance in the middle of that supreme abyss of adventure, I might have groped among the dust of tarnished memories girt in with rows on rows of silent, immovable, resting garments that had long ceased to glorify color upon legs with but little reverence for the laws we know. Helmets lying drunkenly upon armored shoulders, birds' heads whereon not one moth-eaten feather rustled, fripperies and golden bands for heads that rest somewhere in a darker alley, perhaps, upon the sheeting of a skylit room six flights up in Mrs. O'Grady's boarding house.

We looked down into the pit of the empty tank, and Gunga Duhl's heart was greater by a beat. (They call me that on Broadway.)

"This is the pit wherein we prove women," said Voegtlin, "the little, game women that make up a Hippodrome chorus. Down, down they go, with head erect, down into the dark and the cold, while upon the brink stands and shivers, with all the original pathos, the Adam that did not dare.

"No, a girl at the Hippodrome earns her living. There is nothing in it that can give her time to become leisurely, and it's at recess time in the heart when most 'God Bless Our Homes' are folded up and conquerors are down upon their knees searching for lost four-leaf clovers."

"How do you get your ideas?"

We had come out upon a wide-ledged window, and here Voegtlin paused, looking out upon the rain that swept around Jack's and wailed off into the distance of Broadway.

At last a smile that never failed to twist the thin-lipped mouth into a line of lure like the surf at Long Beach answered:

"Upon the elevated—in trains—along the road."

"Is that true?"

"Yes, no."

"Please, Mr. Voegtlin, be nice."

"I am nice, the nicest man in New York—everyone likes me."

"Please, Mr. Voegtlin, I want you to talk about the stage."

"Ah, yes. Nice place, the stage—only, if I had an affection for a cat I would not let it chase a stage rat; if I had a pet flower I would not let it breathe stage air; if I loved a woman I would not let her know me as a stage genius. If I had any love for it, the stage would be very different."

And so it was that at last, I thought, I was going to get

him to talk.

"What would you do?"

"I would produce weird, wonderful, Elizabethan things, with poetry of conception, with wizardry of movement, with a glowing, growing, wonderful lure, like a woman's eyes at dusk gleaming through a dimity curtain of Baxter Street (it's only in the back streets that you get the vampire). And I'd play to empty seats—no, not quite empty, Gunga Duhl should be out front—and there would be no stage manager to remind me that the public would not like this line, and there would be no Lee Shubert. In fact, there would be only me and this Gunga Duhl thing with poppies in her hair, and we would be happy, because we both dream greatly."

"And wouldn't you play for money at all?"

"I would play for the longing that there is in me to create something great and beautiful, something wonderful that would be born of me and which I could be proud of. These shows that I have here are—well, really a study in anatomy played by the masses for the classes. The laboring man as a rule does not care greatly for a show that has nothing on from the floor up—he does not care so greatly for the display of limbs. It's the classes that don't want to think, that love mass work. That's why there isn't much grumbling for places in the Hippodrome production.

"All girls get about the same position, and so there is very little jealousy and also, incidentally, there is no real great acting. Nobody ever was in the Hippodrome who turned out great afterward. I don't know why, but there just wasn't, in spite of the fact that girls have ambition,

as a rule; though there are some who drill like animals.
Men have no ambition at all, and they are left out of the
discussion altogether. We drill the mass, and the mass
masters the drill, and that's about all."

"Tell me about your plans for next season?"

"Well, the play is already named. What is it? Oh, no;
I never tell. Tell you? Well, no; I'll never tell 'you'; and
though I should love to tell Gunga Duhl, I can't, because
if I did Gunga Duhl would have it on Lee Shubert, and
that would peeve Lee very badly. He doesn't know the
name himself. No, I really can't tell you what we are going
to do next season."

"All right, don't; but listen, Mr. Voegtlin. I'm going to
write about you and I'm going to be honest. I'm going to
say that you talked a lot, but didn't say anything."

"That, Gunga Duhl, would be the biggest compliment
you could pay me, and I would be sure then that even the
persuasions of a charming thing with poppies in her hair
could not make me divulge. Come along; I'll show you
the resurrecting room."

There was nothing to do but expect it—and I expected.

Under lights that glowed like oppressed glowworms
trellised in, and under the strain of the hums of many
machines, some twenty tailors and dressmakers sat, backs
toward us, like people in a dream. They did not turn
around at our approach, they never missed a stitch in
the long seam, they never lost a rhythmic pressure of the
booted foot. They turned and sewed and turned again,
and always silently, but for the sound of the wheel—the
machine went on—a half-circle of half-finished garments
for the season of 1915.

The arc lights sweated clammily above and shone in-
gloriously down upon the ceaseless watchers over a thing
not complete, ever catching up to a perfection that would
never be quite understood as it lay in the brain and heart
of the "Silver King."

What he says is law; when he moves, mere plush is
mere plush no longer, the dust is articulate with submis-
sion. Yes, and coming back through a tiny door wherein
Voegtlin cramped and crumbled into a gargoyle twisted
out of sense of shape, and Gunga Duhl dipped and arose
panting—on past the swinging hurdles of the pony barn
and through the haymow, a bitch cried to a litter of pups
and the smell of tall grass was oppressive, and the pungent
odor of disinfectant made you grope back again where
on a slender scaffolding the bowlegged electrician mon-
keyed with baby lights and teetered ominously up in his
spectral height—among broken glass and out again into
the office, still the "Silver King" ruled.

It was "Yes, sir," on this side, and "Yes, sir," on that,
and still I had no reverence for him, and still I was un-
afraid and liked to think that he had said that he was
pleased—and the secretary spoke softly from her softer
framing hair:

"Do I know him? Oh, yes. Come to me some rainy
afternoon and I will tell you. Only you won't understand,
even then."

"Why won't I understand?"

"No one can who has not been with him a long time."

She nodded at the stage manager, a great-figured man,
who smiled in a large way.

"We can't say enough for a man who never goes backstage when there is a rehearsal, who keeps clear of all chorus girls and actresses, who is a member of the Lambs Club and who hasn't been near it in five years.

"Oh, he is so—so wonderful! When he says a thing, it goes. He never changes his mind even if he is wrong; he works by principle, and he is revered and feared and loved by all alike—only, of course, as I said before, we are prejudiced in his favor."

Come to her some rainy day and learn about him, when it had taken me two superb hours to find out, in the end, that he had been mostly interviewing me!

"May I smoke?" he asks, and lights a cigar. Standing by the door, he smokes in a long silence broken only by eyes that speak graphically—if he doesn't.

Mad, Bad, Glad Raymond Hitchcock

From his first performance in 1890 to his national popularity as "one of the storm centers of hilarity on the American stage," the lanky, raspy-voiced, blue-eyed and straw-haired Raymond Hitchcock was a natural charmer—comparable to the Frank Capra versions of Gary Cooper and James Stewart —of theatre audiences, filmgoers, and personal acquaintances.

"Hitchy," as he was known to the audiences of his time, began his career in major roles in The Burgomaster *by Booth Tarkington,* Vienna Life, The Yankee Consul, The Red Widow, The Beauty Shop—*which opened the year Barnes interviewed him—and the film* My Valet. *But it was the on-going revue,* Hitchy-Koo, *which he produced and starred in with his actress-wife, Flora Zabelle, that made him a sensation of Broadway musical theatre. The first edition of the revue opened in 1917 and a second edition appeared on Broadway the next year. The 1919* Hitchy-Koo, *with music by Cole Porter, proved the most popular, and further editions were presented over the next two years.*

In 1921, Hitchcock starred in the Ziegfeld Follies, *singing "Diamond Jim," a song about Diamond Jim Brady and Florenz Ziegfeld, for which both men were in attendance on opening night. For the next several years, Hitchy appeared on Broadway and in films, including* Redheads Preferred,

The Money Talks, *and* An Evening at Home with Hitchy.
He died of a heart condition in 1929.

JUST at what point the Social Pale begins and ends I
do not know. But wherever it may be—either leagues
within the region of the past, where ancestors lie tranquil
under the solid weight of the Ten Commandments unbroken, or leagues in the future, waiting for ancestors
to submit or rebel—wherever it is, sitting with his great
limbs crossed, his arms upon a vest of a pattern wonderful, a smile running across his face, his long blond hair
in his eyes, sits Raymond Hitchcock.

Just behind the pale, he swings his feet and gathers in
the sunlight of a day that finds no problem—and has
found none since the world began—in lighting up the lives
of the dark of deed or reputation.

You cannot get Hitchcock in small quantities; even over
the phone his presence is bulk. When you make an
appointment with him, the whole world knows; those
whom he has appointed to sit tight with him on the last
ride are going advertised.

His life is a series of pictures: his poses are pictures;
his language is as much a picture as any painting hung.
His life has been a picture of a very vivid sort. One
picture stands out in my memory. I had just groped my
way out of one of the little dressing rooms back of the
stage, and halted in my progress down toward the narrow
stage door to look into his dressing room. A million
bottles caught the first attention because of their garish
highlights, one each upon the right hip of each bottle.

And sitting above them and the huge powder box upon a high stool was the inimitable. His face was between his knees, his arms about them, like some gigantic bird, with his brilliant, almost inhuman, wide eyes dancing with some kind of pleasure. That was all. I passed on then, but if I shall see him in ten million poses hereafter, still I shall think back to his first one amid his fragrant bottles, behind him a past full of highlight and scent, of powder and of paint, while he smiled between his knees.

It is not well for a wage earner to be put suddenly down in the center of his Great Neck home, for even the strongest of us have moments when languid grapes and sunny days are stronger than the strongest things in our souls. Looking up from a trellised, red-bricked stairway that leads down to the Sound, your eyes catch the slender, pine feet of the summer house buried in the moss and seafoam—the little summer house with its Plutarch and its Dante upon the table, and its Armond Mangassarian, a lark-eyed, dark-haired, pleasant brother of Flora Zabelle, waiting for the summer to make him well.

Why try to describe it? It is a home-loving man's home, spacious, full of china fowls and pussycats and glazed with dogs.

Having lost Hitchcock for a moment (I lost and found him again fifty times that day), I wandered out along the greenbrier and grass-grown terrace and looked out over a rickety flight of steps and an older boathouse, leaning together, as the heads of the old for the final slide. I had heard that Hitchy upon a certain occasion had a dream; I had also heard that this dream dealt with a ring-tailed rhinoceros, but I had heard nothing about an eight-legged

horse. And there I saw him, Hitchy our hero, like a lost
character never found by Dickens, his head drooped
forward over the $150 padding of a eugenically all-wrong
mare.

"I don't want you to see too much of me," he called
up, removing his hat, "because it will end up like all the
other things if you do. I'll lose my reputation. I'm always
losing my reputation. I've never been able to keep one yet.
I had a good one and lost it. I had a bad one and lost
that, too. I have hardly any kind of reputation left. You've
been told I'm crazy, and if I don't look out you will find
out that I'm not and I shall be ruined.

"That," he said, climbing gingerly up the rickety stairs
and surveying the cameramen, "is the reason that I am
able to make a living. I can think up more different
kinds of reputations than any man in America. Reassure
me, let there be no halations on the dark spot that is
my life."

I shook my head. "I think you are the sanest man
I've met."

"Stop." He whirled around, and the tears almost came
into his wide, expressive eyes.

"Dejunee," he said simply, "don't." He put his hand
out and over mine, and bowed his head.

"Why?"

"People pay to see me because I'm bad and mad and
glad. If you take away the first two, you can see for
yourself that I'll bring about fifty cents in the market."

"But Hitchy, don't you want to stand straight with the
world?"

He sat down then beside me in the mottled light on

his lawn, between the peacocks and the house, and took his knees into his arms. This was the man serious, not the fool.

"Dejunee, I want to tell you something—there is nothing in the world but happiness and the giving of happiness. Nothing else matters, and when they take it away from a man they have already dug his grave. When they put that something into a man's heart that makes him put his right hand behind him when he sees you, they have already thrown the first shovelful of earth upon the coffin. I have got used to the things that are thought of me, but—," here he turned and smiled up at me," —but there's someone somewhere always, Dejunee, who is glad to take me by the hand and call me friend. When hope and ambition go out of a man's life, what's left isn't worth a tinker's damn. You could sit around with the best reputation in the world and be miserable till Hades froze over, if there was no one with whom you could spend a little time and make her smile as I have made you smile. Dejunee, hope and ambition and a smile is all there is in the world for anyone, and if they would only learn that and stop taking themselves seriously, this would be a better place.

"My life has been full of halations since the halation that the first twenty-five dollars made in my memory, when I shook the dust of Auburn off my feet and laid down the razor for the last time; right up to now, because I have been able to make people laugh.

"A halation," he explained, "is something that gets in the way of photographers. It is the sun upon a bald spot, a bright light upon a dark subject, a brilliance that takes dignity from your nose if you don't powder it.

"When I can't get a smile out of my audience, order the pine and coffin-lid screws. In fact, that's the main reason why I closed *The Beauty Shop* a week ahead of time. I was making money, but I didn't believe that I was giving that poor devil out front the worth of his ticket. I was all tired out, so I could not cheat him out of his good money, and closed.

"Look here, Dejunee, there's a lot of people who think I'm crowding them off the stage. That's why they try to poison me; that's why I have learned what a revolver looks like face-on. That's why I grin with the wide mouth God gave me, and wiggle the terrible ears that came from the same place, and sit still and accept the curse of my blond hair. There are many things I got that I didn't want at birth. This hair that I've walked under for forty-odd years wasn't of my choosing; it's the worst thing that was ever held over my head. I wanted black, curly hair, and I didn't get it. God gave me a lot of funny tools with which to go and amuse the natives, and I took those funny tools and smiled and made the public grateful for their own small mouths and close-fitting ears. When they dropped me into the marketplace I had all the qualifications for a place beside the immortals. I was a new joke, and I gave myself unreservedly."

And that is just it. He has never been afraid to be simple. He may have arisen out of the dust, but his arising was a monsoon or a sandstorm or what you will. But though it was dust and mortal clay, it did not give in to gravity.

Seeing Hitchcock at home is not a simple thing. When a man acts and when a man eats and when a man sings songs and when a man puts on or takes off flannel jackets and when a man feeds the parrots and when he gathers mulberries for you—you might imagine that employment was all that changed. And yet Hitchy's employment does not change so vastly, so completely, so astoundingly as does the man. He can be tender or terrible. Bitter or sweet, vulgar or supremely the gentleman. In good company he can be the best in the world; in bad company he can be intolerable, but at no time a bore.

He has gone through a million people on the worst street in the world, where more people have fewer laws than any germ uncatalogued. And having gone through, he knows the follies and the things that he is made of, as well as those things we often blindly imagine we have hidden.

Has anyone ever discovered that Hitchcock is a better Shaw than that person himself? Shaw says bitter things for others to interpret. Hitchcock can tell you just about what you are without uttering a word. Perhaps it is a twitch at his vest; perhaps it is only a sliding along of his pliant, satirical lips; perhaps it is a sudden dousing, over-the-eye movement of his hair. However it is, he's got your number, and he can hate or love you very greatly.

After this we went out upon the piazza.

"Hitchy," I questioned, "why do you work all summer on moving pictures, dodging over country and sea? Do you think that the picture business has even outstripped your humor?"

"Now isn't that silly?" he said slowly. "Of course not. Give the public a good play and they will flock to it like so many bees to a honey pot. Give 'em a rotten one, and they can get something as bad at home watching their offspring aspire. I'm only not letting myself forget that there is always someone waiting to push you off the horse if you are not smart—if you are not right there."

Later he called up to me from the pier. "See that schooner out there? I'm bound for her," he said, nodding in the mists of City Island. "Got to do a diving stunt for these moving picture men. Sorry I can't take you," he apologized as he shoved off, "but there are eight pirates besides myself." Halfway over he howled back, "Watch Captain Hitchy. Brother Armond will take care of you."

And so I went back to brother.

"Armond," I said, "tell me something about Hitchy. I can't make him give up a single interview."

"It speaks pretty well for him that he likes me, doesn't it?" he questioned, turning his large eyes toward me (the poor kid is pretty sick).

"Oh, I don't know."

"Well, it does. Relatives, you know, are seldom loved, but Hitchy likes his wife's relatives and her relatives like Hitchy. That is about the best thing you can say for anyone. Of course, Hitchy has been a devil."

"Eh?" I said.

"Oh, of course. You know that. What actor man isn't? But he's really wonderful—I mean he has such a personality, so different; and why kick about the things that are in the clay, when we all came from the same batch? Don't condemn and don't fly high, but take your brothers and sisters as you find them. They all heave about the same amount of good air off their lungs in the death rattle."

He subsided into a long silence, because speech tires him.

And so the afternoon went. Anyone, if he has read this far, has discovered a couple of columns back that it was not an interview—it was a friendship. He treated me like a sister, or at least like a relative. I had the run of the house. He told me I could swipe his powders, perfumes, grease paint or hair dye, and that if I wanted anything to eat to howl in French at the butler.

And about five o'clock that afternoon we heard him coming back. We didn't see the launch; we didn't hear the kick of the screw; we didn't hear the swash of the water against the sides nor the thump-thump of the motor. It was none of these that told Armond and myself that the crew was coming back. It was the faraway, yet distinct, roaring bass of Hitchy's voice as he sang a song in the coming evening, his men behind him lowered to the status of half-breeds with paint on their faces; his coat off and his body dripping from the plunge.

When the neighbors hear Hitchy coming over the hills, he says, they swear. "Some pirate!" he informed me. "Nothing sacred to me. I have absolutely no reverence for property if it looks like a good piece of scenery. Good heavens! If I am willing to get next to a good lot up here in Great Neck, they should be grateful for the advertisement and let me stand against all property that is for sale. I'm an asset, only they don't know it."

I'm Plain Mary Jones
of the U.S.A.

Upon the deaths of her husband and four children in the yellow fever epidemic of the 1860s in Memphis, and the loss of her home and possessions in the Great Chicago Fire four years later, Mary Harris Jones began attending meetings of the Knights of Labor, and over the next several years forged an identity as "Mother" to laborers and union activists throughout the United States.

As "Mother" Jones, she agitated both for union membership and, where conditions were most deplorable, for strikes. But her great popularity arose from the activist role she took during those strikes, as she cooked and cleaned house for starving workers and their children, lectured—often under harassment and the threat of imprisonment—on the rights of workers, and organized armies of housewives and children to battle against the scabs and police squads hired by the owners of the railroads and mines.

The Pittsburgh railroad strike of 1877, the Chicago Haymarket riot of 1886, the Pennsylvania coal miners' strike of 1900-1902, the Colorado copper miners' strikes of 1913 and 1914, and the New York City garment and streetcar workers' strikes of 1915-1916—all served as battlegrounds for this fiercely independent and unceasing adversary of American industrialists, who feared to directly challenge the "little old woman in a black bonnet," the image she had created for herself.

"Mother" Jones continued to be active throughout the early twentieth century, participating in the West Virginia coal miners' strike of 1923 at the age of ninety-three. Upon her one hundredth birthday, she received congratulations from major figures throughout the country, including John D. Rockefeller, Jr.—her archenemy throughout her more than fifty-three years of union activity—whose greetings provoked from her a fiery outburst, recorded by film cameras. She died in Silver Spring, Maryland later that year, in 1930.

MOTHER Jones stood up in front of me and demanded, "What do you want?"

I stood my ground, though somewhat meekly, and said that if she didn't let me get more than that I should lose my job. It worked. She said no one should lose anything through her.

And after that she sat down. A little ponderous below the belt, but sitting straightly in a high-backed chair, her hands folded in front of her—gnarled, crooked fingers, bent in a lifelong attempt to straighten things. Shadow beneath her lace, her little chin resting on the beads at her throat. Her black dress leaning about her and the ruffles of her bodice curling and welling over her breast— a small Niagara upon the bosom of a torrent.

Her silences are organic bickerings; when she does not speak she is profoundly articulate. When she is not in debate with a person she is in debate with her soul. She is supremely unconscious of her bedroom—where she is,

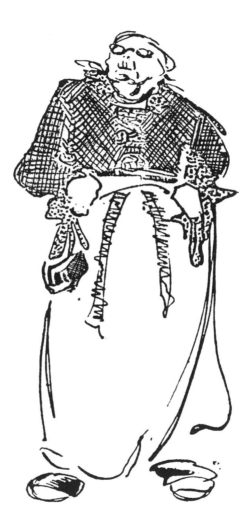

What Do You Want?

all rooms become the council chamber.

In youth one may have been a peacock, in old age one is a sparrow. Mother's movements proclaim her age: it takes eighty-two years to produce activity of the head with the inactivity of the hips. Upon thinkers, death steals from the feet up; upon laymen, from the head down.

Thus Mother proves herself.

The room was a small room in the Union Square Hotel. A bed, a couch, a few chairs—this is her social equipment.

Her clothes ceased to be in fashion when her body ceased to interest her. One may tell the exact growth of Mother's mind—her clothes date back to the fashions of eighty-two years ago.

I asked her what had started her in this work that she had taken as her life task.

It was an unfortunate remark.

She arose abruptly to her feet, she swept her arms wide in a passionate gesture. It was the universal gesture of the powerful person, it proclaimed disgust and contempt.

"And you ask me that?" she said. "That is the question that forty million other fools before you have asked. How does thunder or lightning have its start? How does the world start—it has its birth in the struggle. I was born of the struggle and the torment and the pain. A child of the wheel, a brat of the cogs, a woman of the dust. For even iron has its dust, and when a laborer sweats his sweat of blood and weeps his tears of blood a remedy is thrust upon the world. I am remedy.

"And so how can you ask, and how can I tell when I began to care? You ask because very probably none of you know—you haven't seen our lives as we live them out there in Colorado. We can tell you and you can listen, but no tragedy was ever comprehended that went from the mouth to the ear. It has to pass from the eye to the soul."

She had grasped the back of the chair with her hand and now she let go with a violence that sent her forward.

"Listen," she said. "You are a young woman, you have never seen the beginning or the ending of creation. I've borne sons; I've seen death. I've just come from the inside of the world. I've been on the under side of the watch. I've been breast-to-breast with the ticks, and I know."

Silence came into the room upon this last word and I did not speak. I found suddenly that no word in my world was the right word to say—knew that neither a "tch-tch" of the tongue nor an "Isn't that dreadful?" of the mouth would mean anything.

I just looked at her and she looked back at me, and about her mouth there had settled that subtle something that is a contemplation that has left the mind for the lips. Her mouth is no longer a mouth; it is a sermon.

"And then," she went on, "they ask me where I come from, where I was born. What does it matter? How can it change things if I am Irish from Dublin or Irish from Cork, or that I am Irish at all? It is enough that I am of the world. I'm just plain Mary Jones of the U.S.A. That's good enough for me, it will have to be good enough for you.

"I'm living—God has sent me to do this work and before it's done I can't die, and after it's done I can't die too soon. I don't care which place I go to; I shall serve. They need more than Gungha Din in hell, anyway."

And then she smiled. I thought that I should be safe

here in asking her what she thought of the suffrage question. The query was a little more wrath-provoking than the first.

She snapped instantly: "I haven't enough brains to be a suffragette—I'm too busy trying to locate the left side of the world where the heart is supposed to be."

"By that you would imply—"

"That a vote in a woman's life is like a gun in a nigger's hand. Neither of them mean any particular harm, but neither of them is capable of construction. You have got to send the woman to school to prove her ability; if she's got it, all right; if she hasn't—well, you can see for yourself what a hell Manhattan can be. The most corrupt states in the world are those where suffrage is. When I was sent to the bullpen in a suffrage state I got left there. The women never protested, never tried to free me.

"I saw one today—" She stood up and raised her arms above her head, their long lace sleeves falling like a curtain. "Feathers, feathers, crisscrossed all over her; a skirt about a foot wide! The fool looked like some stuffed horror out of a museum. I hated her, and pitied her. A woman with a skirt like that can't help being an 'incher,' and an 'incher' in life is worth—" She snapped like a man her wrinkled fingers, fingers bent and twisted, seeming to be the tortured bars to her own prison.

"Our women are going blank behind their paint. One hour out of the twenty-four should be used in comprehending the other twenty-three, yet it's not done. There's a trouble in every century and there's a solution. We always acknowledge the trouble; we always fight the solution.

"You have to associate with more than human beings to be a civilian. You have to go through your gutter and your cesspool. I've communed with bullpens, I've sat among the rats—so I know how men work.

"I have wallowed with the vermin, so I know men's minds. Rockefeller is a part of a system that he was born to—that he can't help. Only by going down into Colorado for himself, by seeing the thing on a level plane, by killing

A Skirt
About So Wide

and putting his heel upon the terrible living mass that holds him and the laboring men down, can he help them. God! don't I know what a banquet breeds? No; I've never eaten a banquet, and I never shall. The biggest impulse could be blotted out by a soda cracker. A banquet is not a meal; it's a mockery. It's not a dinner; it's a death.

"I think that Rockefeller wants to do the right thing, but he's blind. How can he see?"

And she droned on in what was plainly the returned ghost of some dream. She held her hand out, and it was shaking.

"It was raining," she said, and her voice had gone from the treble of the present to the contralto of the past. She had slipped down back through a few of the older pages of her life and was speaking softly; for time softens the voice as well as the wound.

"I remember it was raining. I had come down from Trinidad. They were driving me to the bullpens again, and there were others on the road—women and children—and it was raining and cold. Rain never means green grass to me; it always means wet babies and pneumonia. And then, again, I remember how they drove the boys out of their cell in the snow without their clothes at the point of the guns. When a backbone comes in contact with a Winchester, revolution is born.

"And the sons were driven out into the snow before them, and I had to watch them go; but worst of all, I had to watch those that stayed behind. Inside the rats crouched at my feet, and outside Mary was calling to me, 'Did you see my Johnny?' and I stood there and I knew that children are a terrible thing to have, but a more terrible thing to lose."

Mother knows profoundly the shape of creation. It is ragged and vastly irregular—it is a furrow of fear, a pasture of pain, a field of fists. All nature perceptible to Mother Jones is muscle-bound.

It is no longer a question with her what matters; it is why it matters. It is no longer a season of debate; it is the season of redress.

She is no longer satisfied with signs; she must be convinced by conclusions.

" 'What of the women and children of Ludlow?' to put the question in the form that Frank Hayes put it in his poem. What of a mother who gives birth to a child after she herself is dead? What is the significance of life on a morgue basis—citizens from a tomb? Why do we need a President? Because we procrastinate. Why must we have council? Because we are horribly casual. You say let us be unpreoccupied; I say let us be engrossed.

"What do all your so-called Christian Associations amount to? They are run by men who have walked upon the necks of the poor, who have bled money out of the working man to make the foundation, who stand upon the dead bodies of such people as mine in Colorado. All of you who have been born out of the mire stand up and say, 'Isn't she great, the sacrificing lady, the benevolent and bountiful?' and I say it's not a society, but a shambles —it's relief work made possible through slavery, it's charity through chains. It's a rotten system, kept up by your high-class robbers.

"Haven't I been approached with it! Haven't I been given invitation to lunch with the board? Haven't I been sent flowers? I don't want their lunch, I don't want their flowers. I've seen too many deaths ungarnished with the lily, too many births denied not only the frills but the physician.''

The telephone interrupted her here. It is at such times as these that one regrets Bell.

Only for a minute, however. Mother's back tells more than a gossip. It gives her away.

It is a flat, straight back, and broad. It has never had time to become individual. It is not a personal vertebra.

Upon it has lain for many years the burden of burdens. It is not a back; it is a pillar.

However, enough of comparisons. I went to the window and looked out as she stood there and phoned, and below in the soft night light people were wandering about in that aimless way that all crowds seem to have when they are seen from a hotel window three or four stories up and none of them acquaintances. It was like an Old-World village—the square, the odd little shops, the calculating perseverance of its traffic.

Someone has told me that the Union Square Hotel and Union Square are both parts of a whole such as a Thrums town might be. It is not a part of Manhattan; it is a part of a household. Even the barber rarely shaves a face unless it is a face from which he has been removing the stubble for the last ten or fifteen years; and a certain saloon resents a newcomer, even if he throws a fifty over the counter.

It was the exact setting for the little old Mother. No other place in the whole city would have seemed right. Even the carpet upon the floor—a carpet which my eye noted after traveling from the ample folds of Mother's skirt and her immense shoes to the dangling old-fashioned bag at her belt upon a tarnished silver chain—a carpet both red and homely and cheerful, a carpet such as they had in the old Grand Union Hotel—the only carpet in the world, in fact, that any homey hotel would dare tack upon its floors.

I asked her to tell me what she had wanted to be when a child; how she had lived when she was in Trinidad.

But she wouldn't.

And so it was that presently the four of us were talking across the table in the little rathskeller—James Lord, Frank Hayes, and the man who might have been in Rodin's mind when he carved out *The Thinker*.

The boy over in the corner was playing the violin and the beer upon our table was getting flat.

"Now," said I, "you boys must tell me what Mother does when she is not fighting."

I didn't much care whether they answered or not. The atmosphere was perfect: three Westerners (the first I had ever really spoken to), "Traumerei" wailing in the corner, the fat man behind the bar, and myself.

"We're tryin' to teach Mother to be cautious," the giant remarked presently, as you see, entirely ignoring my question. "She is impulsive and gets herself in Dutch saying everything that comes into her mind while she is feeling it. That's the bog temperament; that's the Irish of her. Ah! it's wonderful—for the reporters." He laughed. "It's funny, too," he went on, "how she resents children. I mean she thinks it's a fool business bearin' them, and she lays the devil into any prospective mother. But let anyone lay hands on her boys!

"The world's a common world and Mother, thank God, was born a common woman!!"

Billy Sunday Loves the Multitude, Not the Individual

William Ashley Sunday was well known as a professional baseball player before the religious conversion which led him, ultimately, to become one of the most popular evangelists of this century. Born in 1862, Billy was orphaned by his father's death in the Civil War and his mother's death soon after. By the age of fourteen, he was on his own, drifting from job to job through his home state of Iowa and playing local baseball wherever he went. Spotted by the manager of the Chicago Whitestockings, Sunday was signed by the team and played for the Whitestockings and for the Pittsburgh and Philadelphia teams until 1890. Despite his weak batting average, he made himself a name with excellent fielding and a long-standing record—broken by Ty Cobb in 1915—of ninety-five stolen bases.

It is uncertain what led to Sunday's conversion, but by 1887 he had already gained a reputation for being a "Christian" ballplayer in an age when league players were notorious drinkers, gamblers, and womanizers. Sunday began his preaching as an advance man for evangelist J. Wilber Chapman; but he soon found that his own sermons, punctuated with gyrations and gymnastics, attracted far greater crowds. Ordained in 1903 by the Chicago Presbytery, Sunday "hit the sawdust trail," preaching against the evils of liquor, sexual promiscuity, foreigners, tobacco, motion pictures, and modernism in general.

A typical Sunday performance consisted of his theatrical impersonations of the wicked, from proud society matrons and "phony liberal preachers" to dancing harlots and wobbling winos—at which point in his act, he would stumble to the back of the stage and vomit before his stunned audiences. His most famous "routine," however, was his imaginary encounter with Satan and other sinners, whom Sunday—catapulting himself across the stage boards in a reenactment of his famous baseball slide—would declare "Out!"

Female members of Sunday's audiences were often made ill by his antics—for which poet Carl Sandburg attacked him as a "slimy bunkshooter"—but the crowds grew, and by 1907 Sunday was preaching to audiences numbered in the thousands. So powerful were his followers that he is credited as one of the major forces behind Prohibition. When the new Amendment went into law in 1920, a congregation of ten thousand joined Sunday in burying "Old John Barleycorn, despoiler of man's brain and soul."

The burial of alcohol, however, left Sunday without one of his major causes, and changed the tenor of the times. Only eight years later, preaching at county fairs and small-town prayer meetings, Sunday was nearly forgotten. He died in 1935 of a heart attack.

O NE is instantly disappointed. How does one say such things; how, indeed, does one explain?

Not because he is a little older than you had been led

to expect, not because he is a little shorter, not because he is getting slightly bald—none of these things, for they would but tend to make him more human and by that more lovable—but because upon entering, upon saying, "Good morning," upon extending your hand, he is silent. Silent throughout your entrance, throughout your maneuvers to be seated without spoiling either his coat, hat, gloves, book or pictures; silent after a question.

You had expected the eagle, you find the owl.

In your mind "Billy" was a beautiful ballad. In reality he is not even a tune; he is a rest between bars.

In your mind you had seen him as a center for celestial wires; you thought he moved in wonderfully ordained spasms; had thought that he leaped—aye, plunged—bathed in the radiance of conviction; almost watched him sprawling omnipotently, almost expected to hear, upon knocking for admittance, "Nevermore," instead of "Come in."

You hear neither. He does not summon and he does not banish; he tolerates.

A man with a sudden vision? Not that, while he changes his tie and combs his hair. If one had been tempted to say Bill, and to hold out a hand, one will instead clasp the hand behind the back and say, "Sir."

Yes, one will thrust back the hand where indication always puts it, indecision and defeat, behind the coattail; there will be such a crooked smile as Grimal wore when she "woke up."

"You can have only a quarter of an hour," said Mrs. Sunday, shaking a pillow of the second of the twin beds. "We are due at the Stotesburys' shortly."

I nodded assent.

"I wish you could have gotten here sooner. I know it's just the time I specified, but we could have given you more time."

I assented once more, but inwardly I cursed that hour-and-a-half that I had spent in walking the streets of Philadelphia, a town till then a stranger to me, cursed it heartily, not because it had not been an entirely enjoyable ninety minutes discovering the little red-bricked streets and the sudden doorways and the monuments, but because I might as well have been premature and have got in on Mr. Sunday's silence sooner.

He was looking at me from beneath his rather short, thick eyebrows—fighter's tinder—the first and the last time that day that he looked at me.

Said I, "What has the war done to religion?"

"What do you mean?"

"Hasn't it affected the world's faith; there's more than one fist, they say, that has been knuckles since the war started."

"War has been the best thing for religion in the last century; it has filled the churches, it has brought men to their knees in the trenches. What are they doing in Europe? Filling their guns, yes, and emptying their hearts. There always has been war; there always should be war. There was war in Bible times; the history of the world centers about a musket; its civilization leans upon the sword.

"There's a satire in slaughter; you learn how little you count. You realize God, you know Him."

"Then you are actually arguing in favor of war?"

He Made a Dash
for the Military Brushes

"I argue nothing; I simply say, observe. Through ammunition one attains immunity; through battle one locates the knees. The eyes do not necessarily need to be acquainted with the Bible; the knees must be acquainted with the floor. The jackknife is most dangerous when half-open; the man is a direct contradiction, a man is harmless only when crouching.

"He may spring; it may be into the electric chair, it's likely to be into religion.

"You can't bathe yourself into heaven; there's no bathtub route. You may protrude like a beer drinker and get into society; you can't protrude into heaven.

"As for the war subject, however, that's as far as I'm going to go," he said. "President Wilson has asked me to be neutral, and while I have my opinions, I shall not tell them to you, or to anyone else outside of my household."

"Very well," said I, "so as not to let this conversation waver and fall short of expectations, tell me about the devil."

"What do you want to know about him?"

The answer proved that he not only knew the devil on a basis of anticipation but upon a basis of certainty.

"How is it," I queried, "that the devil is still in the ring?"

"Because you sow good by night, you need not expect to reap it in the morning—if you succumb to the devil at 3:00 P.M. you must reap him. You only plant good in one hill and the devil in the ninety-nine others; how can you expect the ring to hold only one boxer? Good is willing to shuffle off the mitts as soon as you get a divorce from the devil.

"When you hit good alongside of the face, you have taken the sofa cushions out of your future; when you shut your eyes upon it, the electric wires have been ripped from your mansion. If you dedicate your life to evil, you have dedicated your biography to the devil. You're keeping him from his sleep. He hasn't hit the Ostermoor for months because of you. Thousands of years ago he learned to sleep standing up, and let me remark here that if a man is in a business that hurts religion, it's a bad business."

"Is that in reference to your coming to New York?"

"It is."

"Aren't you coming, then?"

"I shan't come to New York until the people want me so hard that it's a call termed unanimous. They have got to stretch out their arms so darn far that their cuff links will slide up to their elbows. And they don't want me there; only a few, why? Because there's the theatre manager, there's the moving picture business; if I come where will their receipts be, where their box office returns?" He laughed for the first time, showing a fine set of teeth. "When I start whistling through Gotham, start arm-swinging for Paradise, Manhattan is going to pass up the rough show and the cabaret artist is going to dance 'round empty tables. The only chin left for her to chuck will be her own, and no one ever banters with their own anatomy. Yes; they are afraid of me, that's why."

"What is their excuse?"

"Too much slang, and I can tell you now—," here he suddenly broke loose, swinging his arms in wide circles and raising the right foot, "—that no one ever got into man's heart when he reaches over a six-inch collar and says 'Aw,' instead of 'Gee!' That grave, reserved stuff may be all right to soothe the nerves; it never hit up the steam, however. A monocle is to the soul exactly as the porthole to the ship: it looks out upon green waves, it never becomes intimate.''

''Then I'm to understand that—''

''The preachers are afraid of me.''

''Because you have set a swifter pace?''

''Naturally. Their pace was all right in the slow days, but you have got to catch up with those crazy, tango-mad, hugging-match-set-to-music people.''

''Therefore, if you got into New York and started this religious movement, it would mean that the other preachers would slide down off the pulpit by a marvelously greased exit and take a splashing movement in the direction of oblivion?''

''You have hit the nail upon the head exactly. They are afraid that after the people get used to good in the allegro they will clamor for that tempo forevermore.''

''Can't these preachers hit the gait?''

''A few.''

''Why only a few?''

''Because every one of them is not trained.''

''What do you advise as a training?''

''One has to be on a one-foot balance; the stork has the right idea. In short, baseball put me on an unequaled basis.''

''But you think most ministers would have to throw up the sponge?''

''Assuredly.''

''Aren't overestimating, are you?''

"Have you ever heard me preach?"

"No."

"Well, hear me."

"I certainly will make a best effort to that end."

"You will have a different viewpoint after you have stood it an hour or so; you will see why bicycles were done away with when automobiles came onto the scene. I've got the argument; I've got the speed and I've got the light."

"When did you first see it?"

"About twenty-nine years ago."

"What were you doing at the time?"

"Running for third, with all the bases full."

"And then—" said I, with the preliminary that all children use before the great climax. "And then?"

"Shortly thereafter I saw the right way and tried to get out of a three-year contract I then held. The boys wouldn't hear of ball without Billy, so I spoke to the Lord and I said to Him, 'If You want me to do your work, Lord, You will see that they give me back my contract. I know You wouldn't want me to break my tie with them to do Your bidding, and so I'll stick, but, Lord,' I said, 'please put a little common sense into them and make them see that it's no longer the field of the diamond that's calling, but the realm of the harp, and, Lord,' I said, 'make them hurry, for I'm starving to begin to preach Your Gospel throughout the world.' "

"And he hurried?"

"He sure did—it was a marathon. I got my contract back within the week—that's how it started."

"How many months do you expect it to take before the

beer glass sprouts geraniums?"

"It is too much of a guess, because for one thing I never expect, I only hope and no one can tell anything about hope. I am not trying to tell the Lord how to conduct His business. I'm not trying to analyze His mind as you and a lot of other fools are doing. I'm simply listening for what I can hear, and after hearing I repeat. There's a lot of you humbugging people who think that you can analyze God, think that you can theorize and philosophize —and all you've got is an infernal swelled head."

"That," said I, "comes from the desire to be literati— we're all a little bitten with the disease."

"There's no excuse."

"Very well, tell me what you think of our nightlife, for instance."

He took off his collar here to place a new blue tie just handed him by "Ma" Sunday, beneath the linen turnover.

"Hells, calcium hells—" Here he made a dash for his military brushes and grabbing "Ma's" hand broke for the front stairs. A few delegates from New Jersey who were waiting in the parlor and who had been utterly forgotten by the Sundays, looked on dazedly as he made his flying exit, as he hustled Mrs. Sunday in first, me after her and leaped in himself. "I'll be back in an hour or so, boys," he called, and the car belched derisive warnings on its way to the Stotesburys'.

And as we shot down South Garden Street and turned in, the murmur as of a resurrection came to me.

About the tabernacle there stood, in one compact, swaying mass, some forty thousand men and women, mostly women, and mostly old women.

Upon seeing this multitude, Sunday's demeanor changed as suddenly and with as little subtlety as the face of a creditor changes into a debtor. It grew radiant, it shone with suburban beatitude; it became on the moment the arc light of the public place; it ceased as suddenly to be the slumbering night light that it had been.

He fairly phosphoresced. He had been looking neither to right nor to left; he had not turned his head. One would almost say that he had been built face forward. Now he took in the breadth, the height, and the circumference of the situation.

It was at this moment that I learned the man. He loves the multitude, not the individual.

He leans upon his wife, but he leans far more upon the people. He needs "Ma's" support in the parlor, but in the tabernacle he needs the support of the public. He can hurl his sermons over the heads of twenty thousand better than over the one bowed head of the individual.

To him undoubtedly, the message of the Bible is bulk—he is morose, silent, even sullen when alone. Put him up in front of multiplied expectation and he bursts into light like a skyrocket.

Before we descended and I should lose my hold on his personality altogether, I asked him one last question.

Said I, "What city in the United States strikes you as the most redeemable?"

"Philadelphia," he answered over his astrakhan collar. "Philadelphia, because it never has got away from the Penn standard and the Quaker faith. It is the most pious, the most worthy city that I have yet preached in. It is full of new ambitions. It has many ideals: it has courage, it has faith. It may speak irreverently at times, but its soul always is saying 'Thou,' and its eyes do not have to turn inside out to catch a glimpse of religion."

He got out now, holding hands with "Ma," and still holding hands, he pulled her past the crowding line, and I, the last link, also holding on to "Ma," got inside.

Against the high-rising background of old and waiting faces Sunday stood a little nonchalantly, hand on hip, and out before him, still longer in their impressive reach, were the thousands. The effect was like a field in fall where in summer have been a million dandelions now gone to fluffy seed—white balls dotting a wide pasture—for only one head in ten broke the white and the gray predominance.

The noise was incessant, a humming buzz, the voice of a congregation taking its articulate survey of its evangelist —appraising his blue tie, his dapper, blithe figure, his laughing eyes, his fine teeth—taking in with an almost passionate reverence every new, jerked pose of this man who was going to do some writhing in the name of the Lord.

Someone, an old woman in the front, grew faint and Billy's appraising eye saw it first. Yelling to the ushers, he had her carried to the hospital, a room set aside for those overcome in the heat of one of his arguments, or should we not say assertions; for, like Whistler, he might as well remark, "I'm not arguing; I'm telling you."

"Rody" at the piano flung his fingers into the keys; a hymn by the title of "Just Trusting" soared out upon the air. Sunday whirled around and in full voice cried, waving his arms, "Not that one, not that one, Rody! It's too darn slow."

There was a wave of laughter that subsided instantly as "Rody" produced another and more racy tune.

"And now, Lord, we pray—" He closed his eyes, and as he closed them the crowd bowed upon its twenty thousand necks its reverent heads.

"And now, Lord, we want You to forgive us our sins and look kindly upon us and treat us gently in that we stumbled and know—" Still with eyes closed he comes forward to the very edge of the platform, spreading out his arms, raising them often vertically—and in this manner finished the prayer.

I had not been sitting there two minutes before I had forgotten, almost past recalling, the Billy Sunday of half-an-hour back, the Billy who had put his nose hurriedly into a tumbler half-full of milk, who had dashed up stairs, who had been discovered by me a minute later peering between the flowers and the furniture, wildly getting a rather irregular parting, making a reverse whirl in the direction of the bedchamber, grabbing his coat, bolting down three steps at a time, coming to a comical halt with his foot upon the top of the balustrade in front of a new bunch of delegates, this time from some other state, who had been invited but forgotten.

Trying to mollify them, feeding them crackers in gulps and dishes of soup at a long table, hearing "Ma" murmur about the importance of some people, who, if they did come, should be satisfied to get even a glimpse of "Pa's" famous coat whether back or front, I myself eating cheese crackers and trying to calculate in which room by minute calculation "Billy" could be reckoned as being at some particular moment at the usual rate of entrance and exit. I had forgotten that he had only met my eyes once during the entire morning, forgotten his little blare of temper when he thought I was trying to "analyze" him. I had forgotten our argument over the soul question of animal versus men. His theory is that the animal has everything over us except the one thing, soul, because he contends, animals know beauty. "Have you ever seen a peacock strut? They have all the senses, pride and courage, but no animal has a soul, because no animal was ever found on its knees." Aye, I had forgotten that "Ma" had been patting and soothing him like an irritable child—forgotten everything, because how can one help it when from this lethargy he wakes suddenly into a man so entirely different, so absolutely genial, so enormously human, so fine a comedian, so willing to gyrate, so ambitious, so light and often so logical?

And when he says such a thing as this: "No Protestant nor Episcopal preacher is worth a damn—," the embarrassed applause stopped in its first swell by the finish of a sentence that they had taken as finished too soon, "—if he does not himself agree—," his turning around and winking at "Ma," at this break of the crowd, and his remark, "They almost got in Dutch that time," and her "You shouldn't make such dreadful pauses, Pa."

As I left, the other half was being let in.

Outside they were selling for ten cents the story of his life.

John Bunny

Comedian John Bunny had perhaps more films to his credit than any other star of the silent era. So popular were the 300 and some Vitagraph films he made over a five-year period with co-star Flora Finch that fans referred to his shorts as "Bunnygraphs," "Bunnyfinches," and "Bunnyfinchgraphs."

Born the son of a British naval officer who, with his Irish wife, had emigrated to Brooklyn, Bunny ran away from home to join a passing minstrel show. For several years he worked as stage manager, actor, and director for David Belasco and others until 1910, when he signed with Vitagraph. His occasional Broadway appearances thereafter were gleefully panned by Variety and other papers, but the same tabloids had only praise for his film performances.

Bunny's screen image was that of a jovial fat man whose life was hilarious and wretched by turns. Off the screen, by all accounts, his wit, contaminated by conceit and irascibility, made others wretched. The public adored him, in part for putting up with his ill-tempered screen wife, who audiences were led to believe was his real-life wife as well; Finch and Bunny were not married, however, and despised one another. One acquaintance said of Bunny, "He wasn't as mean as W. C. Fields, but he was verging on it."

Among his most notable films are A Tale of Two Cities, Vanity Fair, Bunny All at Sea, Bunny's Honeymoon, Bunny's Birthday, and his last film, Bunny in Bunnyland,

shot the year Barnes interviewed him. Bunny became ill with
Bright's disease and died of complications a month after the
interview.

HAVING pieced together necessities of the soul and
the humor that gets past with the solemnity that
holds the two down to earth as ballast, and having attained
with the piecing a weight nearing the 300 mark, John
Bunny, moving picture actor and little friend to the thin,
looks at you out of prolonged almond eyes wherein is
the shadow of the veil drawn aside, and a great sadness
that seldom reaches his public.

Ask him what his nationality is and he will answer half-
and-half, as though he were ordering a drink; ask him
half of what and half of what again, and he will smile,
"Half English, half Irish," and then ask him what he
thinks of the Irish and he will answer, "Now, start something."

For half-an-hour I walked in John Bunny's footsteps,
for he always walks ahead, and you must of necessity
amble slowly behind, like a dog at the heels of a star.

Over his short, sandy hair he wears a cap of a check
diminutive; over his sternum bone a shirt of a stripe
majestic, and over the insteps of his jaunty, slow-moving
feet the best of canvas not used in the making of the tents
of Anthony.

This was the joy of the screen with the screen folded and
laid aside, so I gripped him by the hand and looked into
the face called funny, and wondered to see the mouth
drawn down into the lines of slack net, sadly unfulfilling

the purposes of its mesh.

"Humor," I said, "where art thou—as you live for us in the moving picture house?"

"No," he said, "I am not a humorous man. Many think I must be to get away with my laughs, but it is not because of my size nor because of my face that I have made my life a success; it is because I have intelligence. You can't make everyone understand that; nevertheless, it is the case. If I were merely funny and pounds I would have gone down at five-per day ages ago. It is the intelligence, the brain behind the mass, that makes the populace proclaim and desire. Twenty-six years I've been acting, everything from Shakespeare to a clown; Nick Bottom with Annie Russell to a darn fool with Hitchcock, and I found that it didn't pay.

"Have you ever realized," Bunny continued, in that slow drawl that sometimes broke into a lisp and sometimes into a deep, throaty chuckle, "that actors are merely public toys, playthings for the people to handle and grow tired of, toys that amuse for a time, toys that lure with the brightness of their paint, to be patronized just so long as the paint is new and bright and attractive, dropped and forgotten when it is worn off and the toy is broken and old? Dead, never to be resurrected; discarded and thrown aside for a toy more amply shaded with varnish and crimson, forgotten for a new face, a newer, larger smile, a greater capacity for tears. Who of us ever thinks of Booth? Who of us ever mentions Irving?

"Did you ever stop to think that if some ill-disposed person were to throw vitriol into this funny face that the thousands who had rocked with laughter would turn away and forget all the laughs and hours of merriment, would turn me loose into the realm of the great forgotten; that is, if I had remained an actor of the legitimate stage.

"But I have chosen a better thing. I shall live longer than Irving and Booth, not because I deserve to, but because there is a record of me that they did not leave; the public can have me always the same, so long as the pictures are preserved. To be remembered. To be remembered the feet must move. It is the single photograph that gets put away, but throw me on the screen when I'm only ashes and the people will respond the way they have always responded. Indeed, I would wager that they would rise up and become enthusiastic toward a dead comedy actor who, in pictures, went right on amusing thcm with overcountry rides in pursuit of a runaway daughter. It has a tang of the game in it. Most dead people are dead for a long while, but the moving picture actor goes right on living and loving and laughing and walking, even if he is languidly strumming upon a stringed instrument in another world.

"Oh, don't tell me," Bunny added, wiping his brow, "that the moving picture actor hasn't got it over the regular actor fifty ways. Why, in the mere matter of rehearsing and touring, every well-known actor has had to go on the road, has had to foot traveling bills, has had to listen to the temper which is called temperament of his leading lady, and has to listen to the railing of the stage manager, who is nothing but a clerk out front. He is denied his home, his church, his club. He subjects himself to all sorts of things that the moving picture actor never knows about, and wouldn't want to know, and in the end the play may be a failure. And he doesn't get the big pay that a moving picture actor gets. I get $50,000 a year. How many other legitimate actors get that?"

"But," I interrupted, "moving picture actors are looked down upon by the legitimate actors, are they not?"

"Once," he said, "the regular actor shunned us, until one day, looking to the cause of their slackness of trade, they saw us. Since then they have not crossed to the other side of the street.

"Yet the moving pictures will never take the place of the stage. They are simply a new kind of amusement. Moving pictures give you only two sides of a room, and out of your own imagination you supply the roof and the other sides. You make the actors talk. You are proud of the moving picture, yet it is not the moving pictures that you are proud of at all. It is the amount of yourself that you have put into them.

"And returning to the attitude of actors and public in general toward a moving picture star, I may say that I can pick my friends. Those that I do not like do not know me, because I won't be known. Those that I do not like may speak to me and receive a civil 'How do you do?' but they do not know my house, they do not read my books, they do not look at my pictures, they don't know my dog, they may not take me by the hand and call me comrade. If I dislike a person I don't see him, that's all. There are many that want to know me that I don't want to know. I get hundreds of letters; some of them are very pleasant, all of them are complimentary, and most of them make a touch for an autographed picture—which they get only when the letter sounds sincere. People walk up to me in the street and tell me how I have made their lives a little brighter; people come to me in the cafes and speak of my funny face; others turn about and look when they do not approach."

"What is your greatest ambition?" I asked.

"I hope to improve the moving pictures. Just how I don't want to say, but they are not nearly as perfect as they should be. I am going to experiment and try to make them better. Also, I am going to set out some rules for the improvement of the scenarios; they are often very inadequate. If I light a few more matches," he said irrelevantly, "you will think I buy them by the tree."

"What do you love more than anything else in the world, Mr. Bunny?"

"Baseball and the sea, and my wife and two boys—and my friends. But, best of all, set me adrift on a log." He laughed then and tipped his cap over his only-pair-of-eyes-in-the-world-like-them.

So let us leave him.

Irvin Cobb Boasts He Is Still Just a Country Boy

Humorist, journalist, and raconteur Irvin S. Cobb grew up in Paducah, Kentucky, the son of a Confederate soldier. Forced to support his family because of his father's growing alcoholism, the young Cobb began working as a reporter on the Paducah Daily News, *and by the age of nineteen had become that paper's managing editor.*

It was on the job with the Cincinnati Post *and the* Louisville Evening Post *in 1898 that Cobb was first able to develop his talents as a writer of humorous tales. His column, "Kentucky Sour Mash," set the tone for his witty and dark-humored presentations of Southern rebels, blacks and bourbon-swigging philosophers which were to become his hallmark.*

In 1904, Cobb set out for a job as a journalist in New York City. Unable to find a position in his first two weeks, he fired off letters to the managing editors of the City's several dailies, writing "I was probably the liveliest reporter and the best writer and the ablest editor that had ever come to New York to uplift its journalism to the highest possible level, and yet nobody had jumped at the unparalleled opportunity of hiring me." The gambit landed him a job on the Evening Sun, *and he quickly rose to a major reporting position on Joseph Pulitzer's* New York World.

While on the World *staff, he contributed a daily column and a Sunday section humor page, as well as comic works for several news syndicates and magazines. He also wrote— unsuccessfully—for the stage, including* Funabashi *and* Mr. Busybody, *both in 1908, and, in 1915, when Barnes interviewed him, a dramatization of his popular Judge Priest stories.*

That same year, Cobb was sent by the Saturday Evening Post *to report on the war in Europe, which resulted in several collections of observations—*Paths of Glory, *"Speaking of Prussians," and* The Glory of the Coming—*published through the years of World War I. At the end of the war, Cobb was made a chevalier in the French Legion of Honor.*

After the War, Cobb took to the lecture circuit and became nationally known as a raconteur in the tradition of Mark Twain and Will Rogers. By the 1920s, he had reached the apogee of his success as the New York Herald Tribune *proclaimed him the best writer of humor and horror tales, the best teller of anecdotes, and the most talented all-around reporter.*

The stock market crash of 1929 saw a decline in Cobb's popularity. Over the next decade and a half, his stories began to lose readership, and he turned to films, writing an adaptation of Judge Priest *for director John Ford, and acting in several movies, including* Steamboat Round the Bend *with Will Rogers,* Pepper *with Jane Withers, and* The Young at Heart *with Janet Gaynor.*

Cobb died of "dropsy" in 1944 at the age of sixty-seven.

ONE of the generous catcalls of destiny brought Cobb and myself face to face.

Being face to face with a lot of folks doesn't mean much; being face to face with Cobb means bewilderment.

You can't believe him. You are utterly amazed, totally skeptical: no man ever looked like that.

Still, I don't see why I should say I don't like him, because I do.

Allow me to clench my fist and sketch an impressionistic outline of the writer—we all love outlines, and his is an epic.

But no, I should have to refrain in the end from finishing it up; there are certain things in architecture that are unexplainable. Cobb is of this kind of architecture, and while he is food for the artist he is ballast for flights of fancy.

He has done himself justice.

"I'd much rather watch a summer grow than a city— you see, I'm just a country boy. I still believe in fairies and the arguments in the grocery store. I'd rather grab a fistful of raisins than a fistful of stars—though you're pretty near the one in the other," he remarked.

"A kid?" He kicked a slippered foot at his knee-pant memory, smiled at himself and chewed his cigar. "Let's pretend." He began rolling the cigar from one corner of his mouth to the other and lolling back in his chair until the ceiling was the only thing within range.

"Let's pretend—I'm twelve and catching minnows. Kids never catch any other kind of fish in stories and this is a story. Well, I'm catching minnows and what do I think of myself? I'm Chief Red Moon and a hundred Indians are under my spell. I have feathers in my hair—no—let's skip

that and pretend I'm just raw from the country. I have a
hall bedroom in Fifty-seventh Street. That's the street that
all artists, writers, and country boys locate in when
dodging the R.F.D., and the huckleberry season. Well,
I'm in my hall bedroom—by the way," he said, sitting
forward, "that makes me interrupt myself, I want to say
something about hall bedrooms—they have been sadly
overdone. When a man's famous and he shakes diamonds
around in his pocket as he used to shake fishhooks and
first teeth, he always has a post card picture with a cross
above a window so inconspicuous that the cross has to
have an arrow, and he says, with a fatuous air, 'There.
That's where I wrote *Diamond Dick, Daring Driver; or,
Wading Through Love.* It was in this little cramped room,
suffocating for air, unable to turn around, too cramped
for my typewriter to work without making alphabets over
the rafters, that I became what I am'—bosh, my dear
young lady, bosh. Most of them had just a room without
any hall to it, only they wouldn't admit it for a million
worlds. You see I'm no exception, I'm pulling the same
stuff. I had my hall bedroom period, but say, it was great!
There wasn't anything but a skylight, but then, that's
always been the only light on great inventions. One day
the hall bedroom discovered me, my skylight came down
and sprinkled me with star dust and I shivered so with
ambition that my suspenders rattled like the harness on
a stallion—and I lit out."

"Why," I inquired, "did you leave the little town in
which you were born?"

"Popular vote had something to do with it," he answered, leaning over and dexterously lighting the cigar

with a twelve-inch German match. "Also, after I had become editor of the town sheet—the *Paducah Daily News*—I thought that it was about time that I put Park Row wise to the whopping talented young salmon that had flopped over into the tank of immortalities. Well," he went on hazily, "I flopped—and made the darndest splash you ever saw—but wait a second," he added, thrusting out a level hand. "Don't let any young cub get started on the splash idea too soon. Cheek got me there, but cheek doesn't always pay. Perhaps you can back it up, and perhaps you can't. I don't think anyone is born a genius. Some are born susceptible, that's all. Writing is a thing you can learn; some slowly, some quickly, some not at all. And another thing, don't be afraid to get off the payroll after you are once on. I was afraid until just a short time ago.

"It is better to be on your own at twenty-per than a payroller at seventy-five or so, take it from me."

"But all this," I said questioningly as I waved my hands in appreciation of his den, leather-seated, polished-oaked booky—if one may use the expression—and filled with immortal caricatures of the man now before me.

"It doesn't look much like my role of country boy, does it?" he assented. "Those are things that one can't help acquiring. In this city things will come to you, and once they come, I have to keep 'em. It's not that I cannot get Manhattanized, it's that I won't. What made O. Henry and Bret Harte? Not their city eyes turned toward the country, but their country eyes turned toward the city; it pays, as the saying goes, it pays. Writing is the power to contrast—there's nothing like the eyes of a 'rube' to see the soul of a city; if you are a country boy, you can't afford to forget it.

"I'm trying to remember; I'm always trying to remember. I won't allow myself to become accustomed to sky-scrapers; they are still gosh-darned buildings, and when I see an auto I always say there ain't no such animal—yes?" He swung round in his chair to smile at a little woman who put her head in at the study door. "Will you excuse me a minute?" he said, making a dash, "my wife has an advantageous offer out in the hall." The last words died away as the study door shut behind him.

Now that he is out of the room I can make that outline of him—tall, energetic, human, homely. Some people to be patriotic have to sing "The Star-Spangled Banner"; in like wise, some people to be simple have to get down to one shirt, but all Irvin has to do is to leave the room—he's there when he isn't as much as when he is—said I, addressing the empty chair.

"Now then Irvin—"

"Isn't it the darndest name a nonbelligerent-neutral-souled Southern boy ever possessed?"

He came around from behind my chair and sat down upon his shade. "I come from an old Southern family: all families are old and Southern, just like all samplers are God blessed. Also the family was dead broke: all old Southern families are. Mine blamed it on the war. That's what all old and Southern families who are dead broke do blame it on, and down there at that time they only read two books, *Waverley* and the Bible. That's why I have a name like a passionate lover possessed of a lily hand—my grandmother had been reading through the Scott period. Men had silly names then, so I got mine. There

Irvin Cobb

were perfectly respectable names in the family, any one
of which I would die to possess. Now my father's, Josh
Cobb, can you dream a name that suits me better? Or Con
Cobb, that was in the family once as well, or Hiram Cobb
—anything, anything but this comedy name that's been
strapped to me from infancy. Of course, it has given my
daughter Buff a pretty good pseudonym. The other night
Otis Skinner was up for dinner and Buff marched up to
him, getting him by the buttonhole. 'Are you going to be
a writer, too, when you're grown up?' he inquired. 'I am,'
she returned; 'I shall be known as Irvina Cobb, I've decided on it. And when the next big war comes on and Pa
goes to write about it, his articles will be signed, "I. Cobb,
Irvina's father." ' In this manner she has me under
control."

"What do you think of relatives?"

"A limited number of relatives are all right; it's when
they begin to multiply that one wishes for the freedom
of Topsy."

"Are you satisfied with having been born funny?"

"I wasn't born funny—only, of course, as to contour.
This Roycrofty shape of mine was a scaffolding on which
no one could drape the cloak of Hamlet. I looked in the
mirror and I knew my job. Privately, as man to man, I
will admit to you that I longed to be a special murder
writer. I used to bring reeking columns to the editor. I
was a trifle bilious at the time and I wrote biliously;
in fact, in those days people died to advantage—I made
death worthwhile.

"McLoughlin was the only competitor in ugly looks that
could begin with me—but try as he would I beat him to
it."

Suddenly Irvin Cobb dropped down into seriousness.

"We're not always what we seem to be; we're not always doing what we want to do; we are not always becoming what we want to become. Many a pantaloon has bled to be a Hamlet; Eddie Foy wanted to be a Caesar. How do you know what I have wanted to be? All of us seem to be yearning to become what we were not born to be; it is our tragedy and generally our success. The world asks something of you, and you have to give. The world demanded that I become a fool, and I belong. Yet once in a while the world forgets me for a minute, or I forget the world, and a paragraph is born that would not look out of place if bordered with black. Fame isn't all that it's thought to be—the more fame you get, the more you have to live up to. You get in line for public speaking, and no man who ever had anything to say ever wanted to speak. I'm frightened to death, only I'm used to being frightened. You can get used to nearly anything, or so they say. I got used to Europe, and Europe in the year 1915 is a little harder to get used to than any personal fate."

"I heard an argument the other day," I began. "A man was contending that unless a person could be considered to have done some one or more great thing, he or she should commit suicide, if not murdered by fate before the opportunity presented itself. What do you think?"

"Well, unless you are a master at suicide, can do it nicely without messing the furniture up or spoiling your collar, I should say no, because at some one time a chance to be great comes to us all. Even if it is at the last moment, one has still a chance to change his will or say something in Latin, Latin being the language of those about to cross the river."

"But when one becomes discouraged—"

"No matter. Be anything—discouraged if you like—but don't be similar. For instance, in story writing—you see I'm back on the topic again—never use hackneyed phrases. I'm always catching myself at it. For instance, the other day I used the words, 'the candle guttered.' Now I don't know how a candle gutters, why it gutters, or, for that matter, if it has any guts, but I found myself saying it because it had already been said. Give a genius an inch and he'll make it an epoch; give him a coat and he'll make it a robe; give him a moment and he'll make it an eon—and don't tell him there isn't a chance for him, because there is. There's a chance for everybody, only he must be patient—or, no, he mustn't be patient; let him get mad enough to rear right up on his hind legs and he'll see that the world is waiting. By the way," he broke off, "don't that sound a little regular?"

"Usual, you mean."

"Sort of interviewy," he insisted.

"Certainly not," I said briskly. "Interviews never go off that way. They never tell the young aspirant to get mad; they're always admonishing him to be calm."

"I did start that way, didn't I?" he mused.

"But you didn't finish that way."

"That's because I remembered the incident of the guttering candle," he retorted, laughing and reaching out for another cigar.

"How many a day?"

"Fifteen or twenty; I have to have a limit."

"Don't call that a limit, do you?"

"At least that gets me into bed without a cigar."

Here he gave me one of his books, drew me a picture of himself (so quickly and so skillfully that I greatly fear he has done it not once but many times before) and shook hands.

"Don't give up the ship," he said, "and if you were born in the country be darned glad of the fact and keep hugging the memory of it to you. They say, Hitch your wagon to a star; I say, Hitch your cart to the calf's tail. You'll beat the wagon to it in the swiftest and biggest race of all, and don't forget this either. As soon as the city becomes familiar to you and you can pass by blocks without gasping, it's lost to you."

I was in the hall now, but I wanted to ask him a question.

"Would it be rude if I asked you what your wife had for you in the line of an advantageous offer?"

He looked down at me, and slowly his eyes, then his cheeks, and lastly his greatly amazing and humorous mouth broke into a boyish grin. "Well, you see it's this way. My wife wants a car, and she had an offer at alluringly reduced rates just as you came in, so—"

"Oh, country boy, country boy," I said and shook my head.

Jess Willard Says Girls Will Be Boxing for a Living Soon

Heavyweight champion from 1915 to 1919, 6 foot 6¼ inch tall Jess Willard was one of the largest men ever to hold the boxing title. Born near an Indian reservation in Pottawatomie County, Kansas in 1881, Willard was a latecomer to boxing. Hunter, wild-horse rider, and Kansas teamster, "Cowboy Jess"—as he was dubbed in the ring—was twenty-six before he saw his first fight.

He began his career as an "oafish clown" of a fighter, with little natural instinct for the sport—although his powerful right jab killed Bull Young in 1913. It was the chance to fight black boxer Jack Johnson, set in the racial hysteria of the day, that transformed Willard into a serious contender as the "Great White Hope."

Johnson fell in the twenty-sixth round of the April 5, 1915 match with Willard; but he later claimed the bout had been fixed, and yielded a photograph of himself, sprawled on the floor of the ring with his hand shielding his eyes from the Havana sun, to prove it. Willard remained champion nonetheless, and grew rich in the years after the fight through subsidiary activities, including a stint with Buffalo Bill's Wild West Show. World War I provided a convenient rationale to retire temporarily from boxing, which Willard had never

enjoyed, and he fought only one major bout after the cham-
pionship until 1918. The fury of boxing fans at his reluctance
to defend his title fueled the excitement surrounding Willard's
exhibition battles with Jim Golden and Tim Logan, staged
as practice trials for his contest with up-and-coming Jack
Dempsey.

The Willard-Dempsey match was billed as one of the fights
of the century, with promoter Tex Richard putting up
$100,000 for the winner. But the fight itself was anticlimactic,
as Willard bowed out at the beginning of the fourth round,
exhausted from Dempsey's arm-weary punches.

Financially broke, Willard tried a comeback in 1923 and
knocked out Floyd Johnson, but was defeated in his next
fight by Luis Angel Firpo. Willard died in Los Angeles in
1968, while working on a documentary film, The Legendary
Champions.

"WHAT does the little lady want?" Jess Willard said,
as he came toward me slowly out of the sunlight.

He moves with a certain solemnity, a sort of balanced
tonnage, with a step at once cautious and careless. His
hands seem to be embarrassed. One he left in his lap;
the other he stretched out upon the back of the sofa in
the Hermitage Hotel hallway as he looked at me kindly
tolerant, and even a little sleepily.

His head, having been overlooked by Sargent, is reproduced in every forest where cutters have been—that
gravely solemn thing, the stump of some huge tree staring
in blunt Rodinesque mutilation from the ground.

There is a little, white scar over the right eye. The hair

is black, and it attempts to curl. The eyes are gray. Sometimes humor comes into them, sometimes gravity. They are never quick nor ever very cynical. A man who earns his living with his fist is never bitter; bitterness is entirely a product of disappointed gray matter.

Nor upon his person is there any sign of opulence, no glitter of the man descending from the ropes, no aggressive tie, no glaring spats, no silk shirt, no latest cut, no mannerisms.

What is Time going to do with this ponderous Boy?

"How do you feel?"

"Me? Fine! Why?"

"I just wondered. Aren't you stuck up a bit? Don't you feel hazy about every other individuality other than your own?"

"Not a bit."

"Don't you feel in the least fatal?"

"One doesn't feel any different than a successful businessman. It's an art, that's all."

"Gloves, you mean? Ropes and boxing?"

"Exactly."

"Is it worthwhile?"

"It's the best thing in the world. Nothing like it, since it's come down into the class of scientific playing."

"In what way is it different from all old methods?"

"There, that's what gets my goat. You people are used to thinking back a million years, when a boxing match was only blood set to seconds, murder to minutes, and death to the finish. Why, there hasn't been enough blood drawn in these last few fights to make a transfusion. It's a business now, and the littlest man in the world can lick the biggest into a wail for help in ten seconds if he knows how. It isn't reach and punch. It's brains and skill.''

"Um! The skill part of that goes, but I don't recollect having seen any Hall Caine type of upper frontal bone behind the ropes—''

"What's that?''

"Nothing, nothing. You were about to remark?''

"Why, I was about to remark that women will be doing it for a living next, if it gets much more of an art.''

"You don't mean that, do you?''

"Sure, I mean it. The girls will be taking a whirl out of the mitts soon—you watch. They are great at a fight; they fizz up so easy. All you have to do is to land a punch, wink, look sassy, and you've got them in their hallelujah.''

"Do you receive love missives?''

"Stacks. I'm going to frame them and keep them for my old days, when I won't draw so high.''

"Let's not be frivolous just yet. Now, what about the ring as an uplift? Is it educational, is there anything in it that really benefits the crowd; any aesthetic value?''

"Er—yes—well, say, would you mind saying that over?''

"Not in the least. Is there any aesthetic value behind or beyond the ropes?''

"Why, I should say there might be some of it around. I hadn't noticed. Ask me something else!''

"Oh, certainly. Who is your favorite author?''

"I ain't much on reading,'' he said simply, and I came down out of the interrogation class and lifted up his palm, weighing it on my own, and found it heavy. After that I understood a lot of things.

"Now, on the level, Jess, aren't you plumb proud of

this anatomy that goes with your name?"

He looked over his length as a surveyor over an acre and smilingly shook his head. "It's too gol-darned big! When I'm welcome I'm a feast and when I'm not wanted I'm stomach trouble."

He was turning his hat over in his hands and grinning from between crooked teeth. Such a smile is disarming. It is no longer mere humor; it is poetic blasphemy. One feels sunlight, not creeping through, but shattered before you.

"Then how do you feel?"

"I've just taken the white man out of pawn. Why, what would you expect me to be but sort of sunny-like and cheerful? Yet Johnson made me 'what I am today— an' I hope he's satisfied.' Four years ago I saw him take the colors in his hand and splash the glory of our pride with the lampblack of his skill, and I just grabbed my left hand in my right and made an appointment with myself for a future date when I'd take them away from him again. Up to that time I had never laid my eyes on a mitt. I'd never thought of anything aside from horse-dealing until I thought of the master deal, and say—," he leaned over and placed his hand upon my arm, "—say, the deal went through!" he whispered amazedly. "It went through clean, and anyone who says Johnson wasn't fit is smearing him, that's clear. A man that lasted twenty-five rounds is some man, take it from me. There wasn't much the matter with Johnson. He was fine, he was fit and he was game. I just beat him at his own play, that's all. Other men before rushed him, battled sprawling, and they found the planks face down. But I knew his tricks and I knew mine, and it was skill to skill, and that's why I won out.''

"Must a man be awfully regular, abstemious, and all that sort of thing to be a champion?''

"Sure, but that's not my only recipe for keeping strong. I love the ladies, and it keeps you strong and optimistic.''

"Goodness! I thought you were married. Aren't you?'' I asked, innocently.

"Nope—not a wife yet, but am looking for the job,'' he said.

This is a part of the interview I should like to have left out, but he said it, and so I give it up reluctantly to the judgment of the public.

And in a stage whisper, let me mention, that wasn't the only fib Willard told me in the name of frolic. He said that he had never been licked and that he had never received a black eye nor an invalid nose.

Thus it is that we see the vision looming up but the man leaning down.

"What do you do to amuse yourself?''

"Oh, I eat, sing, listen to music, and sleep.''

"Cabarets?''

"They never got me,'' he answered with something like near disapproval. "I hate to eat with music. A clam can't be manipulated to a syncopated motion. And all those little feet going up and down make me nervous. I feel sure they are going to trip up or stumble or something. Anyway, men look so damn foolish when they try to lose consciousness to music. And, by the way, aren't these'' (he told me not to mention what particular names, as he didn't want to get in Dutch) "a bunch of four-flushers—

these men who go 'round with semi-fitting clothes that
make them look like a rabbit-gored carrot about the hips?"
He struck an attitude and, thrusting out his ponderous
hand, twitched his cuff. "Almost time for a little light
refreshment, Sarah," he mimicked in a high-pitched voice,
looking intently at his wrist bone, which was half-sub-
merged in black hair as some great root in moss.

He shot his cuff down, puffed his chest out and, allowing his hand to droop languidly, remarked, "Don't step
on my cane. It's very young!"

"Tell me about your boyhood. Were you a Willie-boy
or a roughneck?"

He turned the hat over once more and, still grinning,
retorted, "A roughneck, all right, all right. Do I look like
a 'Willie-boy'?" He asked this as a dyspeptic giant asks
the waiter in a growling burst of spleen, "Do I look like
a cup of tea?"

"No," I admitted.

"I should say not! Just grew up like any healthy, bad,
American boy. I'm a Yankee; put that down," he added,
indicating my paper and pencil. "Put it down before you
forget it's 'Yankee' and go and make it 'American' instead." I put it down, and he leaned back with a happy
sigh. "It's simply great to have pretty ladies come and
interview you," he said. "You begin to feel like the reason
for a butterfly net, and I'm simply crazy about the idea—
only I don't see why you aren't attached to a millionaire
or so, you reporter girls; you are all so very much more
than cunning." He placed his arm back from where he
had removed it (this, as will be remembered, was the
back of the sofa), and when he starts draping his anatomy

about any ordinary piece of furniture it goes the limit. Part of me—was using the couch. I didn't say anything, however.

"You're all bright and cheerful and happy-like. What's the reason? And say," he added, lifting my hand up and surveying the glove thereon, "you asked me the size of my mitt. What in heaven's name is the size of yours? How do you hold a pencil?"

"They are really pretty big," I admonished; "only, seen in conjunction with yours, of course they look smaller. But the public isn't interested in me. It wants to hear about you. Now, what do—"

Observe my attempt to get him off the subject, but evidently it is a pet one with him and he wasn't listening.

"I suppose those fellows that say they are millionaires are just a bunch of fakes. It's my opinion most of 'em are walking about in their income, what?"

"You are nearly right, Jess. They are a little overdue and slightly back in the rent—"

"And put the lid on the empty milk bottles on the Harlem window ledge for fear the sparrows will get it, huh?" he added. "Well, it only makes me happier with my profession. I'm glad I'm a prizefighter. I'm glad that there's one thing I can do well. Perhaps I'll last out more than ten years, if I don't get careless, and I hope I don't. You hope that for me, too, once in a while, won't you? It'll help. And I shall say to myself hereafter that perhaps the boy behind the ropes ain't much in the upper story, but he don't have to put comforters on the lower to keep them from becoming patients.

"And remember this: there's only two things that look

better near to than at a distance."

"And of such—?"

"—Is the kingdom of heaven and a dollar bill. Little lady, I'm not pretending anything. I'm out for the dollar, and make no assertions otherwise. And it's a good thing to be out for, if you get it square. After all, we're pretty much satisfied with the S behind the bars. Well, so long. I'm awfully glad to have seen you, and I hope I gave you enough—what do they call it?—dope for a story. I almost feel like repeating myself to a few paragraphs back, when I said that I really don't understand why pretty girls like you reporters have to stick at a dingy job on a newspaper when so many millionaires—oh, I forgot, they're a bunch of four-flushers back here, ain't they? Don't want me to say any more? All right, I won't. But good luck, and remember to pray that I keep going at this same unspoiled pace that I'm keeping now. I want to last more than the usual ten years."

He stood up and held out his hand. Gripping it, I leaned back and looked into his face.

"You're a nice boy, Jess," I said, "but you tripped up once or twice, so I'll stick by you in my prayers."

Ruth Roye, Greatest "Nut" in Vaudeville

Encouraged by her family to go on the stage for financial reasons, teenager Ruth Roye quickly became one of the most popular singers of the day, appearing at the Hippodrome and the Winter Garden theaters, and touring throughout the United States. Her famous syncopated style, compared favorably with the performances of Al Jolson, won her large audiences and a vaudeville record for the longest consecutive run for a one-woman show at the Palace, the most noted vaudeville theater of Manhattan.

During that six-week run, Roye popularized several songs, including "Aba Daba Honeymoon," "Ain't We Got Fun," "Waiting for the Robert E. Lee," and "I Love Mountain Music," which have become classics.

She died in New York in 1960 at the age of sixty-five.

THE joy of being pat, the gaiety of repartee, the tickle of humor, the patter of laughter, have come to Ruth Roye; but most of all, when she serves herself up, she is not *à la* this nor yet *eau de* that. She comes in ungarnished with sauces of France or giblets of England, nor is there a paper ruffle upon her corners, as upon a chop. Ruth

145

Roye is just simple, rough-tongued ginger—the greatest "nut" in vaudeville, eccentric beyond the limits of belief unless you have seen her.

She walks bowlegged across the stage, singing, and through life she goes just as unaffectedly, though straighter.

Upon the stage she syncopates her sentences; off, she is liberal with the commas.

Upon the boards she hitches up her ruff as Old Cy his overalls; in life she is still mentally hitching up something that may be a sentence to a song or a ribbon to a hat. She gurgles behind the footlights, and she sits upon her legs and growls good-naturedly behind the curtain of her dressing room because a "gosh-darned cleaner didn't know enough to do the accordion pleats right."

She pins her hair into a little sharp knob at the back of her head; she smears her palms and her cheeks with cold cream; she drops her slippers off, and then—instead of hissing behind the panel that you cannot come in just yet because "she doesn't look presentable"—she calls out a quick, jolly "Enter," and you are face to face with her as she is to herself.

You are not a visitor, you are a second mirror.

In other words, she does not seduce you; she welcomes you. She does not lure you, she admits you. She does not place before you a finale, but a personality.

She might have come from the Five Towns, she might have hailed from a dairy out in Jersey, she might have been one of ten in Staten Island. She might even have been a farmer upstate. Her accent is frightfully Yankee, her smile Irish, her birth Jewish. You don't know what to make of the program of her anatomy; therefore you expect nothing, and get a lot—that you could not have expected.

She is small. Five feet will easily reach the top pin in her curls. (It's a secret, she says; she's going to get new ones soon, they are so nice to shake.) She can't weigh more than a Scotch oatcake, and she takes up no more room than a vanity case.

"I adore being provincial," she says. "I love being new-mown hay in this city of cut flowers. I like being slangy, incorrect, incautious, and impudent. It makes me happy to chase myself across the stage. I can never quite catch up to that gol-darned little streak of lightning that keeps in front of my feet and dances in my eyes. I'm proud that I'm homely in the same way that a person accepts a birthday present, without looking for the 'sterling' until the donor has departed. Of course, I'll admit that once, a long time ago, I peered into a certain mirror and, failing to find the 'sterling,' I gave up. I accepted instead the assurance that the mirror gave me 'snap,' and here I am. And I'm happy and glad to be alive, and that's about all, please, ma'am." She folded her hands in her lap, ducked her chin and surveyed me.

"Of course," she continued, "one has off days when being funny hurts." Well, it evidently wasn't this day. She combed her hair and talked about audiences.

"I love them in Chicago—"

"That's because they love you," broke in the voice of her sister, who was sitting, Hindu fashion, high up on the top of a Saratoga trunk.

"I know it; that's a good reason, all right. I was second

girl and a nobody a few years ago, and I made a hit—it
was simply great! I put it all down to the fact that I'm
kitchen all the time. People are tired of seeing parlor."

"She has no vestibule through which you have to pass
before reaching her real self," once more broke in the
sister, this time changing her position for one less knee-
cracking.

"Aren't they, your family, dead proud of you?"

"You bet," said the sister. "I don't know where Ruth
gets the nerve. I'd die right in the middle of the stage
if I had to do the fool things she does, and make the
faces she makes, and take the attitudes she takes—"

"I really was shoved onto the stage," Ruth went on.
"I hated it in the beginning, but, oh, gee!" she gurgled
(the only simon-pure gurgle I ever heard outside of a
Chambers novel). "They couldn't get me off now with a
derrick."

She proceeded to get into her gown, a thing of chiffon,
white satin and green velvet, moaning about the accordion
pleats all the while. "That cleaner did it up so wonderfully the first time, and then he sends it like this. Do
you really think it looks so bad?" She fluffed the ruffles
out and turned around.

"Not in the least. Now, tell me, what laugh pleases
your heart the most?"

"The laugh of the man out front. No girl's, no woman's
laugh ever pleases me as much as a man's. When he
laughs—good night! You have got his whole system re-
sounding; the circles you made throwing the stone into
his pond reach the bank. A woman just ripples, and I do
hate ripples—they are the four hundred in the world of

joy, and I hate elite enjoyment as much as I hate the high handshake. When a man laughs it nearly breaks me up. There is a joy loose; they feel it, they let go, and they get their enjoyment across to you, where you can grab it with both hands and feel encouraged. But a woman —Lord!'' Then she laughed—a little, short, fluttering laugh, pursing up her lips. "That's the way, mere shirred mental vacuum.

"Now let's get down to brass tacks," she continued, pushing her pink-stockinged feet into white pumps. "This season is the best in history for the comedian; it ought to produce at least some half-dozen new and great funny men or women. Why? Because the war has taken something out of nearly every family. They want comedy this year as never before. The thing would drive them mad otherwise.''

"Why is it that comedy goes better than tragedy?'' I asked.

"Simple. People come to vaudeville houses to get what they don't get at home.''

"Do you always know when you are going to get across—that is, before you start your song?''

"The minute I land on the stage with a slam, I can taste the atmosphere. And if it's the right kind it simply grabs me by the chin and pushes me into action. But if it's chock-full of bromide and has a brown flavor— oh, well, carry me off, that's all—carry me off.''

"How do you try for effects?''

"I don't try. Why, I thought I had been telling you right along. If you're born funny you know your job, and I was, so why shouldn't I know mine?''

"Do you like popular music?"

"I love it."

"Better than classical?"

"Absolutely. Classical music has no message for me; popular music is a telegram. Perhaps," a little wistfully, "it's because I haven't got used to classical music."

"Don't you think, however, that the public should prefer—"

"Classical music to ragtime, and tragedy to comedy?" she interrupted. "No, the ordinary existence of a person is too classical and too tragical. Change the existence: make the bulk of life comedy and ragtime, and then I'll say let us have *Hamlet*."

"At what point, after all, does ragtime begin?"

"Where Verdi leaves off," laughing.

"I am looking for an actress who will admit or at least says that she stays up late, eats what she likes, loves whom she pleases and goes where her mind inclines."

"Here she is," she put her hand on her breast. "All but two items—"

"Don't strike them out, Ruth. I know one of them is going to be eating."

"No, you're wrong; I eat all the time, what I like and as much as I like. I go where I want to go and I stay up late because—," she pointed her finger at me as a mother to a naughty child, "—because I play in the evening and a play gets out about eleven or twelve, and I like my family."

"I knew you'd do it in the end."

"But how can I say I have stacks of lovers when I haven't a gol-darned one?"

Miss Ruth Roye is a female Billy Sunday. Perhaps that's where she got her original hints.

I have asked her. She says that she never copied anyone; I don't really believe she has.

Just then her cue came, and a moment later she did not skip onto the stage, nor dance upon it. She broke loose, she plunged, she hit the spotlight before it could come to her. She crashed right into the middle of it like a small-powered moth, ugly, alive, vibrating (I'm sorry the word has been used before), daring, saucy, sharp-chinned, windmilling her arms, stamping her feet, jerking her head, flinging her curls about, grotesque, living—and all of it only nineteen.

Lou Tellegen on Morals and Things

Lou Tellegen, the "last of the great matinee idols," the son of a Greek general and a Danish dancer, was raised in Holland as Idior Louis Bernard Edmund Van Dammeler. He left home at an early age, against his father's wishes, to study painting in Paris. It was there he met the great sculptor Auguste Rodin, for whom he modeled, and who helped him gain admittance to the Paris Conservatoire, where the young Van Dammeler studied dramatic art. Upon graduation, he toured South America and elsewhere before joining up with the company of Sarah Bernhardt.

His performances with "the divine Sarah" gained him a reputation in Paris and London and resulted in his traveling with the company to New York, where he performed as Bernhardt's much younger leading man in Phedre *and other plays at the Palace Theater. Lean bodied, with a finely chiseled, dark-complexioned face enhanced by large, expressive eyes, Tellegen became an immediate sensation among women theatregoers. Soon after, he left Bernhardt's company to perform in a string of mediocre plays—among them,* Maria Rosa, Taking Chances, The Ware Case, The King of Nowhere, *and from his own pen,* Blind Youth—*which nevertheless attracted long lines of female admirers at the box office.*

His private life was apparently far from happy. With his second wife, opera prima donna and screen star Geraldine Farrar, he appeared in several films, the most notable of which was The World and Its Women. *He married twice more before his death by suicide in Los Angeles in 1934 at the age of fifty-three.*

A ONE-ACT ENCOUNTER.

SCENE. *A vaultlike cellar, cold, dark, clean, resembling the better class of, let us say, Parliamental minds. At the left a short flight of spiral iron stairs, as deft in shape and as necessary as a curl-paper exterior to an iron-gray grandparent. At the head of these stairs, there is a slight opening in the wall, which at this point has gone from cement into brick. A light shines from the opening, spilling its yellow flood halfway down the stairs.*

To the right of this cavity a short row of men's, or a man's, evening clothes, a washbasin, and a few pappy-toed slippers. To the left of it a dressing table, powder, powder muff, rabbit's foot, nail file, scissors and cold cream, a bottle of perfume, a bottle of wine, a box of cigarettes, a brush done in Stewart Davies.

In the near center of the room a chair; in the chair sits LOU TELLEGEN.

At the rise of the curtain, there is discovered the indispensable PEN PERFORMER, *an interviewer from a downtown journal.*

LOU TELLEGEN *(taking a small sip at the wine glass):* What do you think of this smoking jacket *(touching it with abrupt approval)*? One should call it a smoking episode or a pipe dream—eh, what?

PEN PERFORMER: The jacket is indeed a little more than merely intelligent, I should call it an inspiration. Do you care for it?

LOU TELLEGEN: Care for it? Why, my dear madam, it is the outburst of my life. Do you smoke? *(Offering P.P. a cigarette.)*

PEN PERFORMER *(pushing gold-lined case away)*: No, thank you. I never smoke; purely a matter of economy, however. You see, smoke is always rising—

LOU TELLEGEN: What's that? Surely not a bad pun?

PEN PERFORMER: A very bad one. Will you answer me a question with absolute honesty?

LOU TELLEGEN *(putting glass down and crossing his legs)*: I shall either be honest or silent.

PEN PERFORMER: Do you consider it immoral, or merely indelicate, to enter a lady's bedroom?

LOU TELLEGEN *(with perfect composure)*: Do you remember what Oscar Wilde once said, 'No artist expects grace from the vulgar or style from the suburban intellect'? The entering of a woman's room can be either vulgar or artistic. I admit no immorality. Immorality is what? Your mind's conception of someone else's body. The man who enters Marielle Blondeau's bedroom is an artist. He comes in to prove an alibi. There must be, every now and then, two hours in his life that have been spent with a minister of police's wife—it's his way of completing his art.

That she happened to be a fool was not his fault, and he certainly made it his inspiration. He told her stories as a man tells children fairy tales. He told her he loved her because it was the only way to keep her mind sufficiently occupied to prevent her giving him away. He was an artist and he knew his materials. If she had been any different, he would have filled those two hours quite differently.

Now I'll tell you something else—the sooner you Americans get it through your heads that a play is not indecent because it happens to be connected with counterpanes and bed slippers, the sooner you will understand Shakespeare.

When 'amlet—*(breaking off and trying to make his Greek encompass the H)*—when H-amlet sees his father's ghost one should shout, 'That is impossible, no one ever saw a ghost!'

Certainly not, let us hope. But to make in your minds the scene that passed in H-amlet's, it was necessary for Shakespeare, who knew his business, to bring the ghost physically onto the stage. *(Here he lights a cigarette and after one or two subconscious puffs, holds it between first and second fingers.)*

PEN PERFORMER: Cigarettes are artists, too, aren't they?

LOU TELLEGEN *(looking up quickly, smiling):* Do you think so? I don't.

PEN PERFORMER: But they do know how to come to a picturesque finale.

LOU TELLEGEN: Perhaps you're right. Where was I?

PEN PERFORMER: You were saying that Shakespeare—or no, something about the mind.

LOU TELLEGEN: Ah, yes. If the audience fails to get in its own mind what such an entrance means, it is its own fault, and not the fault of the piece.

PEN PERFORMER *(nodding):* Yes, I see. To be indelicate one must be superficial.

LOU TELLEGEN: Exactly.

PEN PERFORMER: That leads on quite normally to the question of the hypocrisy of interviewing.

LOU TELLEGEN: But that's where you're wrong again. There is no such thing as hypocrisy. You ask questions I'm not supposed to answer, and then I answer them as I'm supposed not to.

PEN PERFORMER *(with a sigh that indicates patience):* That's not exactly the point, you see. If interviews were like that, it would turn out all right. But the interviewer never asks what he wants to, because he never gets the real truth.

LOU TELLEGEN: *(placing his hand upon his chest):* I assure you, mademoiselle, I am perfectly truthful.

PEN PERFORMER: Excellent! Excellent! Tell me what kind of a man you are offstage.

LOU TELLEGEN: Mademoiselle is very clever. Let us even say astute.

PEN PERFORMER: Then you don't answer?

LOU TELLEGEN: Mademoiselle is more than clever.

PEN PERFORMER: Have it your own way. I at least have discovered an artist.

LOU TELLEGEN: Mademoiselle is also vastly sweet. Enormously kind, peculiarly adaptable. So I kiss my hand to you.

PEN PERFORMER: Thanks, Count, thanks, I recognize you. Tell me instead which of the Ten Commandments it's most necessary for a married man to keep.

LOU TELLEGEN *(smiling as he looks into the soul of the* P.P.*)*: That which appeals most to his wife.

PEN PERFORMER: Now, Count, I hand you my Easter bonnet. You have moments of supremacy.

LOU TELLEGEN *(with sudden sobriety)*: It's terrible to be a joker in these times, when the world is carrion. Good Heavens! *(striking the table with his fist)*, it's damnable to have a profession. One almost regrets the arena.

PEN PERFORMER: Ah, that's right, you remind me. You used to be a bullfighter. Now what for? Surely that's the most inartistic thing in the world?

LOU TELLEGEN *(getting up and walking about in a circle)*: Wrong again. It's one of the most difficult of arts. At a first performance the body revolts. It is a horrible spectacle. But you begin to play the thing like a game of chess—so *(making a clear space on the dressing table and putting two articles out)*. The toreador makes a move—so *(moving the nail polish to the right of the cold cream jar)*. The bull acts on that move—so *(following up the move of the nail polish with the cold cream)*. The mind of the man is the active force of the bull. What the man does, the bull is probably more than likely to follow. A bull has a sense of location *(smiling)* but very little of brilliancy. So *(taking a swift turn with the nail polish)* the man becomes the higher civilization, he makes subtle little movements, he takes quick, half-steps, turns in his length and doubles back—he has begun to bewilder. Concentration settles in the bull's eyes; his legs fumble for the mastery of agility. He turns, he stumbles—ah, well. *(He pushes back the cold cream, the nail polish, and chafes his hands.)*

PEN PERFORMER: It makes me think of H.G. Wells.

LOU TELLEGEN: Why?

PEN PERFORMER: Why, he found a 'new force' for 'energy.'

LOU TELLEGEN: That's rather mean of you, to make quotations that I know nothing about. I'll as much as bet you just picked that sentence out without reading another line.

PEN PERFORMER: And you win, Lou Tellegen.

LOU TELLEGEN *(sighing):* Ah.

PEN PERFORMER: I've got to ask it, please forgive me. What is your ultimate ambition?

LOU TELLEGEN: To be a good actor.

PEN PERFORMER: Then you have already realized it?

LOU TELLEGEN: Mademoiselle is facetious.

PEN PERFORMER *(sighing):* Ah.

LOU TELLEGEN: I abhor mediocrity.

PEN PERFORMER: I see.

LOU TELLEGEN: And I don't believe in decency, I believe in art.

PEN PERFORMER: A fine belief, but rather risky in New York.

LOU TELLEGEN: I begin to realize it, since I have been haled to court.

PEN PERFORMER: I'm sorry. I hope you don't realize it too fully.

LOU TELLEGEN: Why?

PEN PERFORMER: One seldom finds one so charmingly indecent, so naively impure, so delicately touched, so— let us use the word profoundly—charmingly soiled.

LOU TELLEGEN: Mademoiselle, there is such a thing as an illicit handling of paints and brush. Also there is dramatic tapestry.

PEN PERFORMER: I shall soon be out of head-covering, Count. Once more, the hat is off to you.

LOU TELLEGEN: Madam makes me regret occasionally my facility. You are supergenerous.

PEN PERFORMER: Having discussed morality and immorality, is there nothing that stands between the two?

LOU TELLEGEN: Yes. The public, with eyes in both sides of its head.

PEN PERFORMER *(rising, holding out hand):* Goodbye, Count.

A PALE CERISE CURTAIN.

May Vokes

Comedienne May Vokes is best remembered for her role as Lizzie Allen, the terrified maid in The Bat, *the play by Mary Roberts Rinehart and Avery Hapwood which opened in 1920 for a run of several seasons.*

Vokes began her career in comic roles such as in The Tattooed Man—*a satirical musical by Frank Herbert in which she played the Fatima, attempting to tattoo the poet Omar Khayam—and* When Dreams Come True, *a musical comedy about immigrants new to America.*

Her interview with Barnes took place a few days after Vokes had opened in A Full House, *a farce in which she played the maid (typical of her roles), Susie from Sioux City. Throughout the last scene, Susie is in comic danger as she positions herself near a hidden ruby necklace and attempts to light a fire in the fireplace in which the thief has concealed himself.*

Vokes died in Stamford, Connecticut in 1957.

SCENE. *A small room in the Longacre Theater. The usual dressing table littered with six or seven powder puffs in various stages of scarlet. A bottle of flesh tint (of which more anon), a comb and brush, a few odd articles that are always*

*in evidence but never in use. At the back to the left is a
leather valise with the words "Sioux City" in large black
letters—such a valise as might be used by a villain to deflect
pursuit, as no one would believe the address to be his des-
tination. On a peg at the center of the stage hangs a ruffled
tango-colored suit, with a small-brimmed crimson sailor hat
above. On the trunk stands* MAY VOKES. *Just above her on
another peg hangs a long, black, tragic coat.*

At the rise of the curtain MAY VOKES *is discovered in conversation with a young woman in black—in other words, the
original* PEN PERFORMER.

MAY VOKES *(leaning back against the wall and twirling a ribbon between two revolving index fingers):* Dearie, please
don't interview me just for a few minutes. It is as bad
to plunge into publicity as it is into a cold bath. In the
meantime let us procrastinate.

P.P.: That's such an unusual order I shall have to think.

MAY VOKES: That's nice. While you're thinking I'll tell you
something that will help you to forget me. I'll make
myself insignificant; I'll dwindle, I'll become illiterate.
The illiterate are never chronicled. Now, I can't count
above three. *(Telling off her fingers.)* So—one, two,
three— *(a long pause).*

P.P.: Go on.

MAY VOKES: That's just it, I can't.

P.P.: Never mind; counting has ever been one of the lesser
necessities in the make-up of a woman. What do you say
about farce?

MAY VOKES: Once a fool always a fool.

P.P.: Meaning?

MAY VOKES: Once a Mark Twain always a Mark Twain, once a Cohan always a Cohan, once a Ford, always a Ford.

P.P.: But you chose it?

MAY VOKES: Chose it? Can you call it choosing when a child is born left-handed? Can you call it choosing when a child is given the measles? Can you call it choosing when a woman is gifted with intellectual vacancy?

P.P.: But you don't mean you disapprove of your mental capacity?

MAY VOKES *(bending down from the top of the trunk and pointing slowly from one feature to another):* Do you call this nose a help to the life of a Venus? Do you apply such lips to a Romeo? Did such eyes ever gaze into the mind of a Macbeth? Yes! But the public doesn't believe it. Of course *(dropping her tone from one of profundity to one of lightness),* I admit I'm not well balanced, dearie. I haven't any mind; I can't count. Now, for instance *(once more going back to her fingers),* one, two, three *(pausing, looking up)*—you see I stop.

P.P.: Nonsense. I like you, you're funny, but you're not an actress. I think you've gotten into the business by a mistake. Why, you are not a bit like any actress in—

MAY VOKES *(twisting up her face):* Don't! Don't! How can you hurt me so? Don't I try to be a good actress? Don't I try with all there is in me to be worthy of my income? Don't I work and work to keep the villains still?

P.P. *(in great distress):* I didn't mean you couldn't act; you must know that. Why, I screamed my head off at you. I mean you're not 'actressy.'

MAY VOKES *(heaving a sigh and placing her thumbs in her*

belt): Now, that's nice. Perhaps it's because I'm old and homely and haven't cultivated moral ferocity. You see, I like Gaby Deslys and Diamond Jim Brady and women. If there weren't any women in the world I'd have fallen down flat and stayed there, associating with the buttercups.

P.P.: Man hater?

MAY VOKES: No, but I've been brought up in a convent, and that's the way you get the sudden contrast. A girl should know all about life in the installment plan; she should go to a regular school, she should live in a regular town and should learn the regular men. Then, believe me, she'll be wise to it that they ain't all cream, extra heavy— Is that my cue?

P.P.: I didn't hear anything. You go on when they scream, don't you? *(Handling bottles and cold creams.)* What's this? *(Holding up a bottle of fluid.)*

MAY VOKES: It's to pink you up, dearie, when you're old and ugly and hate your face, as I do. Say, wouldn't you think they would give me some real straight comedy, dearie?

P.P. *(beaming):* I certainly do, Miss Vokes. I would give you anything you wanted.

MAY VOKES *(deeply touched):* Aren't you the sweet baby. You see, this part is nice, but it's burlesque, and I want so much to do straight comedy. *(Suddenly—)* Did you know it was me that first sang "I'm Afraid to Go Home in the Dark"?

P.P.: Good heavens! Did you, and won't they let you sing any more?

MAY VOKES *(pointing to the dressing mirror, about which there*

are many telegrams and letters): See them! All of them
from people who believed; one from a man out in Ohio,
who calls my attention to the fact that I owe him ali-
mony. I guess he means that song, 'Hang Out the Front
Door Key' he wrote for me. *(As she speaks and as the
time passes, the coat is slowly dislodged from the peg,
coming nearer and nearer its ultimate fall.)* If you live in
the Middle West, dearie, you not only know everyone's
mistakes, you know his conscience.

P.P.: Do you like playing out there?

MAY VOKES *(simply):* I come from there, you know.

*(There is a pause, in which is heard at intervals the wail
of a rainstorm outside, and through it the high-pitched
screaming of a stage cat. At a distance through an open
door to the middle left is seen a woman in lace and chiffon,
a man in shirt sleeves—the characters as they dash on and
off—and at the head of a flight of improvised steps offstage sit Otillie and her aunt from Yonkers, waiting for their
cues; draggled and unhappy in appearance, Otillie with a
perfume bottle and her aunt with a powder rag and an
orangewood stick. Through the thin boards of the stage
house one hears the blustering bawl of Nicholas King, a
stranger.)*

P.P. *(who has slowly passed from one article to the other on
the long shelf and now is gazing fixedly at a picture of*
MAY VOKES *as Phoebe in* The Quaker Girl*): Why! You
know, you are almost pretty!

MAY VOKES *(in a startled half-whisper):* What?

P.P.: I said you were almost pretty.

MAY VOKES *(a little bitterly):* Aw, dearie, that's what lets
a lot of us out.

P.P. *(looking away from the photograph to the figure on the trunk, still stroking the Shavian dog):* Those jewels that you put in your stocking in the first act have slipped down.

MAY VOKES *(stretching out her foot):* They're supposed to. King's got to see them in the last act.

P.P.: Don't you think that it is a rather risky thing to keep money in stockings, as so many of our women do?

MAY VOKES: That's like whiskey and cigarettes. Drink if you want to drink, smoke if you want to smoke, put your capital in your hosiery if you want to put it there; anything, so that you go to your reckoning individually.

P.P.: It's strange to think you can't count—I don't believe that now.

MAY VOKES *(raising her eyebrows):* Why, I never had any mentality, dearie; I wasn't any good in school at all. That's why I was shoved on the stage. They thought that being impervious to algebra I'd be impervious to anything, even contamination and propinquity.

P.P. *(amused):* It's so, isn't it?

MAY VOKES: In a way. It's because I am lazy, the original procrastinator, dearie, the laziest thing this side of death and the most grateful.

P.P.: Why grateful?

MAY VOKES *(irrelevantly):* Don't you love tea parties?

P.P.: I never go to them any more.

MAY VOKES: I mean grown-up tea parties.

P.P.: Oh, yes, once in a while. But it makes one nervous to stretch across a dowager's stomach with a cup of boiling tea and say 'Charmed!' and 'How do you do?' and 'Mrs. Allen's foot got twisted out of place the other day by an irregularity in the pavement.'

MAY VOKES: I love 'em—parties, I mean. I don't see why you can't be human and an actress at the same time. I have tea parties and invite everyone that's nice. *(Aside:)* I'm going to invite you to the next. You must get to be friendly with the world instead of friendly at it.

P.P.: Most actresses say they go straight to bed after a performance.

MAY VOKES: That's just it. I guess they do.

P.P.: But you admit you don't.

MAY VOKES: That's because I haven't any regular mind. If I had, I suppose I'd do things as others do. Some day out of the money I shall have saved by being my own maid, I shall buy a shack. I can never hope to have a real house—they are dreadfully expensive, aren't they? But a shack, why that's within the possibilities of a horse-radish hawker. It will be brown and rough and my family *(the* PEN PERFORMER *gasps)*—only a dog, dearie— shall ever be with me. Isn't that a dream to have?

P.P. *(starting):* I think they are going to scream—

(There is an abrupt silence. Outside the rain can still be heard crying across the roofs and spanking the Broadway taxis into a hurrying line of refugees. The voice of the stage cat has dropped down into a low complaint. Suddenly there is heard a long piercing scream from the stage. MAY VOKES *makes a short, sharp movement, and in so doing dislodges the long, black, tragic coat, which settles down across her shoulders, completely enveloping her.)*

MAY VOKES *(in a whisper):* You see! Poor little bird.

(At this moment the curtain descends.)

A Philosopher Among Russian Dancers

Trained at St. Petersburg's renowned Imperial School of Ballet, Adolf Bolm began his extraordinary ballet career in 1904 as a soloist with the Maryinsky Theater. It was his tour with Pavlova in 1908, however, that established him in the roles of the Chief Warrior in Prince Igor *and Pierrot in* Carnaval. *His fiery and energetic performance as the Chief Warrior, particularly, is credited—as* The Dictionary of Modern Ballet *notes—with "restoring the male dancer to his rightful place in ballet as the equal of the ballerina, not just a* porteur."

From 1909 to 1917 Bolm danced with Serge Diaghilev's Ballets Russes, where his fame eclipsed even that of the celebrated Nijinsky. But following his second American tour with Diaghilev, Bolm chose to remain in the United States to organize his own company, the Ballet Intime, in New York.

Successful as a teacher and choreographer, Bolm was also an early pioneer in film choreography, eventually moving to Hollywood to choreograph Donald Cook in The Mad Genius, *Loretta Young in* The Men in Her Life, *and the dance scenes in* The Life of Cellini. *Bolm continued, moreover, to stage ballet works such as Soviet composer Alexander Mossolov's* The Iron Foundry *and the 1940 production of Serge Prokofiev's* Peter and the Wolf.

He died in 1951, a major force in American ballet, re-
membered as an internationally acclaimed classical dancer.

Léon Bakst, of whom Bolm and Barnes speak in this inter-
view, was the set designer for several ballets performed by
the Ballets Russes, including Cléopâtre *(1909),* Schéhérazade
(1910), and Nijinsky's Le Spectre de la Rose *(1911).*

THE tumult and the shouting dies, the pressmen and
the veils depart—and what is left? Some cosmetic
errors, the sound of the stretching of the arches of multi-
tudinous feet, and Adolf Bolm.

He it is who has discovered himself next to Nijinsky,
now that Nijinsky has gone. He is the pampered, over-
familiar Le Negre, of the chasing of that top-heavy though
attractive, high-hipped Zobeide. He, who is *chef guerrier*
of *Le Prince Igor*, not forgotten in *Les Sylphides* and still
on view in *La Princess Enchantée* and *Soleil du Nuit*.

He comes through the milieu of the Ballet with the smile
of the man who suffers in three languages.

"Bakst—ah, there you have not only the savage, you
have also the artist. I have often thought, how dreadful
to be the picture—you know what I mean? No? I shall
explain. Notice the eye of the connoisseur of arts, then
imagine yourself their goal. See? It is so with the costume.
Therefore, I say, how dreadful to be the picture, but how
still more lamentable to be the costume.

"Bakst is a successful organ; he has a keen appetite,
a nose for cafes, a delightful sense of humor, an impressive style of flirting. His advances are of a marked and
successful nature, considering his natural inborn plain-

ness. Of his retreats one might say they are masterly. He sails a boat and drinks tea with graceful repugnance.

"He has, however, one fault—ah, an immense trifle—his headgear. The hoods, the turbans, the whatnots that he conceives for the heads of his disciples. Beautiful? Yes, as only ugly and vulgar things are, but—"

He paused, knocking his gold cigarette case upon his palm. "But my friend Léon forgets that in the classic arts the feet should have preeminence.

"Is Bakst new, is his art the art of the creator? Often I am asked that, very often I hear others asked that. There is an answer. The tragedy of man—there had been a past. The tragedy of nature—there will be a future.

"Without your yesterdays all would be great today. No, of course, Bakst is not new. Egypt may have been built on the dust of an older Egypt, Rome may have fallen once again on Rome.

"In Russia there are other Russians—better perhaps, and also perhaps not. Bakst happened to come when he was needed, when the world was ready for him.

"It is harder, I admit, to become known for what one has not done than for what one has. Bakst took the easiest way, he became known for what he did. Not for his restraint, but for his vigor. One can say of him what Wilde said of Hall Caine: he creates at the top of his voice.

"Therefore it is that one should not say Bakst dares, one should say, Bakst dares again.

"Some of his designs are purely graphic. From the mind, for the paper. These are the kinds I have reference to, when I say how painful to be the costume. I have had to outrage Bakst, because Bakst has outraged me.

"He invents, say, something he considered decorative, but imagine trying to dance entangled with all the intricacies of Bakst's mind.

"Well, we have made our concessions, each to the other," he added.

When I asked him if America could appreciate Russian art, he answered:

"You are not asked to understand Russia. You are asked to feel. One does not understand death, one only reacts to it."

I said that the whole production had struck most of us as art under the skin. "A matter," I added, "of gastric acoustics, arteries and undressing or overdressing"; also concluding, "but only of the kind we lament because that savage sharpness, that peasant bitterness and vitality given us so richly in the literature of the Russian and in the Russian history, is missing.

"In other words, they seem to be economizing on perspiration," I finished.

"He has fallen into the estate of the man who forgets that destruction is more necessary than construction. The rich perversity of a decaying flower is only transcribable in the still richer, still more perverse flare of the decaying art. The happier midways of life and death. The conception that feeds on itself—that is the most beautiful and the most destructive. Bakst has forgotten, it seems to me, and has instead tried to make something too new, and in consequence has made it too raw. Wounds are all very well but only in that they bleed. Bakst is a wound in which the arteries refuse their waters.

"Yes and no, as the peasant says"; Bolm shook his head.

"I admit that he is not always simple. That is what I tried to point out just a few minutes ago. It is his insincerity that sometimes gets in his way. Nevertheless, his art is a fine thing and the world is coming to know that, and then there will be others.

"Now let me say something that touches America. You want too many doctors. Only people who go around with the assurance given by *medicins* could expurgate so freely your books and shave down to so fine a point your arts. When you have ceased to have stomach troubles, you will not mind the hard and healthy spleen of the children of *L'Après-Midi d'un Faune*."

Wilson Mizner—of Forty-fourth Street

No other country than the United States could have pro-
duced the combined wit and hucksterism of Wilson Mizner.
A disgrace to his old-line, California family, Mizner cashed
in on nearly every available source of legitimate and illegiti-
mate profit available to the conman at the turn of the century.
From hawking for a medicine show to jumping claims in the
Yukon, from managing a flophouse in Manhattan's Tender-
loin to working transatlantic liners as a cardsharp, Mizner
seemingly set out to prove his famous quip, "Money, to be
worth striving for, must have blood and perspiration on it—
preferably that of someone else."

Mizner managed several mediocre prizefighters in the years
of the search for the "Great White Hope" and wrote several
moderately successful plays with collaborator Paul Armstrong.
Shirking the daylight hours and the labor associated with
them, Mizner managed well enough to live by night the
insouciant lifestyle of New York's man-about-town. As he
he once said, "I hate work like the Lord hates St. Louis."
His caricature was familiar to everyone who read the news-
paper, as he nightly caroused with a circle of admiring friends,
who at various times included Diamond Jim Brady, Lillian
Russell (whom Brady was fearful Mizner might steal from

him), Irvin Cobb and II. L. Mencken. Irving Berlin dedicated a song to him, titled "The Black Sheep Has Come Back to the Fold," which the nonconforming Mizner took as an insult. He succeeded briefly in persuading one of New York society's wealthiest widows to be his wife; fortunately for his bride, Mizner's designs on her art collection became clear at an early stage of the marriage, and she showed him the door. Asked once about his famous liaisons with beautiful women, Mizner replied, "To my embarrassment, I was born in bed with a lady."

During the early 1920s Wilson collaborated with his architect brother, Addison, on a multimillion-dollar land speculation deal in Florida. Almost overnight they made fortunes and just as quickly lost them again when the bottom predictably fell out of the market. Few men were shrewder than Wilson at making a dollar out of nothing—or less talented in holding onto it.

Wilson turned to Hollywood for income, writing several film scripts and serving as inspiration for movie creations, including the Clark Gable role in San Francisco *(written by his friend Anita Loos and his associate Bob Hopkins) and the William Powell part in* One Way Passage. *Mizner also prompted construction of the famous Hollywood restaurant The Brown Derby, and presided nightly as wit-in-residence in Booth 50. Indeed, his extraordinary humor never left him. Receiving a wire in February 1933 that his brother lay dying, Wilson cabled back, "Stop dying. Am trying to write comedy." Within three months he also was dead.*

WITH hands outspread in hope of collecting profit, I came into the presence of Wilson Mizner, and therein he threw the tinsel of his wit.

I well knew that, as a moral diver, Wilson would come up covered with histrionic stars, and I well knew that when Wilson went walking for the benefit of humanity—for their uplift—he would take with him one perfect and well-built bomb. Well did I know that, like myself (for both of us have suffered disillusionment), Mizner could

> love now without regret
> And without jealousy—a few slow tears
> Only—

but what's the use of finishing?

If I knew Mizner better and less, I should in all probability refrain from showing him up in an article. But as I know him much and little, I dare, from very ignorance, attempt to lay upon paper a few of the Mizner pigments.

Wilson is a sort of high-hipped epigram. He says he has not been East, South, North or West of Forty-fourth Street in as many years. In fact, he calls it the "real Bowery," and there he says he wants to live.

I had dinner with him not long ago, and over his alligator pear and his liver and bacon discovered that he had not altered much.

Two years ago he had believed in the bed as a national institution, for from bed one never got ill treatment. To this he still adhered; in fact, when he came in at 2:10, he had only been up a few minutes. He was lyrical with the death of roses, and resplendent with talcum. Two years ago he avowed that he was "full of larceny." He said that so far as he knew the larceny high-watermark always kept its date with the ebb and flow tide, and that he had never known a dull season. Two years ago he believed in human nature; he still believes in it. He has a friend in whom he has implicit trust. He always transfers his money to this man's pockets, for "there," he says, "he will never think to look."

Two years ago Wilson was making money, and today nothing very noticeable has happened to his pocketbook. Two years ago he was a master schemer, poring over his friends as Holmes over a case, extracting everything, including evidence, and then calling it a "very extraordinary case, indeed." Today he is as full of schemes. He is betting now. He has a friend weighing something like ninety pounds, who has, he asserts, probably the largest feet in America. He saw this man's possibilities. He intends to hang this man's feet out of a window and make curb bets with whomsoever has the "kale" on their possessor's probable weight. "After that," he says, "I shall retire handsomely."

Has he altered? Not much, you see. Wilson is thinner, due to underexertion. One loses flesh when one does "not stop to think." "And when I stop to think," he adds, "I shall know that it is the beginning of the decline and fall. I loathe, abominate, and detest a thinker. They are always so occupied that the world slips by them, leaving them nothing but its coat in their hands, which they examine and analyze, thinking it to be the man."

And there you have Wilson in his present stage.

Wilson has his old laugh with him; a laugh like a submerged French pastry shop. He has the same happy, carefree, light step of the professional tiptoer. He has grown calluses on the soles of his feet in his discretion with the pasts of his friends, which he edits to a perfection seldom attained by our most expert editorial craniums. He will not leave the world while there is anything in it. He will leave it only when it is begging. In other words, according to Mizner, he can hear a ten-dollar bill fall upon the plush carpet of the tenth floor of any apartment.

His memoirs fall from him like leaves in autumn, leaving only a brazen branch.

He spoke of the war, he spoke of love, he mentioned his personal likes and dislikes, he discussed Bohemia, he spoke of books, he told me of journalism, he conversed on the subject of stocks and racing. In the end he demanded of me, "What do you expect a man to say if you don't ask him a few intelligent questions, such as, 'What kind of tea, Mr. Mizner, do you use in your bath?' and, 'Do you think the moving pictures will make serious inroads on the profitable parts of Shakespeare?'"

Therefore, I chose a subject tenderly, carefully, as one lifts up a lump of sugar for the sweetening of tea. I asked:

"What do you think of the trouble abroad?"

He answered, "I hear they are quarreling."

I sat back, reflecting: if this is the way I am to draw him out, I shall have to be more explicit. I said:

"What would you do if we should get into war?"

He said: "I should lead the boys back. I should lead them so far back that it would take a Michigan search warrant to find us, and that is as long as a Hot Springs drug bill."

I said: "Oh!"

"Yes," he answered, "very oh!"

He added, "It's your turn to pass again."

Therefore, sitting back upon the plush cushions of the Claridge lounge, I asked: "What do you think of journalism?"

He answered: "I have not heard of it. What is it? A sort of paper corpse of reportorial parts of intellectuals?"

So I left that subject.

Next I asked him his opinion of artists.

"Do you mean Bohemians?" he queried.

"Yes."

"The Washington Square kind?"

I said: "Any kind."

"Well," he answered, putting a bit of butter on a crumb, "they are so well fed. Why, I tell you that you don't know anything about poverty, you artists, until you learn to appreciate the sweat on a bakery window.

"Then they all think they are 'devilish' and 'individual.' Why, not one of them has murdered anybody in a still street, or throttled a wench under a cold water faucet. Nor have they practiced thuggery, beggary, or thievery. They don't know what it is to porchclimb, and they have never committed social improprieties—they don't marry, so they can't. You see, they protect themselves from originality, that's all.

"Now," he went on, drawing a plan on the tablecloth, "speaking of thuggery (a nice word, by the way), I probably—but no," he added hastily, "let us change the subject. I have the trained eye of the hunted, and the ear of the bush croucher. Let us talk about writing."

So I told him to begin.

"Well, speaking of myself, it was just a tossup whether

I should be the great man I am, or whether I shouldn't. It was this way. George Bronson Howard kept pulling me by the sleeve, to tell me what a God-given thing his genius was: how pure and how miraculous a thing; how occasionally, in stammering, God brought out a great word; and then he stopped and looked meaning. I got sore, and lanced him where he bled pure English. 'Listen,' I said, 'I can write the same sort of thing you are writing in four hours! Mind,' I added, 'I am not saying this to prove that I am a marvel who has just arisen from the pastures of genius with a four-leaf clover in my front teeth, but merely to belittle your bunk on the God-given gift stuff.' He went quite white, and fumbled his butter. Addison, my brother, was there when I came down from my room with the fruits of my wager. He read it, and said it was not bad. I took it to a publisher, who asked me about one passage in it, running, 'I will pick you some wildflowers, and when I tame them I will give them to you.' 'Pretty rotten, Bill,' he says, and laughs kind of unhappy-like that he had to stick the quill of editorial disapproval so far up to the hilt into my quivering genius. I laughed, too, and told him I guessed it was pretty bad, but that it was a bet. My first—and I was twenty-seven, and probably 'pretty well set' by that time, and could not come out of the final mould of congenital stupidity into a more liquid state where I might be poured into approval. I went away and threw the story into a basket.

"A few days later Addison tossed me a check of $500, and told me that the accepting party wanted me to sign up at once. So you see by what a narrow margin great men are made," he concluded.

Wilson Mizner

I then asked him what he thought of poetry as an art.

"Poetry," he answered, "has never got me where I am deepest. If it had," he added, looking out of the window, "it would never have returned. But occasionally some verse is flung into the pool of my intellect and stays there:

> I'm like some king in whose corrupted veins
> Flows aged blood, who rules a land of rains;
> Who, young in years, is old in all distress,
> Who flees good counsel to find weariness.
>
> . . . .
>
> Whose weary face emotion moves no more
> E'en when his people die before his door—

He touched the corner of his left eye with the napkin. "Now," he said in a husky voice, "quote me something of yours, but make it cheerful." He slipped his fork under a mocha tart, and leaned back. Therefore, I began:

> I came before you when you died,
> I laid the gilded braids aside,
> And peered into your face,
> The pattern of some yellow lace
> Lay on your heart—

"Stop!" thundered Wilson, half rising from his seat. "I don't want to hear another word." He sat down again. "Pure black coffee above the ears," he added, "intellectual cream-puffery. I'm ashamed of you—no, it's good stuff, but I'm hungry."

I subsided. "Why go on with poetry?" he inquired, kindly-like, but firm. "Poetry is all right in its place, beside a log fire, when you have got your slippers and dressing gown on, and there is nobody about to watch you make yourself a fool or something else pagan that poetry is warranted to do. Let us speak of the moving picture business instead."

So I asked him.

"Well," he said, dreamily, "I have just had an offer of $2,400 a week if I will appear in a film of my own life. Now, you know, the Pope couldn't stand two hours of his life on the film. And then again, I am vain. You may not have noticed it, but I am. I freely admit that I am. I also freely and honestly state that I hate to be made a fool of. I don't mind making one of myself, but I object to the kind of a fool that a camera makes me. I take like a bloodhound with the mind of a Pekingese, and am lined over like a state road map. It might amuse my enemies, but I must think of my friends."

"Still," I interpolated, "$2,400 a week isn't so bad."

"Twenty-four hundred is all right when you can spend it without first having lost caste."

"What do you fear—ridicule from some loved one?"

Haughtily he answered: "Love is laughable."

Said I: "Are you, then, so respectable?"

"Not respectable, just unlucky," said Wilson.

"Well, then, let us talk of other things."

We did, for quite a while. His thin and well-kept hands began to stray into a cigarette case. Ovals of opulent opalescence—his nails. I asked him what he was concentrating on.

"Concentrating?" he queried. "I know better. I have seen the effects of concentration on a hen. I took one once and drew its bill along a chalked line for about three seconds. That poor hen just bent down and flopped

over and lay still in a corner for the rest of the morning
without taking its poor, amazed eye off futurity. I know
that if it affected that bird to that extent, merely to con-
centrate on a chalk line for a few seconds, that I would
lie blinking here in the corner until three tomorrow, and
would be a defective for the rest of my life. No, there
are some things that even I won't do, and concentrating
is one of them. If people would stop concentrating, there
would not be enough sustained interest to keep the blood
on the spears in Europe. With less concentration people
might not build houses, but they certainly wouldn't
wreck homes.''

And this was almost all. We finished our demitasse,
we ate the last crumbs of our mocha tarts. We smoked
our last cigarette, and then, arising, we went out into the
chilly street, Wilson with his coat collar well up around
his neck, and I tight-buttoned my wraps. We strolled
along to the corner, where about the Claridge bar entrance lingered all the old part of what used to be the
young theatrical talents. Men in old and faded glory, the
tight-fitting actor man clothes, the arm-hanging cane. A
little Hamlet left in their ears, a little Romeo in their eyes,
and a little Shylock in their hearts. Something of their
past glory still rested in their joints, and there it had
rusted until, halting, like old speeches, they go in good
company to the grave.

Some of them smiled at Wilson as he passed, and one
called out something about the races, to which Wilson
answered something about a game at roulette. Two or
three of them laughed; only one swung his cane, hitting
the top of his boot, looking at the ground. One took out

a pocket file and began to file his nails. It made me think of one of O. Henry's unfinished stories, I think the last he wrote. I turned away. Some luring lingeries in a shop window took my eye, where the ribbons caught at the lace, disappearing beneath a band of silk, to reappear again. I heard Wilson talking at my side.

"Someone should write up Broadway. Really, you know, not just the white lights, and the painted women, and all that bunk—but really write it up from the standpoint of one who knows more than he sees, hears more than he tells, and says more than he means."

"That's just it," I answered. "To know it well enough, one has to have lived with it."

"Ah, yes," he said, "that's the point. And then, when you have lived with it, you do not tell. One treats the place in which one lives as one treats a woman. A kiss, and say nothing. Well, I have kissed Broadway—and I'm a gentleman." He threw his arms out. "Oh, for a peep into the diary of one of its days, into the black book of one of its nights—"

Before letting him go, I pulled him by the sleeve. "Wilson," I said, "tell me just one more thing. What advice would you give to the young and aspiring?"

He turned around, and taking me by the elbow, looked earnestly into my face.

"Child," he said solemnly, "give him a soul full of larceny—make him like the man who offered to buy my copy of *The Last Supper* at a dollar the plate. Make him scheming and indolent—with those things he can attain almost anything without getting the death sweat on every sentence—only," he added, "don't forget to give him a dose of caution. Make him so stingy by nature that he won't let you set your watch by his clock. After which, I should say that the lad would turn out to be a fairly respectable bounder."

And there he wanted to leave it, but, still not content, I stopped him in the middle of the car tracks to add: "That's all very well, Wilson, but supposing he has no mentality; supposing he believes in something or other, perhaps the freedom of the votes, the labor question or anarchy. Supposing he thinks that honesty is the best policy, or that larceny is immoral—what then?"

"Then," said Mizner, and his voice fell into that deep bass men keep for their thoughtful moments, "then— well, then give him a bath." And he sidestepped a Pierce-Arrow that came merrily down Forty-fourth Street West.

"Wait, wait," I cried, running after him. "Tell me what you think of the subject of death and funerals."

He turned around and wiped his forehead. "My God!" he said at last, "am I to be held up for intellectual plunder all the way to my office? The jewels of my speech that I have already lavished on you would make you a pair of suspenders. What do I think of death? I suppose you are writing about that. In youth one always does, as one always writes juvenile plays at seventy. Well, I don't mind telling you: death is the final guffaw of life; the funeral is only a Pullman ride straight through to the last stop. Death is a habit. You cannot break yourself of it—it's rather a good one."

"Then you do not fear it?"

"I fear nothing so safe. Live a hazardous life, and you will slip into death as you slip into a bath—but why end our conversation with anything so tragic?'' he asked, half-way up the block. ''Ask me something cheerful before you leave.''

So I asked him what he thought the national drama should consist of.

''My idea for a national drama is, as I once said, two corpulent gentlemen lying on twin cots: all is sleep.''

And he was gone.

David Belasco Dreams

Born of a father who himself had theatrical experience, David Belasco began acting, writing, and producing as early as twelve years of age. In 1873 he began as a call-boy at the Metropolitan Theater in San Francisco, and by 1876 had become stage manager at Baldwin's Academy of Music nearby. In the same year he served briefly as secretary to Irish-born playwright Dion Boucicault, from whom he learned the talent and passion for the sensational melodramas that were to become his forte, and were to dominate the American stage through his productions.

In La Belle Russe *six years later, Belasco found his first writing success, one which lasted through more than fifty plays, including* The Heart of Maryland, Du Barry, The Darling of the Gods, *and* The Return of Peter Grimm. *Belasco's most lasting contributions to theatre literature were* Madame Butterfly, *produced in 1900, and* The Girl of the Golden West, *produced in 1905, both of which served as libretti for operas by Giacomo Puccini.*

Belasco's major impact on American theatre did not lie in his scripts, however, but in his role as producer and director. With a penchant for spectacular productions and large gestures, and with a particular fascination with theatrical light-

*ing, Belasco produced plays that, as he described it, "Tug[ged]
at the hearts of [his] audience." Full of wicked sisters, exotic
landscapes, unfaithful lovers, and doomed but sexually forth-
right females, Belasco's plays proffered sensationalized versions of the struggles between the good heroine and the vil-
lanous hero which dominated the Victorian stage.*

*A similar conflict between the exalted and the worldly
might be said to characterize Belasco in his own living
style. Through his financial successes, he was able to build
two New York theaters, the Stuyvesant and the Belasco,
and by the end of his life, he had control over several stages
throughout the United States. However, the monastery-
educated Belasco chose to live modestly in private rooms over
his theater in a fabled jumble of theatrical properties and
priceless objets d'art. These surroundings, combined with his
deceptively benign and clerical-looking appearance, complete
with starched white collar band, earned Belasco the epithet
"The Bishop of Broadway."*

He died in 1931.

A T the time when we of the early twenties were
wringing our hands and crying, "Ah! my God!"
David Belasco was clapping his hands and exclaiming,
"Ah! my gods!" In the plural they signify success.

A man of energetic dreams, he had built his hopes of
that material that survives realization. Dreams too often
will not bear rearing in the streets of anything more
tangible than some impatient fancy.

As he stepped out of the inner room of the studio, he
was no longer just the public man that men of genius must

inevitably be, but that more inaccessible thing—the hermit of that same publicity. One hides behind the hat with which one bows to the world. It is through these things that we come by our solitude at all.

A man whose hair is silver and curling like the shavings from some silversmith's machine; simple about the throat, reminding one of some religious order, with quick brown eyes and a little trick he has with his mouth—only this. That is his greatest charm. One can afford to be simple with life when one has acquired the knowledge of being simple with the past. Intimacy with antiquities gives that ineffable something that for want of a better word we call poise.

And it seemed to me then that to break into this thing, this new sense that I had of him, by idiotic questions about the stage and the stars that he had made, as though he were nothing more nor less than a profitable patch of sky—would be not only an inartistic thing, but an unpardonable error.

In this studio there are almost too many beautiful things—a room overcrowded with emotion, as a heart is overcrowded with heartbeats, or a breath overcrowded with small, minor breaths; as Belasco's brain is with new emotions. Rooms which, could ghosts come and could those ghosts speak, would be full of the cadences of pleasure and of pain, mournful with the little exclamations of the dead.

Oh, the impertinence of imperishable dust! Oh, the infamy of consuming time!

"You see this table," he said, stopping before one of those immense boards of the old days, stretched out on carved and ample legs. "This table is dying before my very eyes, and I love it as though it were a brother.

"See these holes," he went on, bending down to examine it, "these are made by that active time we call worms. They eat by day, and by night they eat also the heart of this table; they creep and creep upon it like vultures about some stricken thing. We cannot stop them and, oh," he finished, "it's a terrible thing and a great one, to put men at the watching of antiquities trying to stay their inevitable decay. In spite of me, in spite of them, this table will crumble and fall. A room that typifies all that lives, as it typifies all that dies—for nothing is immortal."

"Not even the world?"

"Not even that. So sure as the bird falls, so sure the world will come hurtling down out of space like a toy balloon. Perhaps it will be a mass of burning fire and vapor, for thousands upon thousands of years—it must be so. Nothing lives forever, and everything changes—yet—," he took up a Venetian tumbler, turning it in the light, "—out of it all will arise that terrible conqueror, worm. Some little hideous animal to give back all that it has taken. And again we shall climb from the caterpillar into the butterfly, and from that into something higher, and up and on until again the fall will set in.

"There are seasons in everything, there is a summer of love as there is a summer of nature, and there is a winter of life as there is a winter of faith.

"Why," he went on, "do you realize that you are—we all are—working on perishable things? That the sheet the author writes upon is maturing under his pen? That the very canvas the artist is laying his brush upon is aging under the stroke? That the very vaults that we hide them in are aging, too, and that nothing can protect and guard anything forever? Ah, yes, it is sad—but then, all things that are beautiful are. Sadness and sorrow are the two most beautiful words and the most abused."

He turned away, setting the tumbler back in its case with a hundred others and leading me into another room. In this room, through the dark, I could see a large, ivory Christ shining, flanked on either side by beautiful thieves with heads hung down—a mystic thing glowing in a mystic dusk.

"I got that altar piece in Italy," Belasco was saying at my side. "Before that I saw a king and a queen bow down their heads, and then—" He passed his hand over his forehead. "And then the very next day they sold it to me for—money. A country that will pluck the very skeleton from its flesh—for what? For gold. Thus is Europe made. They take away, they sell into slavery that penance that was cast before this image; they separate the revered from the reverence. It is appalling!"

We passed on through the heavy drapery of old values and among the glory of historic banners, into the colored light cast by a painted window. Old suits of armor with dull, amazed spaces in the empty helmets, great gauntlets crossed over a heavy sword, spears stacked in a bristling row of thirsty points, battle axes, small cannons looking like little chickens in comparison with the present monsters of destruction—all of the old implements of murder that made war a craft instead of a trade.

"Here," he said, "is a small Japanese garden; those

bamboos are called winter trees. This image over here is the most powerful of all goddesses: see the crystal she holds in her hands? And here is a Buddha watching with cold, relentless eyes the passing of the days." Finally we went back into his own especial workroom; and there amid his tapestries, rare volumes, and quiet cushions, I asked him what he thought of women.

He smiled as though the very thought made him happier.

"Ah, there you have it all," he said, stretching out his arms, "all, all, all. For them everything has been done since the world began, for them everything good and ill will be done until the world ends. Those who say to the contrary do not know what they are saying. Weininger, for instance, holds that women are of less importance than the vegetable and calls acting one of the lowest of professions. It is the highest, the hardest, and the most torturous, for a woman has to give up everything. There cannot be two great passions in an actress's life; she cannot both love a man and her art at the same time. It is impossible! It is suicide! By the wayside so many have fallen, so many of still rarer talents than many who have achieved final recognition and distinction; so many with such great gifts that they were destroyed by their very immensity. Ah, women," he mused, setting his chin in his hand, "what beautiful things women are, what a mess the world would be without them, and yet what a havoc they have made of the world. For a woman Rome fell; for a woman Caesar bled; for a woman rose the arenas and fell the palaces. For a woman the world grew, and for a woman the world will fall. A man is only something at her feet. Alas, not so of all women: there are the coarse and the unlovely. But into each man's life, at some time, some woman has come whom he has idolized and set up higher, much, than himself. And if she falls—he loves again.''

"Then you do not believe in the modern type?'' I inquired.

"I believe in everything from the standpoint of the scholar, but not from the standpoint of the common man in the street. For me, yes; for you, yes. You and I, as all those who love life, can afford to believe in filth as well as in beauty. My advice to such is: Talk with the street girl, talk with the girl of the convent. Talk with the baker, talk with the king—go to the roots. Examine the flower, be not contemptuous of that community of common particles that unites the highest and the lowest—the stem. Be conscious always, be alert; have eyes and use them, have ears and train them; have a tongue and speak little. If you cultivate your silence, your ultimate sounds will be profitable.''

"And the women of the stage—what would you say to them?''

"Always the same thing. Whosoever has a mind, a consciousness, can hear and see anything to his profit. Without books you could not be well read; without life you cannot be—grant me the license—well lived. What tunes could one play on a harp of one string?'' He laughed and drew me toward the mantelpiece.

"People make fun of the realism in my dramatic productions. Well, I believe only in those things that come to stay. Have the modern, wild, high colors come to stay? No. Have the simple things come to stay? Yes. Wherever

Two Tall Women in Strange Headdresses

we may find them. The modern stage? Not so modern; these things have been tried before. Each winter one has a cough, say; it's not new. Coughs have always existed at some time, and then they pass away. I don't presume to think that I can better what God has done."

"You don't believe in the individuality of the artist, then?"

"I believe that an artist should be individual with common God-given things—individual in a common world, not common in an individual conception.

"So when I want a sunset I go out and look at a sunset; and when I want a dawn I stay up all night to get a dawn; and when I want a character true to life I go to life for the character, or I remember back into the lives I have taken note of.

"Isn't this lovely?" He had stopped before an old miniature done in relief—a little woman, sideface, with a kerchief and one of those early Victorian noses that seem to have specialized on the odors of scandal.

He had been so tender and so quiet and so half-melancholy in his slow wanderings about and among his treasures that I, looking for the man of indefatigable energy, put a question: "How is it that you ever happened to get into theatricals at all?"

He turned around, putting the little case back upon its hook, and I saw that he was smiling in the dusk.

"Well, you see," he began, "I guess contemplation, a half-hour a day of silence, and a little wonder would make actors, playwrights or managers of us all. History is all a play, the stage is what? Footlights set before an incident.

"When I was a kid," he went on, "I loved to get away by myself. My one dream was to have a studio. I remember how I spent my first three bits: I bought a packing box and a piece of red cloth for lining, and I put this in the cellar where it wouldn't get too wet, and I climbed inside of it and dreamed for a long time of the wonderful colors I should some day be able to buy and hang about my walls. From that I kept increasing and adding, selling and buying more and more, rarer and rarer things, until now—," he turned quickly on his heel, taking in the whole surrounding opulence,"—I have on the one side swords of Napoleon, couches belonging to Josephine, cups of Martha Washington, carriage lamps torn from a coach in the olden days, and a cabinet of Lucretia Borgia."

I asked him then what he thought the future held forth for American playwrights.

"America has too many lunch counters," he answered, enigmatically.

"Too many lunch counters?"

"Exactly. A man who might otherwise be a thinking man, rushes into lunch, grabs a sandwich, a glass of milk, a piece of pie, and presto—he has killed a Hamlet."

I laughed at the way Mr. Belasco said this and the manner in which he finished up with a snap of the fingers.

"Ah, you need not laugh," he said, "it's only too true. Do you think that it is simply accident that has made all the great names of Europe 'loungers,' as we call them? Was not Verlaine always seen talking over his cup—or at least lingering alone for an hour or so? Here the men and women are too excited and too hurried. If the subway stopped for a week, if the elevated and the car lines got stalled for a month, if all the automobiles and carriages went lame—if all the cogs of modern industry refused to turn—well, we should have had what we are paying so dearly for now.''

''And that is?''

''The awakening to the real things in America. We are awakening, but think of what we have paid: our millions of dead in Europe. Formerly a woman would not wear a hat unless it had a trademark that she could not pronounce. Formerly an orchestra would not play a piece of music unless the name in the upper corner was Russian, German or Italian. Formerly a picture not painted in Paris was worthless. And, worst of all, those men and those women who possessed a little of the divine gift, instead of keeping it for their country, instead of writing about America, instead of giving America its first long trousers—they took the long trousers to a land already overstocked in that size, leaving our child-country to go along in its eternal knee-pants, although America was getting awfully long in the legs.''

''Then you do think that America has a future?''

''Of course I do. It is true that there is more in the present shrug of the Parisienne's shoulder, and more in the smile of a Latin—but America has shoulders also, and she has teeth. Only it is about time that she cultivated her own instead of her neighbor's wits; it is time that she bit into her own historical pie, and time that she flirted with her own future.''

At this juncture two tall women passed through the outer hall, noiselessly, disappearing in a flutter of white headpieces.

"They can speak little English," he said, noticing my interest. "They take care of the studio for me, and of a Sunday you will always see them kneeling before the image of Christ, flanked on either side by the beautiful thieves."

I nodded.

"They do not have to come here Sundays, but they always do. It is for them a private place of devotion and worship. I am glad it gives the place something that it would otherwise lack."

As we talked Mr. Belasco kept on moving, so that in the course of time we seemed to have passed through a score of rooms, each lovelier than the last; each more mysterious with that mystery of the now deserted chair, the cloak long laid aside, the guitar long still. And in the end we came out upon a little staircase that led down again into his particular and favorite room.

Here he showed me a quaint chair that, he said, he had much trouble getting from a rival bidder. He leaned over and opened a little compartment and therein lay some manuscript paper with a blue cover.

"Ah, ha!" said I, "another play?"

"How did you know?" he asked, quickly shutting the drawer again. "Yes, my last play."

He said nothing more, and I did not press him for the plot. He was leading me out again into the room next door, which cuts you off entirely from this retreat. This last room was half-dismantled: in a corner several pictures leaned face inward; a heavy hanging sagged from its ropes. In among a lot of red velvet, a glass case stood, under which arose a figure of Napoleon with his arms crossed, like a resigned cake.

This turned out to be the Napoleon room which, Mr. Belasco explained, was being papered and redecorated. Little figures of Napoleon stood on tables, several miniatures, and as many pictures, while a gauntlet and a sword lay on a chair, and an old cape belonging to another period lay upon a table.

"Half my things are not here," he said as he stood surveying this disorder. "A good many things pertaining to Napoleon are in the other room." He smiled here. "Even a little divan belonging to one of his ladies," he ended.

We passed through into the outer hall at this juncture, the door closing behind us. And there we were in a cold, commonplace day, standing outside the office of Mr. Wendell Phillips Dodge, with its ledgers and its files and its pots of mucilage and pens.

Mr. Belasco sat down here and said:

"Now, what is it you wanted to ask me?"

Was that not charming? He had only just put himself in the attitude of a man who is going to be interviewed and I had already spent an hour with him.

"Oh, yes," I said, as if just remembering also, "I came to ask you about the stars you have made and about the trouble you had with your playwrights bureau."

He looked unhappy all of a sudden.

"No," he said, "I guess we had better not go into that, it seems to spoil things; it's been told so often. As for the actresses I have made—well, let me see—no," he concluded, "I was not going to tell you that either. That would mean nothing but stringing a lot of names together, and that, too, has been done so often. Let us talk about something entirely different; let us talk about you, for instance.''

''Ah,'' I said, ''but that would not be interesting.''

He shook his head slowly. ''No, I think psychoanalysis is one of the most interesting things of all. I believe in spiritual things, in analysis, in intuition, in stars—oh, in everything.'' He stood up and held out his hand.

''You must dine with us some day,'' he said. ''And then we will really have a good long talk. This has been just a sort of little journey, a silent sort of journey through the forests of my collections—yes, some day you must have lunch with me.''

But I know he will forget.

Frank Harris Finds Success More Easily Won Here in America Than in England

Born in Galway, Ireland in 1856, Frank Harris was a precocious youth, earning a scholarship to Cambridge University. Ambitious and romantic as well, however, the boy took the ten-pound award and fled the United Kingdom for America, where he took a series of odd jobs from New York to Kansas and from Texas to Chicago, experiences he recounted —with great literary license—in On the Trail: Being My Reminiscences as a Cowboy *(1930).*

In Kansas, Harris studied law at the recently founded University at Lawrence and embarked upon the promiscuous and lifelong sexual adventures which would later gain him international notoriety through his memoirs, My Lives and Loves. *Banned for several decades, the unexpurgated book was not published in America until 1964, by Grove Press.*

Kansas soon bored the audacious youth, and he left for Europe to report on the Russo-Turkish War, finishing his studies in German universities where he befriended many of the best minds of his day. Returning to England, Harris quickly became editor of the London Evening News. *Brawling and romancing his way into the British literary establish-*

ment, Harris left the News *to edit the* Fortnightly Review *and, soon thereafter, the* Saturday Review. *Drawing upon his friends George Bernard Shaw, H. G. Wells, Max Beerbohm, and Arthur Symons for contributions, he quickly turned it into one of the liveliest journals of the decade.*

In 1898 Harris sold the Review *and, over the next few years, took on a succession of editorships—*Vanity Fair, Hearth and Home, *and* Modern Society—*all of which ended disastrously, and the last of which occasioned a short prison term for libel. His major contributions of this period were his books, including* The Man Shakespeare *(1909)*, The Women of Shakespeare *(1911)*, Contemporary Portraits *(1915), and a study of his close friend,* Oscar Wilde *(1916).*

Returning to the States, Harris bought Pearson's Magazine. *But, as shown in this interview with Barnes, he was sympathetic to the German cause, which led him over the next few years into ever increasing conflict with the U.S. Post Office. Eventually publication of* Pearson's *was suspended.*

In the years following, Harris lived with his second wife in France, writing My Lives and Loves *and a memoir of* Bernard Shaw, *which was left incomplete at his death in 1931.*

I WAS dining at the house of a friend some eighteen months ago when the maid announced Mr. Harris. "Frank, you know," my hostess said as she arose to greet him.

A short man came suddenly into the room, a man with thick, dark hair and a mustache like a mural painting, a decoration to the house of Harris. A man who seemed to be a favorite corridor where life had loved to stroll. When he spoke one became startled: the voice was the deep and rich voice of a large man; let me call it the echo of those who passed.

His eyes were keen at once and kind; not overoften, but once now and again one could see that this man had not flung the harpoon alone.

What more expressive thing can I say to describe him than that life had used him. I like this better than the phrase, he had used life.

This was the only time that I was to meet him and not know him, for he becomes a friend at once or he becomes nothing. He has also the terrible quality that goes with it: he can cease as abruptly and as decisively as he began.

It is a terrible thing that memories of great men die with their contemporaries. For only so short a space can one man say of another, "I knew him well. He used to have a droll little trick—" So soon, too tragically soon, comes the remark instead, "I knew a man once who knew a man—"

This is Harris. With him dies virtually all of the oldest and best in the last century of English letters. An eloquent potpourri of the petals fallen from the flowers of Europe, adding his own fine shower of leaves to the fragrant pile that too soon will pass into the unlimited where all limited things have couch and eternal sleep.

I remember walking up Fifth Avenue one night with him in the fall, and with what awe I watched this man's moods come and go. At one moment running and jumping a brook in the street, and the next denouncing America's insistent crying for "a happy ending." Some editor had got him to change one of his books and he was already beginning to regret it.

A fine strain of piracy runs through the veins of Harris. Like Benvenuto Cellini, he cannot help seeing the beauty of force. Ah, how his eyes shone when mentioning the diamond mines of Kimberley. "There is a living for you," he exclaimed again and again. And even Nellie, his wife, gets a great deal of amusement in watching him, swearing to do her part in holding up the train if he will; both of them amused, but something beyond amusement always in the hot, quick light in Harris's eyes.

I said, "I'll see you swinging yet in Kimberley, see you swinging by the neck in Kimberley."

It had a strange poetic rhythm to it, and Harris looked up and nodded. "That's the way to die," he said. "Go out like a fine, brave fruit, not like a worm."

For me, personally, the social side of Harris is the most charming. He is so human, often brilliant, so caustic, at times so bitter. Undying hate for his enemies and for those who have caused him trouble; such high wrath blazing always for pains brought to the artist's soul by the vulgar bourgeoise; such dynamic contempt for all who cramp and spoil—and yet always so much the gentleman.

This is how I love him, this is where my mind accepts as true the sinister in him.

But there is a business side as well, and to this I had to go also. For when he is being interviewed, he is another man again: not the writer, not the talker, not the host, he is the man who made the *Fortnightly Review* what it was in London and is making *Pearson's* what it is here. And I cannot but feel alienated by the knife that cuts the truth from top to base and lays it a quivering anatomical district before the eye.

Therefore I asked him if he thought he had already reached "safe" with *Pearson's*.

"I believe so," he said. "The circulation manager tells me that the sales have quadrupled in New York in the last four months, and repeat orders are coming in from all parts of the country. Three days after the publication of the February number, we received repeat orders from Philadelphia and Chicago of twenty-five percent—and now another repeat order from Philadelphia for a further twenty percent."

"Success comes running here, where she tiptoes in London?" I queried.

"I can only speak for myself," he replied. "For me, well, I find it more easily won here in America. Let me explain. In England a radical policy is disliked by the classes. Of course, if you get together five or six men of genius such as I had on the *Saturday Review*, an increase of circulation is almost assured. Shaw, Wells, Max Beerbohm, Cunningham-Grahame, and Arthur Symons give a weekly paper distinction and influence, but even in that case the advertiser does not follow the reader. Though I almost doubled the circulation of the *Saturday Review* in the first year, I lost more than half my advertisements. The moneyed classes in England dislike originality and hate all radical theories. The middle-class shopkeeper in England is the most obstinate foe to progress in the world. He is as much the snob as the aristocrat, and has besides an insane love of money and a corresponding hatred of those who hinder him from obtaining it.

"In America, on the other hand, you can reach success through a radical policy. That is, an editor can thus obtain circulation, and advertisements follow circulation. The coming success in American journalism will be a really radical daily paper in New York.

"That is the difference between Europe and America. In Europe you are radical till you get power; then you sell out to the privileged classes and get everything you want for yourself. Like Lloyd George and Briand, who both started as social reformers or Socialists and are now defenders of the privileged classes and money. Mr. Wilson brought in an eight-hour bill while President—a radical reform, a thing unthinkable in Europe.

"America is radical at heart, and if you ever get a Moses, Americans will follow him into the promised land. In Europe Moses' only chance of getting the leadership is to become a lackey of the classes. He frightens everybody by telling them that the Red Sea is a sea of blood.

"My message at present is better than the paper it is printed on," he added, smiling.

Then I asked him if he believed that Lloyd George would be unable to lead the English to success, and if he was not of the opinion that as a popular leader Lloyd George was already lost.

"Completely lost, I'm afraid," he nodded. "He is leaning not on the Liberals, but on the Tories; he is the last hope of the oligarchy. He thinks that energy, courage, and hard work will make the difference between success and failure in this war. Both the French and the English commanders encourage him in the belief that if sufficient munitions are provided, the Allies can break through on the West and drive the Germans back to their own frontier. He is practically pledged to achieve this by next August. In my opinion, he will fail; but even if he succeeds, he will get no better terms from the Germans than he could get now.

"By rejecting the peace proposal and by making exorbitant demands, he has made himself mainly responsible for at least another year of war; and the next year of war will cost more in blood and treasure than can possibly be gained by any or all of the combatants. He underrates his adversaries, or rather, he does not understand Germany at all or Germany's aims."

"And the result will be?"

"A draw," said Mr. Harris, "with the Germans winners on points."

"Do you think President Wilson could end the war?"

"Yes, a year-and-a-half ago when England was dependent for her munition supply on America. The President could then have forced England to give reasonable terms, by threatening to put an embargo on the exportation of munitions; but now American munitions are not absolutely necessary to Great Britain. Accordingly, President Wilson could hardly enforce peace at the present time. By working for it steadily he may bring it about by next September or October, especially if the Allies fail to drive the Germans out of France or to break their lines. I believe that President Wilson will do all in his power to end it all, but I see no hope of peace until Lloyd George has had his trial and failed."

"Then you think that if the Allies win and drive the Germans back to their own frontier, the war will go on?"

"Probably. The Germans will never accept terms the Allies have put forward till they are completely beaten, and that I regard as impossible."

"What do you think will happen in the United States after peace if made?"

"The United States will either have to socialize her chief industries in order to meet the new competition of socialized Europe, or she will have to erect a high tariff wall and keep out competition, which will have the effect of increasing enormously the social inequality inside these United States. I was very glad to see that Secretary Daniels intends to socialize the manufacture of munitions. That is the best line to take. He seems to be doing much good work.

"I should like to see the telephones and the telegraphs taken over by the state, and the railways; but that will hardly happen the next year, and will never happen if the Frank Trumbulls are listened to."

But I was thinking of Shaw and of Moore and of Wilde and those other brilliant minds that Frank had struck fire against. And so I asked him suddenly, breaking in on a reverie which he had fallen into, his hand set in between the first and second buttons of his coat as one sees them in old photographs.

"Tell me," I said, "something about those men who made up the genius of the *Saturday Review*."

"You know," he answered, "Shaw and Bertrand Russell are about the only two men in England who have kept their heads in the general smashup. It is astonishing how infectious is the spirit of the herd in England. In America, too, you have persons talking of patriotism as the soul of the nation."

"And Shaw," I asked, "what kind of letters does he write?"

"Shaw's letters are quite as funny as his plays. You had a specimen of that the other day when he replied to the invitation to come to America to speak. He said he was afraid to come, for he liked riding in railway cars with other men's wives—a home thrust for the way we treated Gorki."

"And George Moore?"

"There is a man who writes letters as well as he writes books. Most men who come to the front are sincere—genius especially."

"And what do you think of America in regard to literature and art?"

"There America has everything to do, and has hardly made a start as yet. In the long run, the composite character of America may be a great help. Every state should have a state art gallery, a state theatre and a state conservatory of music, and, of course, state endowment of scientific research.

"Every big city, too, should have its municipal theatre, municipal art gallery, municipal school of music, municipal schools of chemistry and physics. Art, literature, and science must be endowed and fostered, that is the most necessary thing in America today; that is the lesson Germany and France have taught the world. Statesmen should think of themselves as gardeners and not be satisfied till they can show specimens of every flower of genius in the gardens."

"You believe that the endowment of art produces artists,

and the endowment of literature, writers of genius?''

"The men of genius are always there," replied Mr. Harris, "but if you do not help them, they will not be able to produce the great works. Shakespeare would never have done his best work, never have written *Hamlet* or *Othello* or *Anthony and Cleopatra*, if Lord Southhampton had not given him the one thousand pounds which made possible his high achievement. The popular taste of his day was worse than ours. His worst play, *Titus Andronicus*, was of the popular type, given hundreds of times in his life, whereas *Hamlet* was only given twelve times, and *Lear* once or twice."

"Only when New York has a municipal theatre and a state theatre shall we be equal to Paris, which has the Odeon and the Comédie Française, and we with a population half as large again. We endow common school education in America; but not the flower of education. We must endow genius in America, and every manifestation of it."

He turned suddenly to the mantelpiece and dropping his lower lip, said, "Ah," as only he knows how to say it. The ejaculation of a man who will not weep when his heart is full, the desolate sound of a man who will not permit himself to be disillusioned; a half-sound between a truce and a challenge.

"It's dreadful, dreadful!" he said, clasping his hands behind him, walking to the window where he could see the park.

I asked him, "What," softly.

"The way they treat a man; the way they treat men of talent and of real worth in America. I don't see how you all stand it."

I knew that he was referring to those of us who have been born with a little reverence for the things that are beautiful, and a little love for the things that are terrible; and I nodded my head.

Alfred Stieglitz on Life and Pictures: One Must Bleed His Own Blood

Photographer, editor, and promoter of art, Alfred Stieglitz was one of the major forces in presenting avant-garde modern art in the United States.

The son of a wool merchant, Stieglitz grew up in and around New York City, studying engineering at the age of seventeen at City College of New York. In 1881 he traveled to Germany, enrolling in the Berlin Polytechnic Institute, where he became interested in photography as a career. Experimenting with restrictive light conditions—photographing at night, and in snow, rain, and fog—he quickly became known as a rebel, an image that would dominate his activities as artist and art impressario throughout his life.

Returning to the United States in 1890, Stieglitz embarked upon his pioneer experiments in three-color photoengraving, producing a collection of Manhattan scapes—including his now famous Winter—Fifth Avenue *and* The Terminal—Streetcar Horses—*which demonstrated, as no other American photographer had before, that the camera was a tool of art equal in its aesthetic potential to the chisel and the brush. Over the next several years, Stieglitz argued for this aesthetic principle by presenting his own work and that of others in his journals* American Amateur Photographer, *published from 1892 to 1896;* Camera Notes, *1897-1903; and* Camera Work, *which was begun in 1903.*

With fellow photographer Edward Steichen, Stieglitz founded the Little Galleries of the Photo-Secession two years later in order to show their own photographs and the works of others, beginning with a show of Pamela Colman Smith in 1907. The Photo-Secessionists or "Secessionists," as the artists associated with Stieglitz came to be called, were dedicated, in Stieglitz's words, to "seceding from the accepted idea of what constitutes a photograph." But Stieglitz's anti-establishmentism was not limited to photography, as the gallery (popularly referred to by its address, 291) expanded its exhibitions to include the works of painters and sculptors including Matisse in 1908, Toulouse-Lautrec (1909), Rousseau (1910), Picabia (1913), and American artists Alfred Maurer, Marsden Hartley, Arthur Dove, Arthur B. Carles, Oscar Bluemner, Elie Nadelman, Georgia O'Keefe (whom Stieglitz married in 1924), and Stanton Macdonald-Wright.

The increasing isolation of American artists from their European counterparts as a result of the war led Stieglitz to close the gallery and to cease publication of Camera Work *in 1917, the year in which Barnes interviewed him. Stieglitz headed other galleries in later years—the Intimate Gallery in 1925 and An American Place in 1929—but none could match the impact of "the largest small room in the world."*

Art critic Barbara Rose summarizes Stieglitz's contribution: "Like the little magazines, 291 helped to introduce two notions into American art: that of art as experimental research, and that of quality in art. Both went against the American grain; the first because it threatened the status quo and the second because it seemed to negate the principle of democracy. By insisting that there was a superior or 'high' art corresponding to what had been the aristocratic art of the past, available only to the noble in spirit, Stieglitz and his friends battled against what Whitman termed 'the leveling character of democracy'" (American Art Since 1900).

Stieglitz continued producing his own photographs until his death in 1946.

I T was some time in the early fall, I think, of 1914, that I strayed into the house of Mabel Dodge toward evening, to show her my pictures. At this time I had half of the "old manner" with me and but a slight hint of the new. The nonchalant classes—the poet, the revolutionist, with their heads always on a sort of ball-bearing system, with bombs and other redeeming munitions of a future social order—were entirely new to me. This class struck me at first as entirely charming, not from the standpoint of wishing to cultivate their immediate acquaintance, but from a gratitude arising from the pleasure of being pointed out the way to the future with an index finger that had previously been dipped in gold ink.

These were my grateful days. I was grateful to Mabel Dodge, who let me eat as many sandwiches as my suburban stomach could hold. I was grateful to Carl Van Vechten for having written the introductory card that had given me access to so much.

I remember how funny I looked in the midst of that artistic atmosphere. I remember that even at that time I asked myself the question, Why is it that all similarity of ideas and tastes has the same manner of dress, of speech and mode of living?

Two or three of the older gentlemen paid some small attention to me, and I wondered at the time if it was because of my lack of *sang froid* or because they liked my drawings. I wondered a little, too, why old men have always had a peculiar liking for me where young men are entirely indifferent—and why at the same time for me there existed no man, young or old, who could draw the slightest, faintest word of interest from me apart from my drawing or some abstract thing connected with themselves. Perhaps it was because love had been much discussed in my family circles, because all the old romances of man and maid had already been read to me. Perhaps it was because, and this surely was it, that art had been something that I felt and not saw, longed for and not possessed, to its outward fullness, hoped for and at last approached.

And yet I was in awe of no one; I attempted not to show the arrogance of my upper lip that would persist in an attempt to curl, probably because I wanted to cry and wouldn't. I felt cold because I wanted so dreadfully to feel warm and hopeful and one with them.

But all of this is entirely out of the way, except to give a small pen picture of myself at the time when Mr. Alfred Stieglitz first came into my life. Mabel Dodge was holding up a painting of mine, extraordinarily bad, too, and she was hesitating between approval and disapproval. "Anyway," she said, "go to 291 Fifth Avenue and ask for Mr. Stieglitz, and show him; perhaps he can help you."

Two ninety-one is at the top of an old-fashioned house

overlooking the Avenue. The elevator opened onto a little vestibule and gave a hint of a picture hung well beyond. A man was standing with one elbow on the shelving that runs entirely around this room; his feet were crossed, and he was talking to two or three people, on the same order as those I had met the night before. He did not look up when I entered, nor did he seem to notice me. He was telling some tale beginning, "That makes me remember," interjected with "Well, say."

His hair was longer than usual with men, and turning then iron gray. The eyebrows were bushed, the eyes deep-set and assumed a certain uncertainty. He asserts that he was born in this country, yet I noted then that his mouth had that fine and sudden stoppage of lip seen mostly in the south of Germany. Someone has told me that I have a peculiar habit of noticing mouths. I have, and when I see one that does not merge into the rest of the face, I want the world to know about it, a mouth that is a personality upon a person.

He has a manner of speaking at once quick and hesitating, perhaps a little because he speaks through his nose—I don't know, though I have tried to define and to place it. A very individual speech, an individuality of respiration.

Presently he turned to me and introduced me to those present, at the same time introducing himself to me. They left soon, and he quite naturally took the portfolio with which I was laden out of my arm.

He looked the pictures over and asked me what I thought of them. I had not expected this question, and answered, "I'm quite crazy about them."

He seemed pleased. "You're the first woman," he said slowly, "who has been perfectly frank in that answer. Well, perhaps you're right." He put them back and began to tie them up.

"And what am I to do?" I asked.

"Keep on drawing, if you really care for it, and don't try to sell them or—" There was a pause during which he looked out of the window. "Or keep right on, if you don't want to, and sell them."

That's about the best advice I ever got, and it is typically Stieglitz, though he won't like the word typical. I felt something then which later I analyzed with his help. While he seemed to care for pictures, he did not seem to know pictures; while he gave advice on pictures, he seemed to be giving advice on life.

The type of all his exhibitions has been revolutionary, cubist, impressionist, irrationalist, all of them. There have been Picasso, Matisse, Rodin, Pamela Smith, Brancusi, Toulouse-Lautrec—savage art called "negro," Picabia, Marsden Hartley, Dove, Severini and others, while the newest is a woman, Georgia O'Keefe. Not to forget, of course, the present Marin exhibit and the always on-coming Walkowitz, head down.

Often this man has been called the master faker. I cannot hide behind this statement; I also have thought him the master faker. Many have said, "He must be; he has nothing for sale, yet he has a gallery; he has nothing to gain, apparently, but the futile remarks of those passing." Again I have to confess, but adding, "Well, perhaps he has enough money of his own. In that case, why does he want to amuse himself in such an unamusing way?"

"To meet just such people as you," he said, and laughed.

"Oh," he added, "I'm tired of being America's fool— court fool, jester, buffoon. You have all come here straight-faced, and some of you have gone away smiling, and you did not think I knew. I have been content and patient to know, because that is the only reason for my thirteen years in this garret. You have all thought what you pleased. Why should I enlighten you? Why should I tell you that one must bleed his own blood? It's all right; the other day I thought I had learned all I had come to learn, and the night after, I thought I had learned too much, and I was going to end it. I knew that there was nothing so calculated to expose men as art. They are simple before it or they are the capital liars. What do I know of pictures? Not a thing. What do I know of cubism and all the other things, line and color? Nothing. What do I know of new movements, or old? Nothing. What do I want to know of them? Nothing. But, say, I'll tell you, I've reached the spot where I am about willing to turn down an empty glass. I have had them all here to learn what you Americans are like, and I have learned much. My gallery was only a trap set for humanity, and the trap has worked, season in and out. Who was it who said that he had a gallery, hung on one side with peaceful, pleasing pictures, and the other with horrible and gruesome things, merely to know his friends better? If they stopped before the gentle and the meek representation, he called for his butler to remove the knife he knew would be up their sleeves, but if they stopped at the brutal and the horrible, he had lunch ordered in the green room.

"I have, in other words, had the privilege of laughing at America for thirteen years.

"By their telling me what I am, I have learned what they are. One by one I have lost all my friends to make new ones. They come here and they go away from here, and always I am contented. I do not seek for my life, and that is as it should be. By having open doors the world passes through, and I, I can stand and watch and learn. I have a hunger, a terrible hunger, for that knowledge, and when that knowledge alienates me from the older generation and from the newer generation, I grow afraid, and I ask myself over again, What do they mean when they say no and what when they say yes? Do they have any logical sequence of feeling, is there a before and an after to it? It is the parrot talking in the trees. It is the needle of life reproducing the sounds learned on the mother knee. I do not know."

He went on to talk of women.

"I believe in woman, not in women; I have had enough pain because of them to have made me shut them out of my heart forever, yet I will believe. I can hear 'Nevermore' in the air, and I can outshout it, 'Evermore.' You say I am a perfect gentleman, nevertheless I say that I have been expelled from the Camera Club. I have never gone away from anything; I have let things go away from me. I have never made the mistake of stepping aside; I have always let things pass up and pass on. That is the only means by which one can find anything out."

"And once you told much about trees."

"That I always went to them and laid my heart upon them and told them my griefs and my pleasure."

"Yes, and once you told about the lake, at Lake George."

"The lake is the most human thing of all, it has neither brains nor heart—as my enthusiasm has neither father nor mother."

"Then nature is the only thing that makes humans possible?"

"Nature is the only thing that explains human nature; we expect too much of the one and nothing of the other.

"Now take women, for instance. They are advanced far ahead of the American man—I have told them often about it. Some of the upper classes used to come here and inquire why their souls would not keep time with their husbands? Why, for instance, they loved Rodin, but that if they bought one and hung it on the wall, their husbands would rebel.

"I answered, 'Because you have kept them working on the nickels and the dimes of the world; you keep them down at business so that you may go gadding about.' 'Did you ever hear of a cat?' I once asked one of them. She hesitated, and laughing asked, 'Do you mean a woman or a real cat?' I assured her that I meant a real cat, 'the kind,' I added, 'who catches a mouse and plays with it, and finally eats it.' She said she had. 'Well,' I answered, 'that's the difference. You women play with the mouse, but you never eat it.' "

"People think you have money?"

"And I have not. I have been in the habit, it is true, of taking four or five of my friends out to lunch. That has stopped; it had to. I would rather keep up 291 than have lunch."

"And now that you have confessed that all these years

you have been laughing at us, should we be angry?"

"No—for what? There is no love, there is no art, and I have learned that there are no people. There is only emotional learning, spectacular ABC's and customers."

He laughed.

"And what of thinkers?"

"Brains of insurmountable heights out of which pass incurable thoughts."

"And one should not be in love?"

"One should not be in love, it prevents work; and cool, logical study one should love."

And I thought:

From this place I have been standing eternally, looking out toward the world with my eyes and seeing men pass and look back at me. And I cold and lonesome and increasing steadily in mine own sorrow, which is caught like the plague of other men, until I am full and my mouth will hold no more, and my eyes will see no more, and my ears can stand nothing further. Then do I begin the steady, slow discharge which is called "wisdom," but which is only that too much the eyes cannot see, the ears cannot hear, the mouth cannot hold.

"And so your life from day to day?"

"You see this view from my back window? It is simple and full of a perfect absence of human life. Only a hotel with fire escapes, a lot of blank empty-looking windows, and just lately a few signs painted on it." He began to read, "Hats and gowns, ladies' dresses, A. P. Smith, ladies' cloak maker, neckwear and hosiery." He paused, and I went on, "And petti—"

"Pull down the shade," he demanded. And then we

both laughed. Two or three men had dropped in, and I wondered how Mr. Stieglitz has managed to keep from going mad if he has had to listen to all sorts of people, such as I have often seen there. Great droning bores, like buzzards who have come to earth weighed down with a cargo of the heaviest portions of too heavy souls. Or little murky women who hover, in casual life, over rare editions of Emerson, Longfellow and Riley, wearing rubbers and carrying handbags of uncertain leather and speaking with a hissing sound of all *s*'s as though their words were sliding on a well-tiled floor. Or fat ladies burdened with small dogs, who look admiringly at anything providing it isn't a picture, and say that they "adore" all "trends," it is such a great thing for "progress." Still worse, the tourist type, the willowy man with the pliant cane, and the young women who exclaim enthusiastically, "What conception of line and color!" holding some print off at arm's length. All these things puzzled me, as it puzzles me how he can have the patience to talk to them for the length of time that he does.

In looking it over, the question puts itself, what has he done for others, now that we know something of what others have done for him?

One might as well ask what the image of the Virgin in the corner of the darkest church has done for the casual worshipper; might as well ask what the steps have done for the house; might as well ask what the beggar sitting upon the curb has done for the almsgiving pedestrian. Might as well ask to turn things around, what the casual worshipper has done for the Virgin, what the house has done for the steps, what the almsgiving public has done for the beggar.

But often I ask myself when I think no one will hear me thinking, least of all Stieglitz—what has made it necessary for this man to learn life in this way, and what happened in the lives of the others that makes it necessary for them to form a sort of ''public society''?

Sometimes I like Stieglitz when he talks too much, and often I find myself liking him when he says too little— very much too little.

Recruiting for Métachorie: Mme. Valentine de Saint-Point Talks of Her Church of Music

Although little known in the United States, French poet, novelist, dramatist, and aesthetician Valentine de Saint-Point published extensively in the early part of this century in her home country. Among her many literary works are the collections of poetry Poèmes de la Mer et du Soleil, La Guerre, *and* La Soif et les Mirages; *the prose trilogy* Trilogie de l'Amour et de la Mort; *and the fictions* L'Orbe Pâle *and* Le Secret des Inquiétudes.

Her major contributions, however, lay in her theories as expressed in her book on Auguste Rodin, *in her study of women's theatre,* La Théâtre de la Femme, *and in her argument for a total synthesis of the arts in* La Métachorie. *In 1913, Saint-Point adapted the ideals expressed in* La Métachorie *for a stage presentation of the same name. The production premiered at La Comédie des Champs Elysées in Paris and was performed in New York at the Metropolitan Opera House in April 1917, the time of Barnes's interview with her.*

S ILENCE—dusk. The sound of tapestries swinging against the darkness; an odor of incense; a sense of rest but lately motion; the moan of water dropping far-away in some lonely chamber.

These are the things that greeted me as I was gently pushed out of a day into this sudden night, the twenty-four hour atmosphere of Madame Valentine de Saint-Point, who has come to show us what she means by "Métachorie."

She comes from France, that France that has learned the secret of being beautiful even without its teeth; that France that has made something beautiful out of every-thing ugly, because it took care to place soil beneath the feet of its people so that neither word nor gesture might fall upon barren hate.

And I spoke to her of these things. She answered me in English that threatened every minute to take out its citizen papers and become French.

"You have Picasso and Picabia here and Schoenberg and the moderns in music, and painting in general—but what have you done for the modernism in dancing? Nothing!"

She went on, "It is not that I mind the funny little fox-trotting, you call him? No, it is that I wish to see you doing other things, too." She broke off humming. "What is that little ragtime you have, 'Poor Little Butterfly'? Ah, one should say poor little elephants, you are so ugly when you could be so beautifully angular."

When I looked mildly surprised she went on. "Ah, you do not understand what I mean, you think that I make joke. No, I make no joke with my feet, and now I am talking for them.

"Some people are ideas surrounded by a person, others are persons surrounded with an idea—you see. For me there is music and poetry and painting in dance. When I think of a dance, I think of a poem; you make a little step on the floor now so—and voila, I have a line of poetry. I translate it for you—it always come to me in French." She closed her eyes, and spreading her hand out like one about to slide into rhythm:

> I take flowers to my beloved,
> They shall blossom about his neck;
> They shall spring up between his fingers,
> About him they shall make a wall,
> Within him they shall make a garden,
> For his eyes they shall be as red as blood,
> For his heart they shall be as white as tears,
> And for his soul they shall be as swans,
> Driven here and there by his fancy,
> I take my flowers to my beloved.

"But," said I, "how could you see all that in one little step—there should be a whole dance in that."

She answered, "I saw all that in what you would have gone on doing with the aid of music. If music had been playing you would not have stopped so quickly." Then she added, "They were pretty flowers in the little pot that you must have bought on Third Avenue, toward evening."

She continued:

"I see a line in a picture, and immediately everyone is dancing, everyone standing there examining and criticizing and looking studious and so stupid. They I see making a funny dance, a lovely dance, an eager dance. If I was as much painter as I am poet, I would make a drawing of what you would dance for me. You get what I mean?''

She laughed happily over her knowledge of at least one of our localisms.

''Then perfume, incense—ah, what wonderful things they are. You cannot live without perfume, did you know that? It is why the poor children grow up so quick and abrupt and keen: acrid odors of the East Side, the sharp smells of garlic and onions, the smell of cider vinegar and half-rotten fruits. And that same influence also makes the languid southern beauty. Most people think it sun; yes, the sun drawing out the languid perfumes of grapes and flowers.

''Then there is darkness.'' She leaned a little toward me, and I could see her eyes glowing from beneath a bang of hair, her shoulders sloping into her heavy breast, and I smiled.

''The stage when I dance is quite dark, and I am light. Oh, I cannot tell you how I make myself phosphorescent. That is a professional secret. When you do this the person is the spot of light, whereas when the stage is light the person is a spot of darkness—voila!''

I said: ''Now tell me about your belief in a superdance.''

''A superdance—that which is beyond dancing, is that which is within dancing. You see, what you usually round off I find the angles of, the neglected cube, the ignored triangle—'' She smiled. ''You have that so much in your plays, so little in your dance—see, it is so. There is always something to be made out of everything that has hitherto been discarded. Someone has found a use for sawdust. Well, I am using the sawdust of the dance, picking up the little lost movements dropped, and with them I have made this beautiful theory—Métachorie."

"And just what is Métachorie?" I asked.

"Métachorie," she answered, "is that part of action that is gesture, that part of music that is song, that part of line that is pictorial, and that part of movement that is dance. I do not believe in mimicry, I do not believe that the sight of the singer has ever done anything but harm. I think orchestra and singer alike should be hidden; so I wear a mask when I dance, because my face can only obscure the meaning of my motions. You see," she added, "my face is not dead yet. Only dead faces should be seen. They represent the last divine gesture, the will to conclude.

"For me, dancing is only a part of the great whole, and by that I mean the thing that symbolizes life. Painting alone or sculpture alone, or the voice of the poet or the song in the throat, they are nothing unless collected into a perfect whole.

"True art lies in decomposed forms. That sounds strange. Let me explain."

She moved over to the basket of fruits, and standing erect, slowly bent to gather into her fingers some of its glorious profligacy. Then, rising again, she faced me.

"You see now, many millions of movements went into the drawing up into my fingers of these grapes. Now decompose that action into the one line that would have expressed it, into the one movement that held the basic

Only the Faces of the Dead Should Be Seen

impulse, and you have what I mean."

I said: "What do you hope to do for America with this new dance?"

"First," she said, "let me explain what is wrong with the United States. You have no decadence, no aesthetics. What can you do for art without the seed, which is a passionate desire for art within yourself, not from without? The passion for that art, the love for it, the despair felt in it and the joy, the full blossom. And then—and here is where you almost all tire—the pursuit of that flower into its decay, its drooping of leaves, and finally its charring into dust.

"Too long have you struggled for money and for power, or what you call power: the acquisition of bricks, the domination of laboring men, the ignorance of real religious feeling.

"You go to church to pray. I can pray on the street corner. For me Métachorie is the movement of monks about the cell, or priests about the altar; of knees pressed against the floor. I want a temple built to it, called the Church of Music."

At this I snapped with sudden eagerness.

"Ah, then, you are going to build a theater, a temple—whatnot. Are you going to spread it even to the uttermost ends of the earth?"

"To the uttermost ends," she answered. "To its fullest capacity. I want to see it a religion, a profession, a belief, a passion, a hope, a life work, a school, a library—music, painting, poetry. I want to see it grow up in the generations like a new form for the body. Anyone with an impartial mind will admit that America is not intelligently and spiritually what it should be."

"But tell me more about your plan," I said.

"That is all—it is very simple. I want a fund for the building of my temple—that shall be just outside of some large city, not in it. For it is only that toward which we travel from a long distance that we consider worth attaining. I should want to see Métachorie reach into all branches of life."

"And what about dramas for such a stage, costumes and lighting?"

"The costumes should be bright—I should say brilliant—because the light in striking them would give a different plane of visual pleasure to each pair of eyes, were they a million or only one. The gesture is, of course, always important from any angle. The mask for the face, however, should never be doffed. It is the face and the words that issue from the mouth that make all the wars and all the racial disputes. Covered, nothing would stand in the way of the symbolic beauty of the individual's conception of life.

"Métachorie is a sort of duty—it is a duty one owes to oneself as a thinking unit, and to humanity as to a thinking whole. Realizing that one must renounce pursuit of happiness and gain, willingly going into the silences with tears if need be, sacrificing oneself for the final supreme gesture that shall in the end express all the troubled, multiform movements of life—striking away the roundnesses that hide the supreme angle. This is my one desire; this must be the one desire, ultimately, of the world."

"But do you not think that some of the modern dancers, who have some of this groping for the angularities common to Egypt and the ancients, are important?''

"Not important. Pretty, often charming, even beautiful I will grant, but they are not new; they are the old, the oldest things—and we must get away from the past. We must stop buying old masters and sending our children to Paris for art, to Germany for music, and to England for manners. We must stop thinking of yesterday by creating tomorrow.''

"And what does dancing best express after all? You have written poems on love, on pantheism, on ironies and on war—what do you feel to be the real accompaniment of the dance?''

"All of these things—all of life. But passion must not be merely the kiss on the lips, irony only hard laughter, war not only death, and a belief in God-in-all-things not merely a prayer in times of trouble. No, all these things— and less. I see," she added, smiling, "you expected the usual 'more,' didn't you?''

I did my admitting and asked, "But of what should life consist when one is not indulging in any Métachorie action?''

"In solitude; in nothing, if you like, so far as the outside world knows it. One should cease to exist for everything but oneself until there is something new that can be expressed in Métachorie, and then the person should come forth again for his little moment of enlightenment. What strange faces we should see," she said, irrelevantly.

"Instead of people walking wearily home from work, there would be almost empty streets; instead of children crying in some tenement by the river, there would be silence; instead of the shops opening for trade, there would be nothing perhaps. And down the great stretch of dusty roadway we call the city pavements, as far as the eye could see, there would be nothing but the awaiting air until suddenly, faraway, but a speck on the horizon, moving sadly against a church, we would see one coming with one strange movement that would reveal creation."

I said, "That was rather lovely, but would it not be all rather strange and lonely, if we should stay cooped up in our houses for weeks at a time?"

"Not houses," she answered. "Tents, any open place—in a tree, by a brook, under a hill, beneath the high grass."

"And what," said I, curiously pointing to a crosslike symbol framed on the wall, "may this be?"

"That is the symbol of Métachorie," she answered. "Four colors compose it, red, blue, green and yellow. The yellow symbolizing instinct, feminine passion symbolized by blue, masculine by red, and intelligence symbolized by green."

I continued, "Your poems make one think that you sympathize with war, that you even find something wonderful and beautiful in it. Is this so?"

"Yes," she answered, "I find everything beautiful that has to be, and war has been and war will be. And it must not only be hated and deplored, it must also be loved and gloried in; for all four feelings are common to man, and what is common to man is something that we have no right to condemn from one of the standpoints alone."

"And next year?"

"Even this year I hope to have some pupils and to advance my new art to quite a great extent. I hope to give more performances. My boys, trained by me for two years, joined the army. Two of them are—dead—''

She paused for a second and a new, strange light came into her eyes; and it was a light that had only one nationality, for Madame is French.

''Life is military,'' she said, ''and it is religious. On the one side we see a continual drilling: drilling of the mind for the everyday knowledge, drilling of the hand that it may draw correctly, drilling of the heart that it may be faithful. So I would have my pupils drill. It is inevitable. Military exactness is essential to life and is preparatory for death. And on the other hand, a deep belief in something: men make gods and worship them, they must at once drill and adore. With the one they attain death, and with the other contentment and hope.

''Everything is geometric; we are all numerals that time sets up in a column and adds all together, and leaves the reckoning with—whom, what, where? I see life as figures, as —— designs, as squares, as triangles —— out in a sharp point, the —— cave, the look of hate that is convex, the looks of desire that are oblong and the looks of hunger that are vertical.''

After this I went to see the dance itself.

When I came in, the Metropolitan Opera House was already packed, and I thought, what a night it was going to be for Mme. Saint-Point. A gentle voice arising from the orchestra began in a chant the first lines of her poem:

> I have taken in my two hands, your head and its
>   mystery,
> Your life, that is buried in the shadow of eyelids.
> Then have I circled the dear head

> With the nimbus of my proud renunciation.
> For the skull, sometimes in sleep, I could have
>   crushed.

The lights went out. In the dusk of the stage, away back in the corner, lay something that moved not, something terribly still. The audience, which was bourgeoise, clapped. The voice went on:

> There to find your thought, and at last, to violate it.

Slowly the crouching thing moved up, up, up, two arms and a swaying shoulder rising higher and higher against the blue darkness. The music was seducing this thing forward; it came slowly; again the music kissed it, and again it moved. Then the music broke straight across the orchestra in a triumphant and magic discord, and the thing that had been only arms and shoulders was suddenly a masked head, crouching over two peculiar, creeping feet.

Mme. Valentine de Saint-Point stood before us.

The music proceeded, and so did the figure in its bracelets and its breastplates set with stones, around and around in a crouching step, back and forth and seeming aimlessly, to end in an abrupt and pleasing design in the middle of the carpet, surrounded by mad music.

The curtain did not fall, but by some miraculous system of lighting, the stage grew so dark that only the shining mask could be seen gleaming like an eye.

Again the voice in the orchestra wafted out across the intervening space:

> You have encircled my two feet, naked in your hand
> Upon them you have laid your head.

My two hands, free, I have opened, but in vain
You have taken them in yours, disquieted.
This, that I should be kept from following my road
And laying hold of the invisible.
I have closed my eyes on you, weary, a-swoon at last
Lost is a peaceful dream.
Dead the activity, the action. I have desired
The gentleness of being prisoner.
But the roads are there, elsewhere in the absolute
To the flying goal the bitter mystery.
Then lover, though our pure and mingled teeth
Have bitten into the oblivion,
Insane we will awaken the accomplished abandon,
Believing in some other destiny.
You will lift your head and open your hands,
Accepting the departure.
And we shall go—taking of the two roads.
You—yours, I—mine—indifferent, each one his own.

Again the curving feet of Mme. Saint-Point touched
the floor.

The Rider of Dreams
Is Here

*"The date of the most important single event in the entire
history of the Negro in the American theatre," proclaims
black poet James Weldon Johnson, was April 5, 1917. On
that date three dramatic plays—*The Rider of Dreams,
Granny Maumee, *and* Simon the Cyrenian—*were performed by the Colored Players at the Garden Theater in
the old Madison Square Garden. With the production of
these plays, notes Johnson, "the stereotyped traditions regarding the Negro's histrionic limitations were smashed."*

*The author of the one-acts was Ohio poet Ridgely Torrence,
one of the first American playwrights to write for blacks
and to provide black actors with serious theatrical oppor-
tunities. Torrence's other writings include the poetry collections* A House of a Hundred Lights *(1900) and* Hesperides
*(1925), which have been compared favorably with the works
of Edwin Arlington Robinson and A.E. Housman. But it was
these short plays, argues Edith J.R. Isaacs in* The Negro in
the American Theatre, *that "were the distillation of [the]
lyric poet's long thinking and experience of life. . . . Such
things do not, in the theatre, 'just happen'; but they* can
happen at any time when men and the stars will it so."

*Director of the three playlets, Robert Edmond Jones, was
known at the time of his death in 1954 as the set designer
for some of the most important productions of the American*

stage, including The Wild Duck, Hedda Gabbler, Anna Christie, The Hairy Ape, The Great God Brown, Desire Under the Elms, Mourning Becomes Electra, *and* The Philadelphia Story. *At the time of Barnes's interview, however, Jones had just begun his scenic work by doing the sets for the 1915 season of the Provincetown Players and the Washington Square Players. The same year, he did the sets for Arthur Hopkins's production of* The Devil's Garden, *which led to his long involvement with Hopkins. Over the next few years Jones designed sets also for the Metropolitan Opera production of Nijinsky's ballet* Til Eulenspiegel, *and, with James Light, for Kenneth MacGowan's production of August Strindberg's* The Spook Sonata *at the Experimental Theater, an outgrowth of the Provincetown Players.*

Opal Cooper received special notice for his acting in the role of Madison Sparrow in The Rider of Dreams, *and John Butler portrayed Simon in the third of the short plays,* Simon the Cyrenian. *Emily Hapgood produced the plays, which had a run of eighteen performances.*

SCENE. *The garden of Pilate's House at Jerusalem. Time, the day of the new arising of* SIMON, *the cross bearer. At the moment of the opening in the conversation,* ROBERT E. JONES *sits upon a settle at the right of the stage of his own designing; directly in the center stands a Negro of immense build. Upon his head is a cap of silver. He is* SIMON; *but now he is smiling. A little at one side is* JOE *of* The Rider of Dreams, *that infant who has made stealing a divine privilege. His left hand is in his pocket. He looks continually offstage, as*

*though contact with the human eye would make him a little
less celestial.*

RIDGELY TORRENCE, *author, is speaking to* OPAL COOPER
as I emerge from Pilate's house to left.

There is nothing lacking but MRS. HAPGOOD, *who will be
in later, for out backstage the rest of the Negroes belonging
to the Torrence plays at the Garden Theater are laughing
and singing among themselves—arranging their throats for
the coming of some note of ecstasy which will rest there for
a moment and be heard by alien ears only through those
throaty walls as something too real to be other than hidden—
a song going about its work with the curtains down.*

Here we are, all of us: BOBBY JONES, *the designer and
director,* MR. TORRENCE, *the author and the heart, the sense
that* MRS. HAPGOOD *saw the possibilities, the actors that at
last are coming a little step into their own, and myself—
the interrogator.*

One feels the nearness of the circus; one feels the nearness of spring in the air. One balances between tragedy
and comedy, and a draught runs between the two—it is
called comment.

The story of Simon the cross bearer has come to a close,
the cries of the crucifixion have stilled into that silence we
term the past, but which is the voice of the future. The
cross has been built and has already fallen to dust. The
kneebone of the suppliant is one with the hand of the exe-
cutioner. In the grave of the years they at last come slowly
together eon by eon, till the one closes on the other in the
clasp of time that brings all things together, articulated
by fate.

"Simon the Cyrenian" is now just John Butler plus one superb red cloak by Mr. Jones.

And Granny Maumee is backstage taking the lines of age from her face and the hate from her heart. But the Rider of Dreams is still here, for this is the spirit of the Negro.

R. TORRENCE: And how did you at last feel the part of Madison Sparrow, Opal?

OPAL COOPER: Well—at first I tried to get it in the usual way, Mr. Torrence, by ear—that's no way for a colored man.

MR. TORRENCE: Why not, Opal?

OPAL COOPER: It has to come by way of the feelin's, sir, by the heart. I did it over and over *(he smiles)* this way: *(begins chanting the dream)* I dreamed it las' night, and day befo' yesterday night, and night befo' dat. I heah a voice say, 'Get up and come a-runnin' '—and still I couldn't get off the ground, Mr. Torrence. I was still on de stage and I knowed that the thing should be recited with my feet over the tops of the houses, sung as though I was a-lookin' down on the world for a place to spit without hitting things, and I couldn't do it until—

BOBBY JONES: Till?

OPAL COOPER: Till Sam laughed, my friend who came to hear me out. As soon as he laughed, something let go o' my leg and there I was, away up high against the sun.

VOICE OF THE INTERVIEWER: And what did you do then?

OPAL COOPER: Then I say I looks up and sees a fine white saddle hoss, and the hoss say, 'Ride me right and I'll guide you right.'

VOICE OF THE INTERVIEWER: And how did you feel then?

OPAL COOPER: Miss, it was this way: I had the stars for cobblestones and the nighttime for my car, and I done pour all that was in me out in the high places so that you folk way down low in the world, walking around buying and selling and living and dying, could hear the voice of Sparrow singing, 'Off he goes as slick as a rancid transom car.' Come to a high hill, lookin' down on de sun and moon. Hoss says, 'I bring you heah to give you news the world is yours.'

BABY JOE *(still looking offstage):* Wasn't my work good?

VOICE OF INTERVIEWER *(with much approval):* It was positively wonderful, dear. What are you going to do when you are grown up into a big man?

BABY JOE: I shall be a great actor.

VOICE OF INTERVIEWER: Is this your biggest ambition?

BABY JOE: If I get a good part—a good stealing part. But I can't. Big men do not steal.

VOICE OF INTERVIEWER: Then you think the only hope is in remaining five years old, Joe?

BABY JOE *(in a small voice):* Yes.

VOICE OF INTERVIEWER: One can be more natural then, can't one, Joe?

BABY JOE: Yes; that's the only time. *(He moves off slowly.)*

B. JONES: Isn't he the brightest boy you ever saw? He is acting already. He has acquired all the attributes of a matinee idol.

OPAL COOPER: It's in the blood, Mr. Jones. It's in the blood as thick as daisies in a field. Run him along for a space and he will try to run smooth, but there's no preventing him from hitting one of them flowers in the end.

R. TORRENCE *(to* V. OF I.*)*: You see how they are. You call
   them children—when they are children they are grown-
   up. When they are grown-up they are children; we all
   are—the nicest of us.

OPAL COOPER *(reciting)*: Perchance, by praying, a man shall
   match his god.

> For if sleep have no mercy, and man's dreams
> Bite to the blood and burn into the bone.
> What shall this man do waking?

That were the word of a great poet, Miss. As we pick
   poets for our ministers, so I want to see poets in our
   actors—for the stage could be the right-hand man of the
   church, Miss. When we colored folk get a new preacher,
   we don't ask that he be educated in the regular sense of
   the word. He might rattle the Scriptures offhand, easy-
   like, but it wouldn't be preaching, as we colored folk
   know it. We says, has he heart or hasn't he heart, do
   he lose himself in the Lord or do he just stand around
   on the outskirts a-tickling of Him? Does he ascend, or
   do he just stay where he's put in the pulpit? Do he
   teach the gospel or do he stimulate you into believin'
   what he says? Do he cry, Miss, in the back of his throat;
   do he chant and do his soul sing? Do he be a man standing in a church, or a church standing in a man?

VOICE OF INTERVIEWER: And you want this in your actors?

SIMON *(speaking for the first time)*: We do. If we don't give
   as much to the stage as we do to our religion, how can
   it be worth our time?

R. TORRENCE: There you are. We had hoped to find the
dramatic quality in great abundance in the colored
people. Perhaps we were mistaken; but mistaken or not,
it is something to have done.

B. JONES: For me it is a great awakening. I was fast becoming content with half of myself. To direct a performance as well as to design it is one of the most
astonishing things that has ever happened to me. Instead
of playing around with a color for a bracelet, a shade
for a boot, a certain line for a cloak, suddenly I find
myself interested in an arm, the set of a pair of shoulders, a turn of the head, the position of a mass, the play
of a light, a tone in a speech that is not just right, a
sentence that is too high, a remark that is too low. I
have not one string in my hand, but many. I have not
one art, but all art—I have not one ambition, but many
ambitions.

R. TORRENCE *(in an aside)*: They make a mistake in calling
Negroes children, in thinking that the least praise will
carry them away. It won't, you know—only pleases
them, makes them glad to do their best. They have not
been spoiled—they can laugh from the heart. We have
forgotten how, become blasé on many years of recognition. I want to see this beginning carried out by
Negroes themselves. I want to see a Negro theatre,
directed by a Negro, with plays by Negroes and inter-
preted by Negroes. How soon this will come about
(shrugging his shoulders) I don't know. If it is left now it
will get nowhere. You can't start something as new as
this and drop it suddenly and expect it to stand on its
feet. We have had some plays submitted to us, but,

strangely enough, in the greater number of cases, they were plays dealing with white people. Sometimes they were low comedy, and often they were far too exalted to admit of acting except by a company of the celestially endowed.

B. JONES: Well, you could hardly expect something acted so soon. Later on—in six months time, perhaps.

OPAL COOPER: Sooner than that, sir. If us colored folks can really begin to believe that our plays would be given de chance—we are just a little skeptical yet—we comes forth with fear and much tremblin', sir. We're like the mole, sir, hidin' low and keeping powerful quiet—but our hide is valuable.

SIMON *(peeling an apple)*: We shall yet behold.

R. TORRENCE *(smiling)*: That's right, Simon. I hope you will all "yet behold." I have no greater dream.

VOICE OF INTERVIEWER: And through this you hope to be better recognized?

OPAL COOPER: Yes, Miss, but I don't want to see the colored people change theirselves. I don't want to see them trying to be white. You know, Miss, a race is only at its best when it's being racial. You know what I mean—when it's being itself. I am sorry to say that us colored people have a great habit, a great ability, to copy. Some of us have grown up with little knowledge of the dialect and that, Miss, is a sin, same as it's a sin for the Irish to forget their language. It makes a wheat field poor when redtop runs into it, and it makes a race poor when it does not keep its character clean and pure of other people's.

VOICE OF INTERVIEWER: Then you don't want to become

Americanized, or like the whites?

OPAL COOPER: No, Miss, we want to develop ourselves
and not merge ourselves in another race. We want just
enough space to show everyone what is in us—for what
it may be worth.

R. TORRENCE *(a mischievous look in his eyes)*: Tell her, Opal,
why it is that you all wanted a part in *Simon the
Cyrenian.*

OPAL COOPER: Because what little chance we have had to
show our ability to the theatrical public, Mr. Torrence,
has been as comedians! We wants to play something
tragic and serious like *Simon the Cyrenian* because that
there is the thing we have not been allowed to play.

R. TORRENCE *(with the same twinkle in his eye)*: But what is
it that you love best?

OPAL COOPER *(with a broad grin)*: You knows it, sir—music
sure is the colored folks' strong point.

*(In the pause can be heard the voices of the Cleff Club
band, singing their songs even when they do not "have to."
It rises and swells to a plaintive cry of happiness and
dies down again into a humming as of many bees.)*

R. TORRENCE *(with a new note in his voice, shaking the long
blond hair out of his eyes)*: That's right, Opal, and don't
you ever lose that talent. Just keep a-hugging it to your
heart and nursing it and giving it the encouragement a
great art needs. After all, it's better to be happy and to
sing than it is to be too cynical and silent.

VOICE OF INTERVIEWER: Shall you write any more colored
plays, Mr. Torrence?

R. TORRENCE: I don't know—perhaps. At least I have this
off my mind—I have done something for those people

who have been so greatly misjudged and ignored. Now I am free to do other things. I want to see of what stuff their dreams are made; if they will stand the hard, critical light of publicity or if 'their dream horses go up in smoke.'

OPAL COOPER *[in chanting lilt]*: We are the great black cocks of de world, and we're calling mighty hard upon a sun that is lazy in its bed, but we are a-callin' and a-callin' and a-callin' and when the beak strain, there will come a golden bill all set around that triumphant voice. Perhaps it will be a silver bill, and when that breaks and sloughs off from the strain, there will come a golden bill all set around with rubies and all a-waitin' to be sung into, to call up a new day from the darkness. An' when the golden beak is broke and fallen to dust about the black cock's feet, then a little angel will come, and cuppin' its hands about that song will make it reach way up to heaven, and make it arouse the sun where it lies in a drunken stupor from the revelry of the day before. And risin' slowly like a gentleman gettin' out of bed, the sun will say to the moon: 'Moon, go and get my bath ready and get out my sunbeams by the fire, because it's summer, and I am due to shine upon the cold house-tops and upon the roofs of little dwellings and upon the wheat fields and the roses, the lakes and the quick leapin' fish and upon the tops of little children's heads. For the fields need me to make the seeds grow, and the houses need me to make the home happy, and the children need me to set their minds a-turnin' on what they shall be when they, too, are men. And den when the black cock has crowed and crowed, and sung and sung his little bit in the ravine, and the little hands of the angel have left him, then he will scratch among the gravel and the grass, and you will think it is for grain, but I know it's for his lost beak of gold—for sometimes he's afraid that he had only the impulse, and something else made his song so powerful and tellin'. (R. TORRENCE *has clasped his hands in front of him, and his kind, keen blue eyes are half-closed. He nods his head, but he does not speak.)*

OPAL COOPER *(continuing)*: We mayn't be great and we mayn't be all necessary, we mayn't be powerful and we mayn't be tragic so well as we be glad. But we have de quality if someone will give us a chance to scratch and see if we own the beak or if it's the Lord's.

(B. JONES *gets up slowly with hands behind his back, begins to pace up and down.* R. TORRENCE *remains seated, his hands clasped in front of him.* SIMON *has moved off, leaving nothing behind but the apple peel and a few black apple seeds beside his magnificent cloak of scarlet, but lately fallen from his shoulders. The interviewer has come slowly out of Pilate's house and stands, pencil forgotten in hand.)*

OPAL COOPER: I speaks for my race when I speaks for myself. It's not me only telling you things, it's my mammy and my mammy's mammy before her. What I have forgotten she remembers, and what she has forgotten her mother knows. That's why we linger before we die —to keep alive a little of our heart's blood, a little of our folk song, a little of our dialect and a little of our heritage.

(SIMON *returns with* PILATE'S WIFE.)

PILATE'S WIFE: This way we will find our level.

VOICE OF ACTE AND OF BARABBAS: We shall arise!

VOICE OF PILATE and VOICE OF BATTUS: This way the whites of our eyes shall see across the world!

VOICE OF GRANNY MAUMEE: Thus we shall come a-runnin'!

VOICE OF LUCY SPARROW: For a long time we have been strings curled up in oblivion; now the instrument is stretching us into song.

VOICE OF THE SINGING OVERTURE: At last we are singing up against the cracks of the door. Some day it will swing open.

VOICES OF THE MOCKERS WITH SCARLET ROBE AND CROWN OF THORNS: A crown of thorns for the newborn, a scarlet cloak for a swaddling cloth!

VOICES OF THOSE IN THE GALLERIES: Where's dat nigger heaven now!

VOICES OF THOSE IN THE VESTIBULE: Tickets, that we may see the shell breaking and falling from them!

VOICES OF THOSE IN THE DARK PLACES: We are less by a race!

VOICES OF ROSAMOND JOHNSON AND OF NEGRO SPIRITUALS: Glory, glory, hallelujah!

VOICES OF EXECUTIVE STAFF: To have sewn a bead on, to have mended a broken platform, to have sewn up a torn shoe—this is our share.

VOICES OF THE COLORED PORTION OF THE WORLD *(coming around chair corners and through the cracks of the old theater and down the wings a million on a million)*: May our bow arm be strong for the speeding of the arrow tipped with the message!

VOICE OF OPAL COOPER: I dreamed hit last night and day befo' yesterday night, and night befo' dat. I heah a voice say, 'Get up and come a-runnin'.' An' I looks up and sees a fine white saddle hoss, an' the hoss say, 'Ride me right and I'll guide you right.' On I gets, off he goes, slick as a rancid transom car. Come to a high hill, lookin' down on de sun and moon. Hoss say, 'I brung you heah to give you news. The world is yours to pick and choose.'

VOICE OF BOBBY JONES *(calling offstage)*: I have a new idea for the lighting of that second play, John. Just switch it on and let's try her now. Ready—that's right.

VOICE OF BABY JOE *(far offstage)*: I can't button them up.

VOICE OF INTERVIEWER: I shall try to remember everything.

VOICE OF SIMON: You can't forget, Miss.

VOICE OF RIDGELY TORRENCE: Now we shall see what's in them: if they are great poets, if they are great novelists, if they are great actors, if they are great painters, if they are great producers—or if they are only dreamers singing their dreams over the daily commonplaces that are their lives.

(At this juncture the curtain drops suddenly, blotting out the scene. Then the crooning of many voices singing "Walk Together, Children.")

The Confessions of
Helen Westley

*Born Henrietta Manney in 1875, Helen Westley attended
school in Brooklyn and studied for the stage at New York's
Academy of Dramatic Arts and at Boston's Emerson School
of Oratory. Her first roles consisted primarily of one-night
stands with an Ohio River troupe and in vaudeville. Her
Broadway premiere was in* The Captain of the Nonesuch
*in 1897, and she continued to perform in New York produc-
tions until her marriage to John Westley in 1900.*

*With her marriage, she took a twelve-year leave from the
stage; but upon her divorce she began to actively participate
in the Bohemian literary and art activities of New York's
Greenwich Village. There she directed Barnes's short plays,
produced by the Provincetown Players, and met Lawrence
Langner, founder of the experimental theatre group The
Washington Square Players. Langner encouraged Westley to
join the company, and with other group members such as
Philip Moeller, Roland Young, and Katharine Cornell, she
performed in his theatrical manifesto and a bill of one-act
plays at the Bandbox Theater in 1915. Westley remained with
the Players, acting in a variety of plays from Zona Gale's*
Neighbors *to Anton Chekhov's* The Seagull, *until the group's
demise three years later.*

In December of that year, 1918, Langner invited Westley to help him in founding The Theatre Guild, which would become one of the most important theatrical production groups for the next two decades. Westley performed in the Guild's opening production of Jacinto Benavente's Bonds of Interest *in April 1919, and over the next several years, she became a Guild regular, appearing as Mrs. Muskat in* Liliom *in 1921; as Zinida in* He Who Gets Slapped *in 1922; as Mrs. Zero in* The Adding Machine *in 1923; as Mrs. Evans in Eugene O'Neill's* Strange Interlude *in 1928; as Aunt Ella in* Green Grow the Lilacs *in 1931; and as Frau Lucher in* Reunion in Vienna *in 1931.*

Westley's participation in the Guild went far deeper, however, than performing. As a member of the board, she actively participated in the selection of scripts—often vehemently arguing for or against particular dramas—and in the management of other Guild activities. A Bohemian by instinct, and (according to theatre commentator George Jean Nathan) "begauded like a gypsy queen in an 1890 comic opera," Westley became a powerful and original force in American theatre. As critic Brooks Atkinson has written, the Guild "more than any other group . . . led Broadway into the modern world"; it was Westley's temperament which both created the Guild and led to its destruction.

Beginning in the 1930s, Westley turned to motion pictures, appearing in Moulin Rouge, Death Takes a Holiday, Roberta, Show Boat, Rebecca of Sunnybrook Farm, *and in a film biography of Lillian Russell. She performed her last Broadway role in* The Primrose Path *in 1939.*

"**H**ELLO, is this Miss Barnes?"
   "Yes."
"This is Helen Westley."
"Ah, how do you do?"
"I want to be interviewed again."
"Very well; I shall meet you at three-thirty at the Brevoort."

I am there at three-thirty precisely. I order something "with a cherry in it" and await the appearance of the strange person of the Washington Square Players; and soon she appears, walking easily and wearing another of those adored, secondhand gowns; a secondhand book is under her arm, and she smiles, showing her thirty-two perfect teeth.

"*Toute passe, mon ami*," she murmurs as she takes the seat before me, shaking her earrings and thrusting the book upon the table. It is Murray's *History of Greek Literature*, and she knows it looks well.

"Dusty books," she begins, as she orders oatmeal (which of course can't be got at this hour), "are my one real passion. New books are like young girls—fit for nothing. A secondhand book is like a person who has traveled; it is only when a book has been handled by several persons and has become dirty that it's fit for contemplation. You feel that it has graduated, that it has something larger and more cosmopolitan about it—oh, well!" She began to laugh. "Ah, to be both young and beautiful! Now, I am beautiful and you are young; I can never be again what you are, and you in all probability will never be what I am, so after all I have the advantage of you—no oatmeal? How perfectly preposterous! Very well, bring me a highball.

"To continue: to be young, to be beautiful—how mournful, how sad, how ironical. When I was young I was full of dreams of love, of passion, of idealism, of green, green youth. People called me interesting, but they were a little afraid of me. It is simple enough: I was too eager, too full of curiosity, too vital—too unlovely. Now—," she stretched her thin, long hand out and finished,"—now I am terribly interesting, terribly original, very talented, beautiful, as I said, but—I am no longer a child. Now I have repose; now I can wait, now I can reflect; now I am capable of youth, but not capable of few years—that is the pitiful thing."

"Some advice for young actors would come in here very nicely."

"There isn't any advice. You might as well tell a child to be fifty years old when born. You can't advise, you can only tell of your own case—and anyway, if we are honest, our own case always interests us much more than the affairs of others.

"Well, I shall die as I was born—very thoughtful, full of ennui. That is the one great quality. Ah, Buddhism, China, Persia—races of ennui, not races of men. The history of the world has been one not of conquest, as supposed; it has been one of ennui. Why do we fall in love? Because we are filled with ennui. Why do we fall and break our limbs? Because of ennui. Why do we fall ill and remain unconscious for hours? Ennui, my dear. Ennui sends us to our death; ennui sends us to the battlefields; ennui sends us through the world, and ennui takes us out of it. If this were not so, do you suppose for a moment that we would permit ourselves to fall in love once we had heard of its effects? Do you presume to imagine that we would fight in battle, knowing well death awaited us, if it were not for ennui? The only mistake we make is not to submit to ennui. We struggle against the term, but not against the fact. The greatest people have been oppressed by it. To fall, my dear, is to submit to gravity, to let go, and all the so-called great events of history have been a series of falls. Napoleon climbed only because he understood the value of a greater fall over a lesser fall; that's the real incentive to ambitions of all kinds. In five years I shall be a very famous and wonderful actress, in all probability. I know the value of a long fall; I am a super-ennuian, if I might coin a new word."

"A little faster with your youth, Helen."

"To me Boston is my youth. I went there to study oratory. I felt sure that recitations were my forte. Then I made my first appearance before a Brooklyn city club. I remember to this day the polite and frozen faces in the front rows and the general air of pity that permeated the whole place. I was in despair—and right in the middle of 'The brave house of Tarquin shall suffer wrongs no more,' I knew that I had made my first and last appearance before any audience of that kind under such ambitions. Then I was thinking, feeling. I married; I put my youth behind me at an early age because youth is the age when thinking and feeling have their largest hold, and I wanted to be doing."

"Advice here."

"Well, I should advise young, aspiring women to live their lives first, to get through with their emotional training soon, and to do their thinking and reading. Then, afterward, comes the time for calm, unemotional observation—a snake—''

''A little too early for the snake, I think.''

''No; by all means, let the snake enter here. What is the fascination in contemplating a snake?''

''Well, what?''

''The snake—ergo—there you have it—you philosophize about life, you muddle with your paints, your tapestries and your incense. And so young America, as young France or young Germany did before it, dries up—that part of these countries that indulged in this alone, I mean to say. Oscar Wilde and a few minor poets and poseurs got away with it, but in the end the lesser artificials lose all their knack. Their deftness leaves them with nothing but facility, and felicity is gone forever. Now, go to the snake, a little more Baudelairean and Wildeish than anyone can be, and you find that the snake, after all, is life, is change, and in all its moods is a little more remarkable than such artists can ever be. I say, go to life, study life. Sit on a sidewalk and contemplate the sewer, the billposters, the street cleaners, the pedestrians, anything—but go there before you go to Chinatown to buy embroidery.''

''Do you often sit on the sidewalk, Miss Westley?''

''I do. If doctors would prescribe sidewalks instead of pills and hot water, how much better off we should be.''

''Really, you have a dirt complex, as Freud would say.''

''Yes, a dirt complex. Isn't dirt really wonderful? That sounds like Hermione, but I mean it. She says those things because she is so neat and tidy and smug, and I say it because I am dingy and broad-minded and remarkable and subtle.''

"Can you face real trouble?"

"Absolutely. Give me despair, and I am at my best. Give me sorrow, and only then are my shoulders worthy of me—at renouncing, for instance. Where have I learned this trick of the half-turned shoulder, the cold, drooping eyes? Through sorrows and difficulties. There's nothing like it for developing the figure and making one supple; it's better than dancing or swimming. Oh, yes, I can face all things."

"How do you take death?"

"My dear, place a corpse in front of me, and then—and then only—do I reach my divine height of splendid simplicity. I say, '*Toute passe*—did she die well?' If the answer is, 'No, she died very badly, and without hauteur and finesse,' I say, 'Permit me one moment, that I may disapprove of her.' If the answer is, 'Verily, she passed as calmly and as genteelly as a lady laying down her gloves,' I shall say with a gesture, 'Pass on; she has nothing further to learn.' "

"And joys, how do you react to them?"

"I laugh a little, looking around to see that no one else laughs a little better."

"You are a clever woman, Miss Westley."

"I am, but only within the past years—three or five—have I come to my real self. Apropos of that, poverty is a terrible thing."

"In what way?"

"It hangs before one's soul like a black curtain and behind one's body another equally black, throwing the one into obscurity and the other into relief. That is very bad for the formation of a personality."

"Then you suffered it?"

"Oh, yes, I did not grow under that. Not until I knew for certain where my next meal would come from could I give myself up to ignoring that next meal; I could think of other things."

"What do you think of the theatres of America?"

"I think that our greatest hope lies in the little theatre, though, of course, the regular theatre is improving. The little theatre does give a person a certain impetus, however. An unknown actor has a better chance, as has an unknown playwright, for the simple reason that in the little theatre movement an actor does not have to star and a playwright is only one of three or four other playwrights on a bill—making the risk of a failure nothing of great importance, as it is when the whole evening is given over to just the one performance."

"I see."

"And then there is my future—you want to hear about that, don't you?"

"Yes, I think I know what is in the future for you."

"Do you really?" Here Helen Westley turned her strange eyes on me.

"Oh yes. You say you were born in Brooklyn—good, you will return to Brooklyn."

"Do you consider that my future? How horrible!"

"Not so fast. Brooklyn is only the beginning of your future; I am positively certain that you will take to wearing shawls and comforting yourself with hot water bottles."

"More horrible and more horrible!"

"Exactly, but that is not all—in the end you will return to that same thing that you had your beginning in—

religion. Am I right?"

"Yes, you are right. But it will not be the usual religion; it will be something oriental and mystic."

"Probably one has to suit one's religions to one's complexion, and yours is oriental."

"Thank you, you are probably right again. Yes, religion, but it will be something Chinese—perhaps Buddhism— or any religion that has the occult turn to it. Religion is the only practical end for me."

"You see, I knew it."

"You have your moments."

"Thank you. What started you originally on this stage career—I mean after you had married and were beginning to bring up a family?"

"I don't know. Probably it was the easiest thing for me to do. I had acted, so I returned to acting. Perhaps this is not the great thing I was cut out for; the next five years will tell."

"What else have you in mind?"

"Well, I am taking up the study of English. I may be a great writer like the Russians, or perhaps an artist or a thinker—you never can tell. I took out a book on mental derangements from the library, but everyone in it seemed so natural that I gave it up. I believe too heartily in the vanity of all things to take up such a thought permanently —but it serves to pass the time, and it gives one a culti- vated sensation while going through with it. Then I have other habits—chocolate almonds for instance—and you have probably noticed my oatmeal passion."

"Yes, I noticed that long ago when someone pointed to you and hissed, 'Vampire'—I thought it very funny."

"It isn't funny at all, that's where you young people make a mistake. You think vampires have to smoke cigarettes and drink absinthe and live on larks' tongues, whereas vampirism thrives on oatmeal. I wouldn't be a bit surprised but that it has its very roots in oatmeal and wheats and such nourishing things; after all, one has to be pretty vital to vampire one's life to a close. You can't do it on nothing."

"That was merely a trap—then you do consider yourself a vampire?"

"What do you call a vampire?"

"Anyone who can break a habit easier than acquire one."

"Then I am indeed a vampire."

"Very well, multiplication always adds up to a vampire anyway."

"Really, Djuna, you are sort of clever, aren't you?"

"I am only a little less conceited than you yourself, Helen."

She burst out laughing. "We are a funny couple to be sitting here talking a lot of nonsense, aren't we?"

"We are."

"Well, let's stop it."

"We can't, not yet; I have at least three pages more to fill."

"Have you been making notes?"

"I don't have to. My memory always makes a paragraph out of a note automatically."

"What shall we talk about now?"

"Anything you like."

"Suppose you describe me, and finish the article in that way."

"You would love that, wouldn't you?"

"Yes, but you have done it already two or three times, so I suppose I can't expect it again. Waiter, the check please."

"I often wonder if you are contented."

"There you go. That's the trouble with you all. What is contentment, what is happiness? I admit the existence of nothing excepting ennui, and that only gets us back to the beginning of our story."

"Contemplation and that sort of thing?"

"That's just it—let the world go by and watch it going, that's all. We take it too seriously. After it is all over and the procession has passed, there remains just exactly what remains after a carnival: a little more dust, a broken bottle or two, and some colored confetti. Is it for that you worry until your hair is gray and you lie down in death? Oh, how vain, how vain."

"Yet I have heard you crying out because you had lost a handkerchief."

"Because I wished to wave adieu to the procession with it, that's all."

"And have you now come to the end of all you have to say? Think well, for I shall never again write you up for any paper in the world—this is your last chance."

A look akin to horror crept into Helen Westley's eyes.

"You don't mean that?"

"I do."

She remained silent for a moment only, then smiling amiably she said: "Impossible! You will run out of material sooner or later—then enter Helen again." She leaned back comfortably, crossing her feet—terrible zebra spat upon zebra spat.

Sitting thus she contemplated herself for a while silently in the mirror.

"Do you know," she said suddenly, "I am really the original for *The Sphinx*. Am I not like some rare exotic marble, for ages standing in an ancient, desolate mood, overlooking some fathomless desert?"

"Perhaps, yes, if you don't let your eyes wander down until they rest upon those horrible spats."

"Don't you like them? I got them for thirty cents on Second Avenue—by the way, that gives me a lead on a little further advice. More people should dress from the secondhand clothiers than do; you can have the wardrobe of a lady for the pittance of a waitress."

"My dear Helen, you are the only woman in the world who can wear them and still be asked out. You are Time clothed in Age."

"Yet I am really a young woman."

"That is your big mistake: you are ten thousand years old and make an idiot of yourself by being thirty-odd. For you to be thirty-odd is an impertinence—and a slander. You probably knew Columbus when he was contemplating the great discovery, and doubtless you gave him some valuable information as to location and worth of the said country."

"Yes," she said slowly, "I am really wonderful."

"When you laugh you are like a Mephistophelian lizard—very uncanny."

"Like a cloak model—very exclusive." She laughed again, drawing on impossible large and yellow gloves.

"I have only one complaint to make," she finished, reaching for an old worn umbrella. "That is this: the

Helen Westley

theatrical profession for one of my facial attainments is hardly all it should be in the way of accessibility. I am too far away from the public, they can't appreciate my full value. Every line, every muscle of my countenance is worthy of study. Yes, I shall have to take up something confidential with the public, that as they lean forward to say, 'Would you really advise this or that?' they will become acquainted with the peculiar worth of my extraordinary and individual features. Adieu."

Stepping easily out into the avenue, she hailed a passing carriage and seating herself, leaned back, gazing with pale strange eyes into the descending dusk.

Yvette Guilbert

"You little monster! You've made me look a horror!" de-
claimed Yvette Guilbert upon seeing how Henri de Toulouse-
Lautrec had portrayed her. Guilbert was the subject of
numerous Toulouse-Lautrec drawings and caricatures in
which he pictured the tall, emaciated French singer in her
habitual yellow dress and long black gloves; she had worn
them originally because of poverty, but they became her
distinctive trademark.

Performing as a comic singer in Les Bouffes du Nord in
Paris, in the leading cafes of Germany and England, and in
vaudeville in the United States, Guilbert became famous for
her risqué songs of the Latin Quarter, sung with an almost
spiritual innocence but filled with double-entendre. In later
years, Guilbert changed her repertoire to include historical
ballads and songs of the French peasantry, interpreting these
with great subtlety and dramatic expression.

In the mid 1920s, she began performing in films, including
Faust (1926), L'Argent (1929), and Pecheurs D'Island
(1935). Guilbert died in Aix-en-Provence in 1944.

THE room is not large. An odor of a city autumn is
in the air. Not that autumn which brings death and
decay and trampling out of flowers, but that Manhattan
autumn into which alien blossoms suddenly thrust their

pink and purple opulence: the spring of the year for hot-house blooms.

The pink chair of gray enameled wood rests on a carpet still a little heavier with shades of rose. The high screen, with its false plumed birds and its great rusty dahlias, stands aside just enough to expose the portrait of a small Parisienne in white gown and cupid-shaped straw hat, who, lifting her skirt ever so little with that conscious coquetry that always goes before an ankle, smiles at the gentleman leaning out of the latticed window.

Suddenly the pink and gray chair is obliterated, the screen and the grisette forgotten, for Madame Yvette Guilbert has swept into the room and is leaning forward, her two white-clad arms upon the glass top of the table.

She is a large woman with low-curling blonde hair. Her years sit on her kindly indeed, more like a decoration than a calamity, more like a friendship between her and life.

Her smile is quick and broad. I remember once hearing her sing something with "hips and haws" as a refrain; and now, looking on her some ten or twelve years later, I saw the same intelligent eyes, the same mobile but thin lips and the large, slightly tilted, clever, cynical nose; and I knew that one is bound to be at home wherever this singer is.

It is impossible to catch and render on paper her manner of pronouncing English; it is not a matter of letters, it is entirely a matter of the back of the throat. Therefore, I shall not attempt it at all.

"Sometimes I think," she said, leaning forward, "that the world does not understand anyone. The artist, no matter in what country, has so many terrible and pitiful hours to pass through, and if finally someone does pay attention to him and does give him a chance, it is only to have him grossly misunderstood.

"You ask me about my songs; you say, Madame Guilbert, are you not sorry that you can no longer sing the little saucy songs you used to sing—ah." She throws up her expressive hands, draws her lips together, bows her head. "Ah, ah that such a thing should be said, that anyone should misunderstand me like that. They were not naughty songs, mademoiselle, they were life. They were flowers tossed from the gutter into heaven; they were strands of martyrs' hair blowing across the centuries; they were drops of blood from the heart; they were human passions and all-too-human forgetfulness. For alas, alas, the world forgets so soon and so easily.

"No, mademoiselle. They were irreverent and they were sarcastic and they were cutting—they were never risqué. They were the little penknife blade with which one cuts the wrist of malice and deceit—this and nothing more.

"I am not a tragedienne, nor am I a heavy and emotional actress who tears her hair out in teaching a truth. These things I cannot do, but this other I can. I want to be like Pierrot, to play the fool, the gay one; and as I smile, appear to weep, and as I live, appear to die. If I pull out one single strand of hair, it shall seem as terrible as if I tore out the whole; if I make one shake of the head, it shall be as if some hand took all humanity by the ankles and shook it loose eternally from life.

"When I appear this winter at the new French theatre,

the Théâtre du Vieux Colombier, I am going to present
a Pierrot that I have based on the poems of two brilliant
men, and then I shall prove to you all that Pierrot is a
gay blossom, but that his roots go deep and are wound
about the eternal corpse of the world, as a ribbon is
wound around a lovely gift.''

She laughed, tossing her great head back, and suddenly
I knew that she was beautiful: the crooked smile, the
bright eyes, the sensitive under-curve of the nose. With
these things Madame Guilbert is as clever as with her
songs.

''I am always trying to teach someone some few things.
Is it silly, impossible? I do not know. You see, I was ten
years before my time. I set out to destroy deceitfulness
by truth, and the future shall see such things attacked;
not in their reality alone, but in their spirit.

''You see,'' she went on, bringing her hands back from
a last gesture, ''we need to know each other better,
America and France. We have always made mistakes in
judgment about each other. You think we are naughty
and off-color and trivial, and we think you are giddy and
cruel and ignorant. We think of you as society women,
who have a flower trained to your corsage as we train
flowers to our verandas, who carry about little dogs and
spend your hours in idleness. Now it is time that we know
what is in the heart of the other. We are allies fighting
for the one cause, and we should not be strangers to each
other in life if we can be such comrades in death.

''The Théâtre du Vieux Colombier is such an attempt—
a medium through which we can learn to know ourselves
and to know you better than through any one other

thing perhaps. But ah—'' Again she tossed her hands into the air. ''What is one going to do if you insist that our writers are 'naughty' and our entire life a little what it should not be? But I tell you—,'' and here she brought her fist down upon the table top, ''—there is not one indecent song in France, nor one immoral poet.''

''Tell me about France,'' I said.

''Ah, France—can one speak of it?'' She lowered her lids slowly, looking at her hands. ''You know, I have had some letters, many letters from the *poilu*—I am godmother to many of them. Ah, mademoiselle, and such letters, such letters! One wrote me, 'I had hoped to keep a thumb or two to press buttons with when I came back from the war, but, madame, will you believe it, they are dead; they will push nothing further. I am sorry; there are so many things I will no longer be able to do.' And another—a man unable to move his legs, with one eye only a blind groove where sight had been—he said, 'It is well, I shall go back to the trenches when they will let me.' ''

There were two spots of wet upon the table, and Madame Guilbert put her crossed hands over them quietly. ''And there are others, mademoiselle, many others. No, they do not say, 'Ah, the Germans, how we hate them.' Instead they say nothing. One cannot say anything; one can only die. Europe is an immense field of fragments, and these fragments are moving. Some of them still have eyes, some of them still have mouths, some hands, others feet; but they are terribly scattered. They lie in the four corners of the earth, piling up slowly, and always as dust gathers in a forgotten corner.''

She looked out of the window, turning her head. ''One

of them said to me, 'There was a parade, a charity parade or something—you were not there—that is right. We knew we could trust you, we knew you would not disguise yourself in the carnival patriotic.' "

She repeated it and laughed a hard, quick laugh. "Ah yes, mademoiselle, so are our men; they cannot stand any hypocrisy longer—any more lies, anything false. God! If anyone can know where things begin and end, it is they.

"When will it end?"

She turned to me. "Have you read *Le Feu*? That man told the truth—he knows. We who do not know should keep our peace, should be still. It is only an insult to our dead."

"And what will be the end of it all? Will there be a revolution, or will there be nothing changed?"

"There will be a great rebirth of religion, mademoiselle. One needs God."

"Do you mean by that universal brotherhood, without revolt?"

"I do not know; all I know is that after this, one will no longer dare to hate."

"And do you see anything happening that portends upheaval?"

"Again, I do not know. Somehow I don't see how there can be any more energy for revolt. One must be angry for that, and the people are terribly tired."

"But love by fatigue is not lasting love."

"It will be more than that—infinitely more than that; but you who have not been there cannot know."

"Yes, I think a few of us know—those with intelligence."

"Ah," her eyes snapped, "there you have it. With intelligence even stupidity is understood; with intelligence

Europe could have had this war without a single dead man."

She continued, "No, no, no, after this no one alive will be the same person he was before. You go through the 'face hospital,' you see that 'thing' lying there, a red slanting plane for a face—out of which, in the place where the mouth should be, oozes a little saliva and blood—a cross section of flesh. There are no ears to hear with, yet they have heard all; there are no eyes, yet this body that we call a 'thing' by its very sacrifice, sees all; and shorn of lips, it speaks in such a thundering voice that it must be heard to the uttermost ends of the earth.

"One's parents and children, husband and lover are in it. In peace one may be an individual, but in times like these one is only that flesh which is a little to one side of the wound.

"You know," she said, "I am quite angry at your society, at the society woman. They are very ignorant of the proper manners. They assume that money makes up for everything, instead of having discovered that money pays for everything, even an education." She laughed in a good-humored way, very generously and forgivingly. "I have had some funny—what do you call them —run-ins with society when it wants to give a benefit and does not seem to know enough to take the same amount as they would make out of their own pockets, instead of making all that fuss and show for a few dollars. But then," she shrugged her shoulders, "I suppose one must have misfortunes, or where would they get their 'benefits' from."

She stooped and, lifting a handful of manuscripts up, began to turn the leaves over.

Yvette Guilbert

"I have composed a few songs in my life, mademoiselle, and I made out very well and seemed to please. But lately I have found two artists that I love to sing: Rictus and Laforge. One poem—ah, so splendid, so magnificent—to Christ. He says to him, 'Do not weep, old chap, yet there is nothing else for you to do.' Ah, ah, ah, such men as these in all countries alike are left to starve and to break their hearts—and then to die understanding, but mis-understood."

"What of the artist in America?"

"If you Americans would only be patient in the presence of life it would be well, but you won't. Every-thing real shocks you. Not all of you, of course. I mean the crowd, the poor tragic crowd; when will they know—will they ever know?"

She stood up. "And now, mademoiselle, let me see what you have been drawing." She came up behind me, placed her arm about my shoulder and said:

"It is like an antique, a carving in wood. Perhaps it is like me, and perhaps it is not."

"No," I shook my head. "Something is wrong."

"It is the nose," she said, and tilted it a little, laughing. She walked away from me again, her hands behind her back.

"And do you, as an artist, find anyone in your life who understands you?" she inquired, looking at me search-ingly.

"Yes, yes, I see," she said, quickly smiling again and, putting a hand on my shoulder once more, she said:

"It is nice, is it not, even if there is only one who really understands."

Guardabassi, Soldier, Singer, and Artist

FROM Gorizia has come Signor Francesco Mario Guardabassi, Captain in the Second Regiment of the Grenadier Guards.

For him the tumult and the shouting has died, and verily the captains and the kings have departed, each on his separate errand, for he has left the battlefields for an hour under the orders of the Italian Ambassador, Count Macchi di Cellere, as a representative of the Italian American Society.

Coming into the cool and the quiet of a Vanderbilt Hotel room, with its chairs of soft blue cushions and its fire screen of red, one sees the figure of Signor Guardabassi, tall, well built, gray of hair, in a uniform of splendid lines and colors. Silver braid goes about a throat that has many times sung in opera, and scarlet cord at the cuffs shows off to advantage the hands that have put upon canvas many smiling or severe profiles and full faces of royalty.

And one says *"Bonjour"* and one bows, and bowing in kindly pleasure the Captain leads you to a seat.

He sits down also. There is the faint metallic sound of spurs, the murmur of wrinkled leather, the whisper of braid sliding along braid. Looking across the room the better to focus the eyes, one sees an Austrian belt and knife hanging from a candlestick on the mantel.

Leaning forward, he gives his face to his visitor for perusal. Kind brown eyes that too easily might go out of their sphere of Italian sympathy into the realm of severity, a long nose with the flaring nostrils of one who has breathed warm air, and the somewhat too flexible and sensuous lips of those who sing good songs and who know the *joie de vivre*.

And one finds oneself saying: "So you have seen the war," as one might say: "So you have arisen from the dead."

And he answers:

"Ah, signorina, you people in America do not understand what the Italians have done and are doing in this war."

He goes on to explain: "You think here in America of the Italian as of the wine-loving, rose-kissing, languid people of the South. For you his languors are laziness and his love of music and of splendid warm life is sensuous indulgence. No."

Just that word "no" and he stops, looking at the large linked fingers of his hands. "The most beautiful act of this most unlovely war was that act of the Italians by which they severed themselves from Austria and from things German. This meant very much. In every family in Italy that could afford servants and nurses, there was at least one among them of Austrian or German descent.

"In my own house there was one who had been with us for forty years. When the war started she began saying: 'The Germans are misunderstood.' In a few months she was saying: 'The Germans are not what they are painted to be; this is a war of protection, not of aggression.'

"I said to her: 'What blood runs in your veins?' and she answered: 'Austria is in my veins.'

"I said to her: 'There are some people in whom justice can flow, but not in the veins of an Austrian.' I went from her to my brother and I said to him:

" 'You must turn our old nurse out of your house,' and he answered:

" 'Aye, we must turn our hearts out until there is no furniture in them that is not of Italy.' "

He got up, walking to the window.

"Will you have an orange?" he inquired, smiling a little. I shook my head.

He came back to the mantel, and lifting up a long club on which a steel end with spikes was riveted came toward me.

"You see this? That is a mace, or in trench slang a 'head masher'—it is German."

"Don't all belligerents use them?" I asked.

"When they can. We do not invent them, we inherit them. There are a lot of things that the battlefields bequeath. There are things called common law and there are things I call common wills, and these are the things that come to one after a combat, that the dead leave as a legacy behind them. A legacy of hate and the utensils for making hate. The workshop that only turns out its tools after death. Ah, well," he sighed, "it is all in a death's time, I suppose."

"Had the Germans such a strong place in the financial world of Italy?"

"But yes. Do you realize that Germany was Italy's

commercial mother? The banking was German. They controlled the electrical plants. There were Germans in the journalistic world that made any Italian venture either in commercial lines or in banking unsafe. They would stop at nothing in the way of caustic comment and abuse. Their power was subtle but absolute. Control the finances of a country and you practically control everything, for the life of a people is based on finance, and if the finance is in the hands of a neighboring country there is bound to be trouble.

"It took several months for us to enter the war. Why? Simple enough is the reason why. If we plunged in at the beginning with our hearts, nevertheless our roots would be in the ground that Germany had placed there for them to grow in. We had to loosen ourselves by degrees. We could not throw our bread and butter away and say, 'We will fight to a finish for our ideals,' because without bread and butter there is nothing to go on with.

"You will ask how Italy got into this partnership with the Prussian. That is also an easy matter to answer.

"France had always displeased the Italian. Napoleon III we considered very weak and grossly eager. When Nice and Savoy and Tunis were fallen upon by this man's following, Italy turned from France in heart and mind. England had never shown any love or interest in Italy, and therefore there was nothing left for this people to do but turn toward Prussia."

"And how does Italy stand now? Is she capable of maintaining a national industrial life of her own, or is she again to be at the mercy of another country?"

"Italy can survive only if America helps her with

finances and raw materials."

"And how long can she hold out?"

"Until her stomach is empty. This is a war of the stomach, signorina. When the world starves, then the world will stop fighting, and not before."

"And what do your artists think of it? What does d'Annunzio think of it?"

"D'Annunzio is a great poet, but he likes to blame Italy for many things. He tries to imagine that she drove him out.

"It is true that while we Italians realize d'Annunzio's genius we do not sympathize with his personal indulgences, those same cruelties and laxities that caused one great woman's heart to break along with Italy's respect of the master, for he is a great man.

"But he has largely redeemed himself. He has fought for the country which he really loved. At least if it was all a pose, and if it is still a pose, we must give him credit for being a master at his own life, a man who can back up his untruths with truth."

"But does he feel that his life is over, or is it the genuine sacrifice of a man who still feels himself capable of being the artist?"

"I don't like to answer that for fear I should do him injustice. He says he loves Italy, and that he has proved by aerial service. He says that he has given Italy his brains and that he will give the Adriatic his body."

"And what of Marinetti?"

"Ah, the crazy boy! A friend of mine, a charming fellow, but those futurists—" He spread his hand out in a gesture of amusement.

"Then let us speak of Enrico Ferri."

"The Socialists in Italy have caused a great deal of trouble. They are the poison left back home while the men fight. They have time to be active with their propaganda and they fill the women and children with ideas which may be all well enough in times of peace, or well enough even if socialism were accepted simultaneously by all nations, but which at a time like this are no less than treason. The women, wishing the war at an end, longing for the safety of their husbands and lovers, sons and fathers, write to the soldiers letters tainted with the ruinous peace suggested by the social fanatic."

"And how does the common soldier take it?"

"How does a man feel at the front?" he inquired.

I nodded.

"It is very strange," he answered, and his eyes half closed. "There is a trench language as alien to the mother tongue as is imaginable. It is a conversation between life and death. I don't know how to explain it in any better language.

"It is neither pessimistic nor gay, it is neither laughter nor tears. It is the language of those who are dead, though they have not acquired death. The man in the trench often speaks jokingly, but it is a joke quite devoid of humor. He often speaks sorrowfully, but it has nothing of melancholy in it.

"It is a strange language, spoken by a tongue that moves neither in the here nor in the there; a patois of indifference and excitement. It is above sorrow and grief and expectation."

"But, then, does not the soldier hope to come through

alive?''

''The soldier does not hope, signorina. The soldier fights when he is expected to fight, dies when he has to die, and lives while he may.''

''But does he not think back to his home and family and of the time when perhaps he will see them again?''

''Sometimes, yes, but not with the kind of hope that you know of. You see, signorina, when a man you have loved and fought with side by side for days and nights suddenly bursts beside you into the flame that rises and into the blood that sinks, you stand and stare and stare, and feel nothing. It is only afterward, provided you are lucky enough to have an afterward, that you care.

''Most men are dazed with the things that will hurt and numb with the knowledge that their time for realization of these things may never come. It is like hiding a letter in your pocket that you want to read, waiting for a moment when you can slip away from the rest and open it. They are waiting, knowing that they will never be able to slip away where they can open it.''

''And religion?''

''Religion is for the man who is either very happy or very unhappy—it is not for the man who is neither of these, and this is the soldier.''

''What is the thing that the soldier fears the most?''

''The gas.''

''More than shellfire, more than going 'over the top,' more than overhead fire?''

''More than hellfire, more than going over the top or into the very pits of the inferno. Gas takes away the breath, you can live a few moments while you realize you are dead. Nothing is so diabolic as the gas."

"Who invented it?"

He smiled a little crookedly. "They say Cellini did."

"And still people recover?"

"Oh, yes, to go insane or worse. The most terrible sight I have seen in warfare is that of the gas-smitten soldier. His brass buttons turn black, he spits up his lungs, blood spurts out of him like soda water from a bottle, and then he begins to run. Ah, God, that is terrible!"

We were quiet for a little while. I could hear the watch ticking on the Captain's wrist.

"And then—?"

"They run and run, terribly, in circles sometimes. If you run you know you can keep alive, it keeps the lungs moving, but a man has only strength for a little running, signorina, and he knows that the moment he stops he dies. And I—I have seen men running like this—I have seen their eyes—and then they fall."

I heard the little watch ticking against his wrist.

"And you—?"

"And I?"

"You rose from a common soldier to the rank of Captain in two years, did you not?"

He nodded. "Say that I am proudest of that."

"Not prouder of that than of being a good opera singer, a fine artist?"

"Prouder of it than of anything I ever did."

"And the Grenadier Guards were formed in the year 1659 and all of the men are at least six feet tall?"

He said: "All of them six feet—the best-looking men in Italy. My regiment has been reformed seven times, signorina. Forty-five thousand men are lying dead—forty-five thousand men six feet tall.

"But," he continued, "work of reconstruction is going on. We have in Italy the National Federation of the Committee of Assistance to the Blind, Crippled and Mutilated Soldiers. It is a tragic thing undoubtedly that men have to build themselves back into human beings, but this is war, signorina."

"And shall you return to painting or singing when the war is over?"

"I am too old to sing—I was too old for service, but when my brother went I had to go also. I couldn't rest. No, I shall never sing again in public. I shall take up painting perhaps—perhaps some other art will take my attention.

"I have taken from life all that it had to give me. Some people think that no two things can be done well. Perhaps they are right, but I have amused myself often and others at times, and what more can a person do who is not a world smashing genius?"

"You are a strange mixture, Captain," I said, laughing at his quickly raised eyebrows and down-drawn lips.

"I am still a bit proud of having risen from common soldier to Captain in two years."

"You should have been satisfied to remain a common soldier," I retorted. "You could do no more than die for your country, could you?"

"Who wants to remain a common soldier, an ignorant fellow? One wants to prove that he has intelligence even in battle."

"Now," said I, "tell me a few incidents of battle."

"What do you mean?"

"Those little things a man does that bring the war before one's consciousness as nothing else can. Do you remember that passage in *Le Feu* or *Under Fire* by Barbusse, where the soldier told of his going back to see his wife on a day's leave—how he reached there late in the evening and how it was raining and they had to take in some soldiers out of the wet? How the home consisted of one room and how in the morning the soldier's wife gave him a package of food saying, 'This I saved for you, it was to have been our supper, there was not enough to share around among all of us. Now you are to keep it—we have given them enough.' "

He answered: "Duplicate that book and its incidents ten, twenty, thirty thousand times and you will have the anecdotes you want."

"But there must be a million new ones."

"There are, but somehow we do not like to tell it. It makes things seem more and less terrible than they are, and we who are fighting for Italy cannot afford to stop to think—to think of such things as I have witnessed. A shell falling into a graveyard returning the dead, the dead who always return dead. The sights are too awful, the sounds too horrible—and the stench, the heavy warm air full of the aroma of the mutilated, the tragic bareness of everything! Not a tree, not a flower, not a blade of grass—nothing coming out of the ground, but everything going into it."

"And now?"

"I left Paris and my studio to go to Italy; now I have left Italy to come to America—my job is a difficult one.

I must try to make America realize what Italy knows. I must try to show America that she has something financial, intellectual and commercial that she can give to Italy, that she must give to Italy if she would see the war won, if she would not have Prussia again take hold of us, and not only us but the whole world. For I say to you all that if Italy fails the Allies will fail, that America will fail."

At this moment the bell rang and a messenger boy brought in a letter. The Captain sprang for it.

"From my dear General," he said, holding it up to the light. Slowly tearing it across the end, he added:

"America must rise above her slang—her judgment that is backed up by a phrase. The Italian has been called a 'Wop,' a 'Dago,' and in those two words you have a more subtle knife than the dagger of war, a more terrible weapon than the mace, for it is on a slang word at times that a nation has gone down into oblivion."

Dempsey Welcomes Women Fans

By the end of his career, heavyweight boxer Jack Dempsey had won sixty-four of his sixty-nine bouts and had gained a popularity among his fans that would not be matched until Mohammed Ali's long tenure as the poetry-quipping champ in the 1960s and 1970s.

Born in 1895 in Manassa, Colorado, William Harrison Dempsey dropped out of school in the eighth grade and, while working at various odd jobs, trained himself in the art of boxing. He fought for the first time under the name of "Kid Blackie" in 1914, and the following year he adopted the name "Jack," which led to his ringside epithet of "Jack the Giant Killer." By 1917, under the tutelage of manager and promoter Jack Kearns, Dempsey had begun his climb to the heavyweight championship. He captured the title in his 1919 bout with Jess Willard, and for the next seven years he retained the crown.

The Carpentier-Dempsey bout of 1921, for which Barnes interviewed him, was promoted as the "Battle of the Century"; but in reality Carpentier was not championship material and had little chance of winning. Writing in the New York World, *H. L. Mencken described the fight as being "simply a brief and hopeless struggle between a man full of romantic courage and one overwhelmingly superior in every way."*

A far more serious contender was Luis Firpo, who fought Dempsey in a savage battle in 1923. But it was Gene Tunney who finally stole the title by decision in 1926 after a near-knockout by "The Manassa Mauler."

Dempsey attempted a comeback in 1931, but a year later he retired from the ring, performing over the next several years in movies—among them, The Prizefighter and the Lady, Off Limits, *and* Requiem for a Heavyweight—*and opening a famous Manhattan restaurant which for decades bore his name.*

"OF course, the women will all be on Georges Carpentier's side," said Jack Dempsey, pausing with his golf club in midair on the green meadows of Fred Welsh's training camp.

The champion heavyweight paused as if to let that sink in, then continued:

"It's no longer enough to have speed and a good right arm to be the favorite. You have to be good-looking, too, now that ladies go to the fights. Well, I am willing to do my bit."

He grinned a broad and happy grin. "What am I doing? Why, plucking my eyebrows."

The golf club came down, and the little white ball went spinning up into the sunlight.

"Then you think," I asked, "that in the future the ring is to see a great change?"

"You bet. The old days of cheating and cursing have passed," Jack retorted. "I suppose it's due to women.

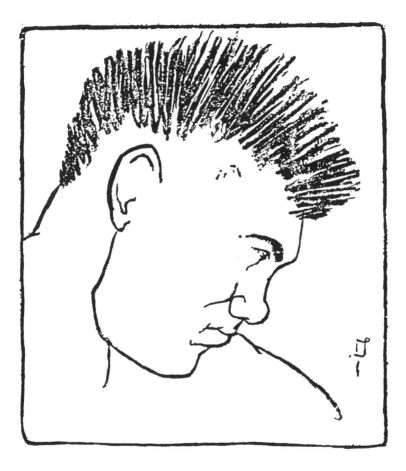

Jack Dempsey

"But—it's right queer how much more excited women get if the fighter has a pretty bridge to his nose, and a right fetching smile. Women are—what do you call it— perverse, you see. They like to see a head punched, but they want the head that's punched to have a smattering of seven languages in it and a taste for poetry. I suppose they really like destruction. The more a guy's got to lose the louder they yell."

"With a man?" I queried.

"He is satisfied with just physical skill," Jack answered.

"And so you wish they had never let women in on prize fights?"

"Oh, gee, no!" Dempsey said hastily. "I like to see different things in the world. I like to watch them grabbing at their fellers' arms when a guy makes a strike. I like to hear them howl. A woman howls twice as convincingly as a man. It's longer and higher. You can get it above the pounding of the blood in your ears. And then I like to hear the feminine sigh when it's all over; a man just grunts."

"And why do you think Carpentier is better looking than you are?"

"Well, ain't he? Look at the long fine line of his nose. I had the bone cut out of mine so I could breathe when it gets smashed. Then Carpentier has that look of cold steel in his eye. Ladies are great on the cold-steel look. By the way," he inquired abruptly, "do you speak French?"

I said that I did not.

"Glad to hear it. A French gambler, who has some few thousand bet on Carpentier, sent out a couple of staggerers —French beauties. They came creeping up the path here one evening at dusk, and said: 'Dempsey, eet is well that you are strong man, because we have come to invite you to a leetle party wiz us tonight. There is music and wine and dancing, yes?' ''

Dempsey laid down his golf stick.

"Now what do you think of that?" he questioned.

"Did you fall for it, Jack?"

"Say," he answered, turning about and pointing to the gateway, where two dogs sat on their tails in the dust of the road. "Those dogs have been posted there ever since that night."

James Joyce

*James Joyce needs little introduction to readers of twentieth-century fiction. His primary works—*The Dubliners *and his longer fictions,* A Portrait of the Artist as a Young Man, Ulysses, *and* Finnegans Wake—*are among the most important contributions to modern literature and have had a major impact on writers of this century.*

Barnes's interview with the great Irishman took place in 1922, the year Ulysses *finally appeared in book form. With the publication of that novel—which Barnes first read in the pages of* The Little Review, *where stories of her own had also appeared—she despaired of ever attempting to write fiction again: "I shall never write another line. Who has the nerve after this!"*

Just how close Barnes's friendship with Joyce was is difficult to determine, but it is clear that she saw him often in the early 1920s and that she got on extremely well with Joyce's wife, Nora. Joyce quite obviously thought highly of Barnes as well, presenting her in 1923 with the original, annotated manuscript of Ulysses. *According to Gertrude Stein, Barnes was to have introduced Joyce to Stein, but she showed up at Stein's apartment without him.*

What is apparent is that Joyce was a major influence upon Barnes's writing and that she was an influence—evidenced particularly in Finnegans Wake—*upon him. No matter that she felt it fruitless to write "another line" after* Ulysses; *during these years of friendship with Joyce, she produced the picaresque* Ryder *and began work on her own master-piece,* Nightwood, *published in 1936, three years before* Joyce's Wake.

T HERE are men in Dublin who will tell you that out of Ireland a great voice has gone; and there are a few women, lost to youth, who will add: "One night he was singing and the next he wasn't, and there's been no silence the like of it!" For the singing voice of James Joyce, author of *A Portrait of the Artist as a Young Man* and of *Ulysses,* is said to have been second to none.

The thought that Joyce was once a singer may not come as a revelation to the casual reader of his books. One must perhaps have spent one of those strangely aloof evenings with him, or have read passages of his *Ulysses* as it appeared in *The Little Review,* to have realized the singing quality of his words. For tradition has it that a singer must have a touch of bravado, a joyous putting-forth of first the right leg and then the left, and a sigh or two this side of the cloister; and Joyce has none of these.

I had read *Dubliners* over my coffee during the war. I had been on one or two theatrical committees just long enough to suggest the production of *Exiles,* his one play. The *Portrait* had been consumed, turning from one elbow to the other, but it was not until I came upon his last work that I sensed the singer. Lines like: "So stood they both awhile in wan hope sorrowing one with the other"; or, "Thither the extremely large wains bring foison of the fields, spherical potatoes and iridescent kale and onions, pearls of the earth, and red, green, yellow, brown, russet, sweet, big bitter ripe pomilated apples and strawberries fit for princes and raspberries from their canes"; or still better, the singing humor in that delicious execution scene in which the "learned prelate knelt in a most Christian spirit in a pool of rainwater."

Yes, then I realized Joyce must indeed have begun life as a singer, and a very tender singer. And, because no voice can hold out over the brutalities of life without breaking, he turned to quill and paper, for so he could arrange, in the necessary silence, the abundant inadequacies of life, as a laying-out of jewels—jewels with a will to decay.

Yet of Joyce, the man, one has heard very little. I had seen a photograph of him, the collar up about the narrow throat, the beard, heavier in those days, descending into the abyss of the hidden bosom. I had been told that he was going blind, and we in America learned from Ezra Pound that "Joyce is the only man on the continent who continues to produce, in spite of poverty and sickness, working from eight to sixteen hours a day." I had heard that for a number of years Joyce taught English in a school in Trieste—and this is almost all. Of his habits, of his likes and his dislikes, nothing, unless one dared come to some conclusion about them from the number of facts hidden under an equal number of improbabilities in his teeming *Ulysses.*

And then, one day, I came to Paris. Sitting in the cafe of the Deux Magots, which faces the little church of St. Germain des Près, I saw approaching out of the fog and damp, a tall man, with head slightly lifted and slightly turned, giving to the wind an orderly distemper of red

James Joyce

and black hair, which descended sharply into a scant wedge on an out-thrust chin.

He wore a blue-gray coat—too young it seemed, partly because he had thrust its gathers behind him, partly because the belt which circled it lay two full inches above the hips.

At the moment of seeing him, a remark made to me by a mystic flashed through my mind—"A man who has been more crucified on his sensibilities than any writer of our age"—and I said to myself, This is a strange way to recognize a man I never laid my eyes on.

Because he had heard of the suppression of *The Little Review* on account of *Ulysses* and of the subsequent trial, he sat down opposite me, who was familiar with the whole story, ordering a white wine. He began to talk at once. "The pity is," he said, seeming to choose his words for their age rather than their aptness, "the public will demand and find a moral in my book—or worse, they may take it in some more serious way, and on the honor of a gentleman, there is not one single serious line in it."

For a moment there was silence. His hands, peculiarly limp in the introductory shake, and peculiarly pulpy—running into a thickness that the base gave no hint of—lay, one on the stem of the glass, the other, forgotten, palm out, on the most delightful waistcoat it has ever been my happiness to see. Purple with alternate doe and dog heads. The does, tiny scarlet tongues hanging out over blond lower lips, downed in a light wool, and the dogs no more ferocious or on the scent than any good animal who adheres to his master through the seven cycles of change.

He saw my admiration and he smiled. "Made by the hand of my grandmother for the first hunt of the season." There was another silence in which he arranged and lit a cigar.

"All great talkers," he said softly, "have spoken in the language of Sterne, Swift, or the Restoration. Even Oscar Wilde. He studied the Restoration through a microscope in the morning and repeated it through a telescope in the evening."

"And in *Ulysses*?" I asked.

"They are all there, the great talkers," he answered, "them and the things they forgot. In *Ulysses* I have recorded, simultaneously, what a man says, see, thinks, and what such seeing, thinking, saying does to what you Freudians call the subconscious—but as for psychoanalysis," he broke off, "it's neither more nor less than blackmail."

He raised his eyes. There is something unfocused in them—the same paleness seen in plants long hidden from the sun—and sometimes a little jeer that goes with a lift and rounding of the upper lip.

People say of him that he looks both sad and tired. He does look sad and he does look tired, but it is the sadness of a man who has procured some medieval permission to sorrow out of time and in no place; it is the weariness of one self-subjected to the creation of an overabundance in the limited.

If I were asked what seemed to be the most characteristic pose of James Joyce, I should say that of the head, turned farther away than disgust and not so far as death. The turn of displeasure is not so complete; yet the only

thing at all like it is the look in the throat of a stricken
animal. After this I should add, think of him as a heavy
man yet thin, drinking a thin cool wine with lips almost
hidden in his high narrow head, or smoking the eternal
cigar, held slightly above shoulder-level, and never moved
until consumed, the mouth brought to and taken away
from it to eject the sharp jets of yellow smoke.

Because one may not ask him questions, one must know
him. It has been my pleasure to talk to him many times
during my four months in Paris. We have talked of rivers
and of religion, of the instinctive genius of the church
which chose, for the singing of its hymns, the voice without "overtones"—the voice of the eunuch. We have talked
of women; about women he seems a bit disinterested.
Were I vain, I should say he is afraid of them, but I am
certain he is only a little skeptical of their existence. We
have talked of Ibsen, of Strindberg, Shakespeare: "*Hamlet*
is a great play, written from the standpoint of the ghost";
and of Strindberg, "No drama behind the hysterical
raving."

We have talked of death, of rats, of horses, the sea;
languages, climates and offerings. Of artists and of Ireland.
"The Irish are people who will never have leaders, for
at the great moment they always desert them. They have
produced one skeleton—Parnell—never a man."

Sometimes his wife, Nora, and his two children have
been with him. Large children, almost as tall as he is himself, and Nora walks under fine red hair, speaking with
a brogue that carries the dread of Ireland in it; Ireland
as a place where poverty has become the art of scarcity.
A brogue a little more defiant than Joyce's, which is

tamed by preoccupation.

Joyce has few friends, yet he is always willing to leave his writing table and his white coat of an evening, to go to some quiet nearby cafe, there to discuss anything that is not "artistic" or "flashy" or "new." Callers have often found him writing into the night, or drinking tea with Nora. I myself once came upon him as he lay full length on his stomach poring over a valise full of notes taken in his youth for *Ulysses*—for as Nora says, "It's the great fanaticism is on him, and it is coming to no end." Once he was reading out of the book of saints (he is never without it) and muttering to himself that this particular day's saint was "a devil of a fellow for bringing on the rain, and we wanting to go for a stroll."

However it is with him, he will come away for the evening, for he is simple, a scholar, and sees nothing objectionable in human beings if they will only remain in place.

Yet he has been called eccentric, mad, incoherent, unintelligible, yes and futuristic. One wonders why, thinking what a fine lyric beginning that great Rabelaisian flower *Ulysses* had, with impartial addenda for foliage, the thin sweet lyricism of *Chamber Music*, the casual inevitability of *Dubliners*, the passion and prayer of Stephen Dedalus, who said that he would go alone through the world. "Alone, not only separate from all others, but to have not even one friend."

He has, if we admit Joyce to be Stephen, done as he said he would do. "I will not serve that which I no longer believe, whether it call itself my home, my fatherland, or my church; and I will try to express myself in my art as freely as I can and as wholly as I can, using for my defense the only arms I allow myself to use: silence, exile and cunning.''

This is somehow Joyce, and one wonders if, at last, Ireland has created her man.

The Models Have Come to Town

Best known today for her long artistic and sexual liaison with Dada artist Man Ray, Alice Prin—known as Kiki of Montparnasse—was born and raised in a small French village in Burgundy, to which she claimed throughout her life she would return one day to "raise pigs."

When Ray met her, she was already working as a model in Montparnasse and was well known for her wit and talent for singing erotic folk songs, somewhat reminiscent of those performed by Yvette Guilbert. Singing nightly at the club Le Jockey, Kiki introduced Ray to the artistic avant-garde of Montparnasse. He found in her, moreover, an adventurous companion and an artistic inspiration and created, during their tempestuous relationship, several of his most important photographs, films, and paintings.

The most famous of the photographs featuring Kiki is Violon d'Ingres *of 1924—the year of Barnes's interview with her—in which the turbaned Kiki sits with her back exposed to her buttocks; on her back Ray has superimposed the two sound-holes of a violin, playfully suggesting all the standard clichés and metaphors attending the notion of comparing a woman's body to a musical instrument.*

Two years later, Ray featured Kiki and his friend Jacques Rigaut in his first film, the satirical Emak Bakia, *in which Kiki dances the Charleston with a pair of eyes painted upon her eyelids, which, as she opens her own eyes, gradually vanish.*

In response to a showing of Kiki's own paintings in 1927 at Galerie du Sacre du Printemps, Surrealist poet Robert Desnos celebrated the artist and model by writing: "You, my dear Kiki, have such beautiful eyes that the world, through them, should look so good. What you must see! A thick, broad prairie in a calm valley at the edge of which there is the murmuring of the sea. In the blue sky the trees are asleep, in the green grass the women are nude, in the air there are simple songs which, with melancholy, speak of love, and whose refrain is sad like the summer street sun of Quartre-Septembre when it reaches us in Paris. . . ." [Translated from the French by James Wine]

In 1931 Kiki and Man Ray separated, and she began seeing journalist and caricaturist Henri Broca. Broca encouraged Kiki to write her memoirs, which he published in French with reproductions of her paintings. Ernest Hemingway wrote an introduction for the English language version, but when Bennett Cerf attempted to import the book for Random House, it was seized at Customs and banned.

Kiki continued to live in Montparnasse until her death, shortly after World War II.

The other models mentioned in this interview, Bronja and Tylia Perlmutter, arrived in Paris from their native Poland around 1923. They posed for several Montparnasse artists, including Moishe Kisling and Nils Dardel. Bronja played Eve to Marcel Duchamp's Adam in Francis Picabia's Cinesketch, *performed on December 31, 1924. Witnessing that performance, French film director René Clair fell in love with Bronja and married her soon after.*

"LIFE," murmurs Kiki, "is, *au fond*, so limited, so robbed of new sins, so *diabolique*—," she raises her mandarin eyes, slanting with kohl, "—that one must have a mouse, a small white mouse, *n'est-ce pas*? To run about between cocktails and *thé*."

Holding the little thing upon her rouged fingers, the favorite model of the Montparnasse turns its warm dexterity toward the Boulevard Raspail, where with sharp, sparkling eyes it gazes on all men, without prejudice, knowing nothing of the comforts of "good and evil." A shade of the same unconcern is in the eyes of Kiki, who, among other lovely women models, has come and conquered France.

In the old days a model was simply a model; she broke men's hearts but not their traditions. She stood for hours upon the model stand, saying nothing, while the painter measured and planed her and got her down upon canvas for the autumn salon.

But times have changed. The model is no longer the monopoly of him who deals in colors. Musicians, yes, and writers have fallen under the sway of the "personal and living enchantment" of the models themselves. Musicians employ them, arranging them in octaves and themes. A girl, they say, may change the tempo of an opera at any moment; a trill may turn into a dirge, a dirge into a war song, a war song into a sonata, a tragedy into a comedy, a comedy into a psychological thesis, and a sermon into a—confession!

It has even gone so far that a group of the four arts calling themselves "Super Realists" have sworn to lay aside their inspiration forever unless it comes to them through the "*belles femmes*," and in turn the model demands her long-subordinated personality, she will no longer be the decor, she will be the actor, too.

And with it all she must have her fancies. For Kiki it is a white mouse, for others it is a tiny monkey no larger than one's sense of humor; a *l'oiseau jaune*, a half-meter of snake, and for others the movies.

Man Ray gives Kiki the credit for one of his best marines. She stormed into the room, so dark, so bizarre, so perfidiously willful—crying, "Never again will Kiki do the identical same thing three days running, never, never, never!"—that in a flash he became possessed of the knowledge of all unruly nature.

Truc to her word she flung herself into the cinema, appearing in *La Galerie de Monstres* with Catalin, in *L'Inhumaine* with Georgette Leblanc Maeterlinck, and a few nights later on the boards of the Gaiety—only to leave the Gaiety, the *L'Inhumaine* and *La Galerie de Monstres* as she had left Man Ray!

Bored with painting, bored with acting, bored with *le monde*, bored with Poiret, with Lanvin, she shut herself in and designed a dress that took the Quarter by the throat!

But would she speak to anyone? No. Laughing, talking in a cascade of rebellious French, like an unrecorded fountain in a noisy city square, she delivered up her judgment to her mouse: "*Bate! toujours infidèle, vous avez blessé mon coeur? Non,* most certainly *non!* My heart is ticking away regardless of you! Voila! Let it tick, it amuses, it is so—how do you say it—so personal, so French, so me!"

From Holland come the tiny sisters Bronja and Tylia, eighteen and twenty. They speak four languages, they have sat to Marie Laurencin, Princess Lucien Murat, Boussingault. Indeed one entire exhibition of Boussingault's at the Galerie Marseilles was Tylia. These sisters have also been in the movies, but that is not all. They are part of the movement *Cigale*, the *"Boeuf sur le toit."* For the Cigale they are the most rapt part of the audience, for they know how everyone "got that way." They call Cocteau "Jean"; they talked with Radiguet as he dropped and replaced his monocle in those days before his death. They danced to the rhythm of the jungle beaten out by a "dusky" on the drum; they sat in their capes at the bar drinking *Yvette* and *Menthe* for its color, discussing Belgian poetry with the bartender, or were overheard saying to Marcel Herrand, the Romeo of Cocteau's *Romeo and Juliet*: "A high lace collar, a pair of tights, and immediately you are almost something else! Isn't it?"

"America!" Tylia opens her eyes, sighs and lights her tenth cigarette. "America for me is the only *volupté*. Why? Because in all the pictures that I seen of your American life, everything is arranged so symmetrically, the trains have space, the space is full of buildings and your buildings full of money. Isn't it?"

If you tell her it isn't, she will not believe you, for the model of 1924 insists on believing what she likes, and so it is that she is held responsible for cubism. Was it not she with her peacock laughter who broke old rules into a thousand pieces and established the cubes and the angles? Was it not she with her mischief that threw representation into a fever and brought it out into a convalescence of futurism? They say it was, nor does it stop at that. It is more than a whisper that free verse was by her freed, that in her cyclonelike pass through the established world she razed and emptied it of dust, and set it a new measure.

It might well be, for as Oscar Wilde says, she is "not a serious purpose!" No, she is superbly irrelevant, magnificently disconnected, triumphantly trivial.

Ask "La Choute," darling of the "Quartz-Arts," Metzinger's muse, with her Spanish mantilla and her irrevocable eyes; ask Suzanne, ask the "Queen of the Montparnasse," Mlle. Michelin, who wears the Cleo de Merode coiffure; ask Yvette, *Folies* girl and athlete, ask the turbaned Myrka from the blazing Indies, who is, the painters say, just the right shade of obscurity. Ask any of them and all of them, they will answer, *"Mais oui!"*

How do they live? The same as you and I. And how do we live? Do we ever tell?

You never see them before two o'clock. Perhaps this is your fault, for do you ever get up before two o'clock?

Drinking your coffee (as deadly as the rapier of a D'Artagnan), eating your *petit pain* (as hard as a woman's heart), you raise your eyes and meet their eyes. They smile a little, and you smile. You will not see them again until dinner time; then there they are in just the same cafe that you always frequent, drinking their cognac or pale ale, and smoking dreadful French cigarettes. You meet them in the Bois, you go to the play, and while making ready to clap for some joke you do not hear but understand (French jokes are like that), you are drowned and done away with by the multitude of her white-gloved hands, held high before her like frantic doves' wings, thundering your approval down to oblivion. For the Montparnasse model is everywhere you are and are not. That is their life, their life is their "confession"— the only one they make. Any other would be unnecessary.

Then Sunday comes, wending your way to church, not because you are a good Christian, but because you are a good tourist. Following the bells of Notre Dame, of St. Sulpice, of St. Germain, or of Sacré Coeur, there you find her buying long, thin candles to burn for the heart (touchingly, not for the soul) of *petit Grace* who died of slow consumption in the Henri Merger style—for he must be kept immortal—bending the knee, sighing before the altars. Saying her prayers with its yearly difference—for no man prays this year as he did last—bowing her head.

Back again in the Boulevard, sipping her liqueur, there is Kiki holding her white mouse out on her hand, smiling her mandarin smile. "They have broken my heart? Not at all, I keep it for me. What will you have—*thé? Bon!"*

Do You Want to Be a Movie Actress?

Son of a Civil War hero of the South, David Wark Griffith grew up in a household reduced to poverty by Reconstruction. In Louisville, the young Griffith helped his family with income from a number of odd jobs while dreaming of becoming an actor.

In 1897 Griffith joined Louisville's Meffert Stock Company and played in supporting roles for two seasons before touring with various companies throughout the South and Midwest. Frustrated with the low wages and desultory lifestyle of the traveling actor, Griffith turned to writing, finally placing a poem in Leslie's Weekly *in 1906 and selling a play,* A Fool and a Girl, *as a vehicle for actress Fanny Ward.*

The play, however, was a failure, and the dejected Griffith shifted from the theatre to the new medium of the movies. In 1907, Edison company director Edwin S. Porter rejected Griffith's idea for a film based on La Tosca *but hired him for the leading role in his upcoming film,* Rescued From an Eagle's Nest. *Biograph Studio bought several of Griffith's stories the same year, adapting them as* 'Ostler Joe *and* At the Crossroads of Life—*films in which Griffith also appeared as actor.*

Within a few months, Griffith was given the chance to

direct his own film, The Adventures of Dollie *(1908); and over the following five years, as head of production at Biograph, he directed an astounding 450 movies, including the four-reeler* Judith of Bethulia *(1914).*

Griffith was a natural at directing, introducing techniques such as intercutting, crosscutting, closeups, pans, and other innovative devices. But his major genius lay in working closely with film actors and actresses—from his wife, Linda Arvidson, to Lillian and Dorothy Gish—in a manner more akin to the theatre than to film "factories" of the day.

These talents were made most obvious in his film masterworks of 1914 and 1916, Birth of a Nation *and* Intolerance *—the first of which was a commercial success and both of which influenced film directors throughout the twentieth century.*

*Over the next several years, Griffith produced a number of classic films—*Broken Blossoms *(1919),* Way Down East *(1920), and* Orphans of the Storm *(1922)—and a greater number of artistic and commercial failures that forced him to contract with a string of film studios and independent corporations. By 1930 he was bankrupt and without supporters. He was able to produce only one more artistic success,* Abraham Lincoln—*his first "talkie"—before he was forced to retire, a bitter, nearly forgotten man.*

The great pioneer of the cinema died in a Hollywood hotel at the age of seventy-three.

D. W. Griffith, when I interviewed him on the subject of what chance any talented young woman has to become a movie star, declared: "No woman is ever too old. She must not get the 'old idea' into her head. No woman is ever too experienced; she must not be afraid to live and to live dangerously, for it all counts to the good in pictures. There is absolutely no age limit. All that is necessary is an agent, indomitable will, some experience, and a knowledge of the requirements of the screen.

"Struggle is inevitable. Despair is inevitable—but if you go through what must be gone through, not foolishly expectant but wisely intent, there is no reason why the goal should not be reached.

"Still, every girl cannot be another Gish. The Gish girls went on the stage when still babies. This was their great advantage. They became inured long before the average girl even thinks of a career. Now they are famous and rich while still young enough to enjoy it.

"A tall woman has less chance than a short woman. The public likes to think of itself—if masculine—as defending a small woman; it's easier. And the public—if feminine—likes to see itself coming up to the heart, and no further, in the love embrace. It looks better; there is no doubt about it.

"It is rather difficult to tell what the requirements are. The season's taste changes with the leaves on the trees— at one moment it is the baby doll with a head full of curls; the next it is the vampire with the calculating look. Just now the people are a little tired of both the baby doll and the vampire. They want neither unsophisticated youth nor crafty experience. They are looking with more interest at the woman who is still beautiful but wise, sophisticated yet tuned by experience.

"In regard to men, it ran first to roughriders, then the

mounted police, then the silk-dressing-gowned and long-cigarette-holder type. This is the last stage—what next? No one knows.

"I never select girls. I haven't the time. They come to my attention only after they have gone through the hands of the agent and then through the hands of my casting director. When they secure a part, no matter how small, I never forget their work, their face or their name. And if, ten years later, the story I am about to film requires a character like one of these extras, I will recall her in every detail, and make every effort to find her for the part.

"This was the way Mae Marsh got the lead in *The White Rose*. She is married, has a baby, and is neither a child nor what is called beautiful. She wears no mass of golden curls. She brushes her hair straight back, and she creates no illusion of unsophisticated youth. She belongs because she can create—simply, directly, and effectively—the woman who has no longer her teens with her nor knowledge before her. She was every year of her age, but she was those years with art and with abandon.

"Of course we all, audience and individual, court youth or the illusion of youth. It is only natural. It is an inborn instinct to love the sound, the new, and the pleasing. It is foolish, and it is nearsighted, but so it is. Personally, I respect a person with her years upon her because each year holds its separate dignity, and such things are truth, and truth should be of value to the man in the street, and it is—a little.

"Nazimova is no longer a young woman, but she preserves the appearance. She has taken care to do so. It is her bread and butter, and she must. If you are famous enough you can take risks, and standing in front of the camera is the most hazardous risk a woman can take because the camera does not lie, or not much. Sarah Bernhardt was old enough in tradition to get away with it; so was Mrs. Fisk. But then, you could not lose on them; the crowd would come to see a picture of Mrs. Fisk if it did not understand a move she made, and it would flock to see the divine Sarah just because she had lived herself into an immortal fame.

"It is quite another thing when, being mature, you offer yourself for the first time to the scrutiny of the people. A man may love a fading mistress, provided she fade before his eyes; he gets accustomed to it, but would he love this woman if he saw her for the first time at the age of, let us say, fifty?

"So youth must come first here as it does in life. It is best to begin young for any trade, that of letters, pen, or stage. You can't begin anything too early. There is not enough time in any life to get to that point of perfection which might really have meant something. We are all mortal too early. Pull and push count, of course. Push in getting pull, and pull in getting in.

"I know I am missing some potential Mary Pickford and Charlie Chaplin, but I am helpless. I simply cannot hunt out these people. And no young girl can get into my pictures without experience."

How the Woman in Love Should Dress

One of the most popular opera singers of all time, Mary
Garden was born in Scotland and brought as a child to
live in New England in 1880. She began studying piano,
violin, and voice early, continuing her voice lessons during
her travels to France in 1895.

Five years later, Garden made her operatic debut in Gustave
Charpentier's Louise at the Opéra-Comique in Paris. Over
the next few years, she played in La Traviata and numerous
other operas. A statuesque beauty and a dramatic actress
as well as a gifted singer, Garden was chosen in 1902 for
the female lead in the premiere of Claude Debussy's Pelléas
et Mélisande, and her interpretation made her famous.

In the next decade Garden sang internationally in numerous
roles, the most famous of which were those in Le Jongleur
de Notre-Dame, for which Jules Massenet rewrote the tenor
part for her; Thaïs, in which she made her New York debut;
and Richard Strauss's Salomé, a role described by critics
of the day as "bloodchilling and revolting."

In 1910, Garden joined the Chicago Civic Opera and
starred with that company until 1931, serving as general
director in 1921-22. She retired from the stage in 1934,
lecturing and judging musical competitions until her death
in 1967.

I F anyone in the world knows the gestures of love, if any woman knows what dress is and why the woman in love cannot give too much attention to her appearance, that woman is Mary Garden.

For has she not only sung all the great love operas, but dressed the part? From the haunting Mélisande to the passionate Salome and the little, stricken, hemstitching Louise, not to mention the irresistible Thaïs? What then could she not tell of the very threads that make the garment of romance. Wearing her smart, close turban of gray, with its slanting pins of pearl, with two pearls in her ears, and many on her fingers; encased in a faultless tailored suit of blue, with a mannish and immaculate silk shirt, sounding the bracelets of amber and tortoise shell and ivory, she rolls back her suede gloves, tucking the fingers in, and leans forward, her elbows on her writing table, and says without hesitation:

"If you are in love, dress with passion!"

The eyes burn; the whole body, in one flexible, feline movement reestablishes itself to its most comfort. "Do you know what love means? No? Then you do not know what dressing with passion means. You *do* know what love is? Voila! Then I do not need to continue."

I said: "Yes, but you do. Many, many women who are in love are too much overwhelmed to know what to do, too immersed in their emotions."

She shook her head, she ran a pen clear through the blotter, she tore an envelope across and flung them into the fireplace, pen and all.

"Never, never, never! No woman in the world, old or young, rich or poor, handsome or ugly, has ever felt the approach of Cupid without making an offering to that god, if it be but a bunch of ribbon, or a rose. But if you are talking of the sophistication, the perfection of that offering, if you mean the ultimate essence of fitness that conditions that ailment, then yes, there is much for women to learn. Love is never quite honored unless the person in that beatitude is, shall I say, dressed for the part. Love is a part that we all, at one time or other, are called on to play; then why is love's make-up so badly practiced, so amateurishly adopted, so faulty in its construction? I'll tell you why—because women, and men as well, have not learned that falling in love is a condition, keeping in love an art.

"Take the wild fitness for love exemplified by Salomé. She knew that display of the body kills the dream of desire. She veiled. Take the splendid Thaïs; a red-haired woman they say, loved by a hundred men. Well, contrary to the long-established rule, when I personified her, I dressed in red. The red-haired woman never looks so glowing, so ravished by ardor as when gowned in some tone of red. Then she is like a brand plucked from the burning. Her person is one entire glowing whole.

"Do I not hear you say, Well, but what of Marguerite with her high-bosomed dresses, her girlish simplicity, her implacable austerity?" She smiled one of those smiles that have made more than one man in the audience wish he were stronger, richer and younger. "Well, is that any less dressing for love? There is love of the virgin, and there is love for the experienced, and there is love for the old; for some women who have been masters of their art have been loved to the coffin's edge.

"It is exactly because of these different ages and different conditions that the question of dress is so complicated, so difficult. A young girl must dress to youth, and a middle-aged woman must dress to experience, and the old must dress for the acceptance of the conclusion.

"Personally I admire no woman so much as that woman called 'false' and experienced, but I mean something quite different from what is ordinarily accepted by these terms. I love that woman who has wrestled with life, who has triumphed, and who shows it. I like the deft carriage, the quick, capable, dauntless bearing, the maneuver of the flesh—the experience that sits on the body like a decoration, every ounce where it belongs. This woman is always called 'false,' that is, always prepared for an attack, dressed for the part, armed for the conflict. You'll never see such a woman with a rumpled collar, soiled gloves or run-down shoes, just as you'll never see a warrior with a rusty sword.

"In the day, wear only those things that repel creases and dust. There is nothing that so becomes almost all types of women as the smartly tailored suit. Some think that men do not like women so dressed—they are wrong. Ninety-nine men out of a hundred will look at a fluffy creation, but they marry the tailored girl. Then dark colors for street wear. Dark colors make you a part of the city, you don't stick out, you are not too conspicuous. And don't, oh don't," she added, "wear a cape unless you are tall and slender. Why will women cut their line down! A cape carries out the width of the shoulders—almost no woman can wear one. And now that we are on the subject of 'why do women'—what about hats?

"Personally, I almost never wear a hat that is not close to the head, a turban. They can be made of the richest material, in any color; they are good taste because good taste is symmetry. You are a whole when you are compact, no flying ends, no flouncy brims, no unguarded material about you. No useless pleats and insets.

"In the evening! What may not a beautiful woman wear in the evening! Any color in the world, except brown. I do not like brown at night. Why? Precisely because it reminds me of the day. And that is a thing to remember. Never wear in the evening anything that can carry the thought back into the workaday world. Jewels, flowers, lace, satins, little flashing slippers, beautiful furs.

"Black velvet!" She drew the paper cutter through her hands with a slow pleasure, testing its keenness, as if perhaps black velvet and daggers were one in her mind. "Men, you know, cannot resist black velvet. There is something regal, austere, triumphantly sad about black velvet. It cleans the lines of the body. It makes you absolutely not to be denied. It mails you. It is at once victory and surrender, denial and acceptance. If—," she laid the paper cutter down and began buttoning her gloves. "If you can wear it—and if you can not only wear it, but can wear it tight, body-fitting—there's nothing so lovely as the sculptured body, and nothing sculptures it quite like velvet. After that, brocades. In the bouffant you are expressing the material, in the clinging gown you are expressing your body. But, of course, you must have a beautiful body to express.

"For the young girl there is nothing more delightful than organdies, voiles, sunny effects. A little lace but not much ornament—these things are for those sophisticated women who can play with decoration, young girls can never quite do it. They are always a little afraid of jewels and a little ill-at-ease if too beleaguered by many things.''

I rose as she rose. ''And what of shoes?'' I said.

''Tell women, especially the woman in love, to choose only those shoes—those slippers, those *pantoufles*—that look charming not only on the floor, but coming down stairs. That is the hard moment on the foot—in fact, the hard moment on the entire ensemble. If you can come down stairs and still look beautiful, everything is well. You may be sure that you have achieved the almost impossible perfection.''

And so I left Mary Garden, she who walks down stairs more like a bird than a woman.

American Wives and Titled Husbands

A DAY in June, a bower of roses, a blare of publicity—and another American girl has captured or been captured by a titled foreigner. Then a luxurious suite aboard the *Majestic* or *Leviathan*, the waving of a lacy handkerchief in farewell, and one more American girl has been lost to her native land. Except for an occasional visit, she will not return unless heralded by the publicity which attends a divorce suit as faithfully and as frantically as it does a marriage. But what of the American brides who marry coronets—and even crowns—and then are lost to sight, who reside abroad, who cling to home and husband, and who are apparently content and even happy? Have they truly found themselves? Are they genuinely at home in their foreign surroundings?

While in Rome, I took the opportunity of calling on the Principessa San Faustino, lady-in-waiting to the Queen. The Principessa, who was a Miss Jane Campbell before her marriage, is American born, and through a long life spent outside her own country, involving close contact with a tradition alien to her own, is eminently qualified to advise the American girl.

Lying among her laces in the Palazzo Barbarini, laces

that submerge her a little more each day, like a pitiless surf—for she is frail with years and worn with royal obligations—the Principessa said: "The American girl who marries outside her own nationality is casting off a known mythology for an unknown. Throwing away a tradition that is herself, for a tradition that she can never comprehend. Traditions, customs, manners cannot be acquired. They are in the blood of a race, and only the race that is tuned to them can be their perfect medium. The music of a violin sounds only through a violin, nor can it transact the business of a harp, nor sing in the harp's voice. A country is an instrument, and no music comes from it but of its fashion.

"Let us speak of the American girl in relation to the Italian, for that," she said quietly, "is all that I am an authority on. The Italian is supremely unfaithful, his *liaisons* sing, because they are a part of his orchestration. It is his way of life, he does not know what "unfaithful" means to an American girl; he cannot understand the horror that runs through her at the word. He is amazed to see with what a shudder of outraged feelings she accuses him of a condition that is, to him, not infidelity but custom, manners. Let me explain. Manners rule his life: he marries for manners, it is good form to have a home and children, and it is with the most exact punctiliousness that he renders to his wife the courtesy of that position. He never fails, no matter what the occasion, or where his erring heart may be, to accord her the deference due her as his wife and mother of his children. If she needs him, he is there, he is the perfect host. When she is ailing he is the most tender, most solicitous nurse; if she dies,

he will be truly the most bereaved of mortals. But—,"
she rose a little from her encircling laces, and for an
instant a thin arm appeared in a profusion of cambric,
"—is he a moment faithful as we know the word? Is he
dedicated, body and soul, to that girl who is his partner
in life? Never. He sees many beautiful women—there are
so many in Italy—and it is a part of his breeding that
brings him to his knees, to do homage to the beauty of
the world. This an American girl will never understand
nor forgive, because it is his music and not hers. She is
plunged into misery, she argues, she quarrels, she up-
braids him, and in the end she loses him, either by
divorce or, though still bound, through his lack of respect
for an emotion that he thinks supremely vulgar. He cannot
understand her psychology, her lack of what he thinks is
an essential in the gentlewoman and the wife: manners,
his manners. Yet if, (and it is a rare thing), she can train
her ear, if she can close her eyes, if she will not 'forgive'—
for that of itself is an intrusion—but if she can accept, she
can be a very happy woman. There is no kinder man in
the world than the Italian. He is accused of marrying an
American solely for her money; I do not think this is a
just accusation. He marries that woman who appears to
him kind. An Italian will lose a world for gentleness and
affection.

"The American woman is essentially unfit for international marriage, more unfit than the woman of any
other nation, because she has cast out the one thing which
the world at large can understand. She has done away
with the mystery of sex; she has come out of the great
and divine shadow of religion; she has flaunted herself

in the world. In other words, she is a businesswoman relying on herself for her own maintenance, demanding equal rights, whatever they may be, and almost entirely indifferent to motherhood. All this might have made her a good influence in Europe if it had not been carried so far. Italians, like Frenchmen, are in need of 'go,' of 'dash.' Thirty years past, the American woman had such influence. Now she has gone so far that no one can cope with her, not even an American. I admire her, I cannot help admiring anything so strange and so individual, but what is to become of her and her after-life if she marries abroad?'' She paused. A bee, flinging himself crisply from crystal grape to crystal plum, searching for the essence of that nature so exactly reproduced, sounded in the silence.

''There,'' she said, watching his perplexity, ''you have the whole matter nicely pictured, the bee searching for honey where there is none. So will the foreign man search in vain for the feminine tincture no longer an integral part of the American woman, and be amazed, lost and frustrated.

''The woman of forty,'' she said, ''*there* is the really distressing traveler. She is of another generation, made mad by this, a mid-Victorian heart flung into a world of jazz and excitement. She is ridiculously sentimental and silly. She has a mental picture of foreigners that is simply outlandish. She thinks every Spaniard a Valentino, every Frenchman a Don Juan, every Egyptian a sort of un-crowned king. So, she makes a perfect fool of herself. She leaves her good and industrious husband slaving in America that she may make herself ridiculous in Monte

Carlo, in Florence, in Paris. She flirts outrageously with the first Argentinean she meets; she thinks any foolish creature who speaks French ravishing, and she is positively overcome by the dark eyes of some nobody from Algiers. She makes herself a byword; for no foreigner takes up with the married woman of forty for anything but her money, and such are the lowest of any race. She becomes a laughingstock, shaming herself and her innocent husband.

"Oh," she said, "it is very pitiful when women forget that home and children and religion and a little difference in their rights are what make life worth living. I married a foreigner, I had children, my husband is dead, but I have my children still, and I have kept my traditions and my faith in spite of the fact that I met my husband on his and left it as I found it. Courtesy, children, God, that is life. Yes," she smiled, "my son has married—an American. A charming girl, handsome, clever—will she be clever enough?"

I put the same question to Countess von Bernstorff, also an American, a Miss Vivian Thomason before her marriage, and she, perhaps because she has youth, spoke with amusement.

"Foreigners—Germans, well, they are charming to talk to, they know everything you know, they are perfect at the opera, at the museum, they remember when everything was written and painted, they are even most delightful to be engaged to—but to marry—" The red, red rose on the Countess's shoulder flashed in a shrug. "What do you think, my dear?" she questioned, turning to the exceedingly lovely Manolita, Baronne von Oppenheim, a glowing child of Spain. "Let us ask her first, because we Americans are supposed to be so hard to please, and the Spanish so easy," she added in English, not to disturb the composure of the little creature who speaks only her own and her husband's tongue.

The Baronne's smile faded. *"Gemütlich!"* she exclaimed, condemning the race in its own phraseology. "Vain, egotistical set. If you want to hear everything on all subjects that no woman can possibly bear, marry a German. They are sentimental, ah yes, very sentimental and you are *schoen, schoen,"* she said mimicking the race, "but after you are married it's 'Do this,' 'Don't do that'." It was evident that in the back of her mind there was a very definite idea of what a husband should be, and had not been.

The Countess was delighted, she pinched her cheek and gave her a chocolate. "What a darling! What could a German do with such a little doll of a girl. They are so material, you know, in spite of their enormous, rumbling flights of fancy. A woman must be a good wife, voila! She must have children every year. Now I have been married three times, still I don't think that all the fault lies at the foreign husbands' door. I think American women have become too fond of pleasure—and drink, yes, drink. I must speak frankly. They no longer know how to behave themselves, especially when they come to Europe, though licentiousness set in long before Prohibition made it smart. Men and women have become too 'chummy,' too 'pallish.' Do you know what that means? When an American is a pal of an American, it is all right perhaps, but try to be a pal with a foreigner! He simply thinks you have gone mad, and will treat you with the pained courtesy, tinged with apprehension, due a lunatic; but he will not comprehend you for a moment. If, on the other hand, a German girl married an American man, why there you have a horse of a different color. She will be amazed at his 'chummy' proclivities, at his fantastic efforts to make her equal. She will be in the seventh heaven of happiness, until some dark and rainy day she will take her bedspread, and tearing it into a hundred strips, will hang herself on the highest limb of the tallest possible tree, because she will have had just one day too many of not being able to fathom this protracted palship. She keeps waiting for the master, and having waited in vain, she will think that perhaps she has done something charming and different in marrying him, but sadly against nature, and she will, as I have said, inevitably climb that tree and go to an adjusting God.

"Americans, you see, are no longer people, they are what they call in biology a throw-off. Look at the case of Anna Gould and the Marquis de Castellane; he could not understand her, nor she him. He was used to that life in which women figure as good mothers, though of the highest social cast, in which they adore their children as the greatest thing in their lives; where even a dowager thinks first of the ingredients in her son's supper before those of the family tree. American women live for pleasure, foreign women for duty. I also have my opinions of American men. I married one. I don't think they are half as chivalrous as foreigners fancy. They are nice to a woman as a person is 'nice' to a mummy. They don't know what she is made of, and worst of all they never think that they don't know. They imagine she is just like themselves. This accounts for their 'pal' attitude. It is also the reason that marriages do not last. Well, you say, who then is the perfect husband? I've come to the conclusion that possibly the Englishman is. I've never had one, so perhaps it's an illusion, but he seems, from where I must inevitably regard him, to be the most considerate, in that he does not 'watch' you. He does not give you freedom, precisely because he does not know when you take it. He is so divinely oblivious, and a little oblivion is essential to the peace of any two people who elect to live together.

"I know, per se, there is no such thing as freedom when two people are bound in wedlock. Freedom is a nice, impossible dream of those persons who do not know how to adjust themselves to life. It is a word for inadequacy, a symbol of a lack of power. Anyone can be just as free, and no freer than the general condition of life. But that freedom comes of courage, and American courage and foreign courage are so dissimilar! A gazelle and a buffalo hitched to the same car would draw most exceedingly different."

The Comtesse de Chambrun, who was Clara Longworth, spoke briefly and to the point.

"People," she said, "who are happily married do not talk, they do not feel the need, they have nothing amusing for the public. This is my case. Nevertheless I will say that as a rule, I am not in favor of international unions. Why? Because in difference of nationality one overlooks too much and sees too little. If they find fault, they will do one of two things, they will say either 'He or she acts so because he or she is French, and therefore the things should be forgiven'; or, 'He or she acts so because he or she is French and therefore it should *not* be forgiven.'

"With the right people the fact of their difference will work for the best, not because they fundamentally comprehend each other, but because they don't, and therefore pass it over. Yet after all, this is a blind sort of felicity, it does not lead to a real community of feeling, it simply overlooks the nice points of a psychology for a nice oblivion. If, on the other hand, the couple are ungenerous, it will be this precise inequality that will bring them to a hurried breach. The marriage will split on the very rock which for the other type was a refuge. Othello did not smother Desdemona because she was unfaithful, but because she was a Venetian. He did not kill unfaithfulness; he killed a pattern of unfaithfulness that ran counter to the pattern of his own blood."

The Duchess of Clermont-Tonnerre, on one occasion when I spoke of the increasing number of young American girls abroad as possible brides in the foreign market, made some sentient observations to the effect that the old race needed the vigorous life force of the American.

"If," she said, "an American could have knowledge of the foreigner, could learn him from the heart out, as only a lover can, she would be vastly improved physically. He would value the beauty of energy. The French are always putting off until tomorrow what should be done today. A Frenchman is always hoping to have something better to do than business. If he is a bootmaker, he will make you boots, but not this month, next month will do. So Americans are annoyed, and with this annoyance they might teach him the value of immediate action, in which he is sorely deficient. But marry him—never! A Jew, yes. They make an ideal marriage the world over, because they have no land. You say, well, the American is the outcome of so many races that she too should be easily assimilated. Yes, but the mixture is too new, like some new wine, not yet justly proportioned. She is always popping out of her bottle, she is too heady and too violent. The question is not so much what of the present generation, but what of the future? The children of the international marriage are the ones who will suffer most, they will neither lie quietly in their bottles, nor will they be able to escape in a burst of effervescence. They will simply ferment.''

Lord Alfred and
Lady Lynn

*Alfred Lunt was born in Milwaukee, Wisconsin in 1893; and
Lynn Fontanne, born in 1887, was raised in Woodford,
England. For more than forty years, Lunt and Fontanne performed together and, occasionally, in separate stage roles,
recognized as two of the most gifted actors in America.*

Lunt first saw Fontanne in the New York production of
The Wooing of Eve *in 1917, but they did not meet until he
was appearing in Booth Tarkington's* Clarence *two years
later. By 1921 Fontanne had risen to stardom in her role of
Dulcinea in George S. Kaufman's and Marc Connelly's*
Dulcy; *and a few months later the two sneaked away by
subway to be married at New York's City Hall.*

The couple first appeared together in Sweet Nell of Old
Drury *in 1923. Recognizing the duo's appeal and romantic
potential, The Theatre Guild quickly signed them for* The
Guardsman, *which brought them rave notices and was the
first in a long string of theatrical successes. "They have
youth and great gifts and an unmistakable attitude of as-
cent," wrote Alexander Woollcott of opening night. And
ascend they did, performing over the next few years in more
than eighteen dramatic successes, including* Arms *and the*
Man *(1925),* The Goat Song *(1926),* Pygmalion *(1926),* The
Brothers Karamazov *(1927),* The Doctor's Dilemma *(1927),
and* Caprice *(1929).*

Over the next two decades, the Lunt-Fontanne name ap-
peared over the marquees of productions of Design for Living
(1933), Reunion in Vienna *(1934),* The Taming of the
Shrew *(1935),* Idiot's Delight *(1936),* Amphitryon 38
(1938), and several other plays both in New York and London.
Their last official appearance on the stage was in The Visit
in 1958, the year the Broadway Theater was renamed the
Lunt-Fontanne in honor of their achievements.

Lunt directed plays for a period after this, which culmi-
nated in his 1965 production of La Traviata *at the Metropol-*
itan Opera. The same year, the couple temporarily came out of
retirement for the "Hallmark Hall of Fame" production of
Magnificent Yankee. *And in 1967 Fontanne appeared alone*
in a television adaptation of Anastasia.

As a performing couple, the Lunts brought romance to the
stage, yet they acted with realistic clarity, delighting in all
the nuances of movement and gesture. As playwright Robert
Sherwood said of them, "They always seemed to have a better
time at a play than anyone in the audience."

Lynn Fontanne lived five years beyond her husband's death
in 1977.

BELIEVE it or not, the drama is no better than it
should be, because the actors are not married!

Or so we gather, now that we are back from an interview with ye Lady Lynn Fontanne and her Lord Alfred
Lunt; for we went to inquire of this matter (we always
go editorial when we interview), pen in hand.

We found Lady Lynn looking extremely royal. She has
the high, hounded lines of a queen. In a dressing room

to her right we heard Lord Alfred was making up for
Meteor—for though they are married, rehearse and act
together, they are interviewed alone. The Lady Lynn
being the most nearly dressed, we presented ourself at
her door.

"Do you think the fact that you are husband and wife
makes your scenes together—your love scenes—you
know, more or less convincing?"

She turned on us a handsome but an haggard eye. Phil
Moeller had at that instant entered the room. He answered
promptly, "To be married is a far, far better thing than
not to be married, for then the lovers may add to reality
the overshadow of imagination!"

The Lady Lynn held up her hand. "If I might be allowed
to speak," she said, in the voice of one who has seen
fact stabbed in the back before by the master hand of
wit; "I shall now tell the truth. The fact that we are man
and wife makes our custom facile to a touch, the rule
forgotten in the mastery. And yet, if either Alfred or
myself, when on the stage, committed the unpardonable
error of recalling it, the play would go to pieces; absolutely and positively to pieces. Any life we portray in public,
any lines we speak on the stage, any glance we cast in
a professional capacity, must of necessity be impersonal.
Otherwise irony would be cast upon our personal relationship. We would be undone. Never again would we dare
to set our feet upon the boards. Do you see what I mean?
Suppose I have the lines to speak: 'Do you think I married
you to be left lying about the garden like a parasol?' (a
very proper, and quite natural question, perhaps, set in
its text). What would happen to Lord Alfred? He would be

shaken out of his part; for in that instant, that speech would become a veiled personal reproach. Startled, he would think, 'Egad, have I treated her like a sunshade indeed? Does she not seem to suggest by her eye that I, in some unpardonable slip of the marital obligation, have acted toward her as one umbrella toward another? Ah, my life, how shall I explain it when we get home. Or was she merely jesting?' ''

"Just a moment on that," we cry, "we must interrogate the master himself on this nice point!" And hotfoot we turn to his chamber. "What ho!" we demand, "what ho, Sir Gaffer! Your Lady has it—but no, we will have your unsullied impression on this question!" And to him, fair enough, we put the case.

"Does the fact that we are married make our love scenes more, or less convincing? Why *more*, of course! How otherwise could I improvise to my heart's content? How otherwise get that subtle interlocking of lines that makes everything seem so natural, and which an actor does not dare essay on one who is not known to him! Where is such a field for the life-giving interjection and interruption! What an opportunity for the word-braiding of lines that makes a living unit!"

"Where else," we muse, "that beautiful disregard for what the other fellow is saying, that the best of us must feel when we are having the right to time, in another fellow's space?"

"Whom else," he says, laying on a fortification of umber No. 2, "could play, say, Grushenka to my Dmitri, in *The Brothers Karamazov*? Half an actor's fame lies, not in his ability to say the lines just as they were written down for him, but with that charmed by-play known as the pinch in the right place, a liberty that one takes only when the heroine is also a wife. With other women, when I crush them in my arms, I always feel, between their breast bones and mine, the crackling of the law of 'Thou shalt not.' But with my Lady Lynn, when we are in an embrace, we are not merely bosom-to-bosom, we are heart-to heart—''

''Halt!'' we say, ''we must get us back to the chamber of the lady herself, for here is the very corpse of discrepancy!'' We charge back. ''It is observed by your Lord,'' we report, ''that marriage is not only far from fatal, it is in very deed the breath of the act!''

''He is not feeling well,'' said the Lady Lynn, ''or he would know better; or perhaps it is that you do not read

We Rehearse in Bed

him aright. That we are married in truth makes the act the better; but did he, the great loon, say we dared think on it when on the stage? Saving, of course, in the subconscious?"

Again we hurry back to the room on the right. "Did we understand you to say, my Lord, that while holding the lady in your arms (where, we believe, we left her) you were base enough to recall that she was your wife? Or did you say she was a cue alone?"

"I said she was neither maid, wife, nor widow at that moment, yet all things in one, and no one thing apart. In fact, on opening nights we shake hands like strangers. If, in the future, plays run for seven or eight hours—in other words, slightly longer than *Strange Interlude*—we shall have to marry all over again."

We arrive at Lady Lynn's. "He admits that, on the stage, he does not know you, and yet somehow he knows you well."

"It is most true. We act as strangers who have known each other in a forgotten world. We are like duelists, fighting for an ideal, clasping hands when the duel is over, having learned to respect each other's fanaticism."

"And nicely put," we observe. "Now to the matter of rehearsing together. Do you take each other's criticism, without going into those rages common to one improving another who is, in his own esteem, letter perfect and in accord with the universe?"

"We rehearse together with the anxiety of matchmakers officiating at the marriage of our stage selves. We accomplish it the easier because it is the second ceremony. We can rehearse at any time, day or night. We rehearse at breakfast, at dinner, in taxicabs, and in bed.'' She sighed a little. ''Often I am awakened in the dark of sleep to a 'Hist! my love, are you awake, and if you are not, why then waken. I have just thought of an improvement, and want your reaction. Now don't you think that if I said, ''Were I in power alone,'' instead of, ''Had I the power,'' that scene would be twice as effective?' And there we are, awake the rest of the night, trying to determine the very marrow of power, trimming it and turning it about until it is a kidney to our liking. Now you know yourself that no two people, unless married, would take that much trouble with a phrase; would give up a life for a thing of fancy unless the fancy were a thing of their life. Working together we have become flexible; we know each other, as a player knows the keyboard. Before we present a drama we have, like the Moscow players, become wedded to the script. In these times of hurry, what company makes preparation for a career as those Russians did? No company; they can't—unless they are married.''

''The very thing!'' we cried. ''It is perhaps the answer. Let everyone who wants to be an actor or actress get married as quickly as possible, have half-a-dozen or more children, and ergo! a native art theatre. The Italians do it. Certainly no one who has seen Italians can say they act constrained.''

''I have rehearsed so constantly,'' mused the Lady Lynn, chin on hand, ''that I talk to myself crossing streets. One day a policeman spoke to me about it. He said, 'Lady, you have money in the bank.' I was dumfounded. I said to myself, 'Is it possible that I have met a psychic member of the force?' But I demanded sternly, 'How did you know?' He answered, 'Because you were talking to yourself, and anyone who talks out loud, when alone, has money in the bank.' "

"Would you go on playing were Lord Alfred called away to a better land? Would Lord Alfred continue his career were you but dust?"

Lady Lynn marked in her mouth, which is an excellent foundation for any scarlet. "Were I to pass into the wings forever, possibly my Lord Alfred would be found stark and cold, and again, he might not. But a pox on such contemplations. What a head you have for horror! My Lord and I are alive and together, and we seek the perfect play."

Of this we then inquired.

"I would," said the Lady Lynn, turning her curls upon an iron, "that I might portray a rowdy, *moyen âge* Duchess before I die. A play of love and thunder and blood. A play of wit and wisdom. A play with such hearty stuff therein that Alfred and I would not have to forget that we are married. A play where it would be safe to remember, a play that we might add to our condition. A play in which we could act both what we are, and what we might be: a very hair-raising vehicle!"

"I ask no better than to be your cry for mercy!" exclaimed Lord Alfred, striding into the room. "One of these days, my girl, you shall be a titled hussy, and I your charlatan!"

Donald Ogden Stewart Confides the Secret of Worldly Success

Born in 1894, Donald Ogden Stewart lived one of the most fascinating and charmed lives of American writers of the 1920s and 1930s.

Stewart attended Phillips Exeter Academy and Yale University and worked for the American Telephone and Telegraph Company before enlisting in the Navy in 1916. Upon discharge, he returned to work for AT&T in Minneapolis, where he befriended his Saint Paul neighbor, F. Scott Fitzgerald—at work on This Side of Paradise.

Other professional positions followed, but in the early 1920s Stewart decided to abandon his business aspirations and traveled to New York City, where he renewed his friendship with Fitzgerald, now married. Stewart became acquainted with Edmund Wilson and John Peale Bishop, who together helped him place his newly written parodies in Vanity Fair. *Writing for* Vanity Fair *and the* Bookman, *Stewart honed his comic talents and published the series of witty pieces as* A Parody Outline of History, *a book in the style of other humorists of the day such as Ring Lardner, Irvin Cobb, and Dorothy Parker, and of Fitzgerald's short stories.*

It was in France, however, that his American writer friends were relocating, and Stewart decided to join them. He arrived in Paris the year Ulysses *was published in book form, and he immediately began to assimilate the literary excitement around him. For* Vanity Fair *and* Harper's Bazaar, *he penned parodies of etiquette books—collected as* Perfect Behavior—*and began work on his most ambitious project, the satire* Aunt Polly's Story of Mankind. *In the same year, Stewart met Hemingway, Dadaist poet Tristan Tzara, and composer Darius Milhaud—and revived previous acquaintances with Bishop and John Dos Passos.*

He returned to the United States to complete his satire; but with playwright Philip Barry and his wife, Stewart sailed back to Paris in 1924. During this stay he traveled with Robert Benchley to Vienna, and with Lady Duff Twysdden, Harold Loeb, and Bill Smith he joined Hemingway on the trip to Pamplona of which Americans would read in The Sun Also Rises.

Disappointed with the critical reaction to Aunt Polly's Story of Mankind, *Stewart returned to light parody in* Mr. and Mrs. Haddock Abroad *(1924) and* The Crazy Fool *(1925); for both he received positive reviews and for the latter a Hollywood movie contract.*

Over the next few years, Stewart continued to write light fiction, but he also shone in several other careers: as a stage actor, appearing in the Holiday *role his friend Philip Barry had based on his life; as a movie star, playing Dulcy in the 1930 film version of the play which had made Lynn Fontanne famous; as a playwright, authoring* Rebound *in 1930; and as a screenplay writer, winning the Oscar in 1940 for* The Philadelphia Story.

It was, perhaps, the glibness of Stewart's success and his opting for lighter parody over his earlier attempts at more serious satire which so galled Barnes in her interview with him during the run of Rebound. *In any event, Barnes was never so revealing of her own art and aspirations as in this piece.*

Stewart's later years, however, held some surprises for admirers of this master of quick wit and quipster of the Algonquin Round Table. In the late 1930s and 1940s he became a Communist sympathizer, and divorcing his wife, Beatrice Ames, he married Ella Winter Steffens, the widow of activist writer and journalist Lincoln Steffens. Blacklisted for his political activities in 1951, Stewart and his wife moved to London, where he composed his autobiography, appropriately titled By a Stroke of Luck! *He died in 1980 at the age of eighty-five.*

"**A**LAS! alas!" we sighed, turning our back on Donald Ogden Stewart as he made his change from first to second act, "that life should be so hard, and that you should be so fortunate!"

"It's just a matter of getting the breaks," he muttered, fumbling for a stud. "Getting the breaks and knowing Phil Barry, and having Hopkins in the world, and being in Minneapolis in 1921, trying to get into the telephone company, and having Crowninshield suggest advertising, and writing a parody on the *Old Oaken Bucket* to prove my talent, and having *Vanity Fair* burst into hearty laughter, and giving up the thought of getting into the bank, after looking about at their faces, and deciding to be a sad,

sad fellow known as a humorist, and never being sad for a minute, and having a ripping time with Benchley, and playing in *Holiday*, and having a wife and kids and living on Long Island, and never really trying to be professional, and taking everything as it comes along, and shamelessly reading my press clippings in the middle of Broadway, and loving it all, and reading them some more, and standing where I can get the best view of the lights spelling my name and the title of my own play, and reading the clippings again and catching a train outward bound, and getting into the house and saying loudly, 'My dear, Donald Ogden Stewart is with you, and isn't it simply perfection it happens to be me, and there's going to be more of mc tomorrow!' ''

We looked at him in a profound and melancholy silence, noting the wide smile, the terrible smile that puts gall and wormwood into the heart; the bright, happy eyes, slightly protruding with success—eyes that make the best of us reach down with that primitive gesture that once, in better days, spelled a dagger by the hilt, and in these degenerate times means the finding of a last, disheveled cigarette.

We lit it by a wavering match, saying, ''Are you happy?''

''Happy!'' He was now a man again, listening, tense with anxiety for his cue. ''I'm jittering! I'm all of a deep contentment and a wild delight! Things are absolutely jake! I'm sitting on top of the world, singing in the rain, rolling up hill and ready for life!

''Did I want to be an actor? I did not. That's all a lot of nonsense invented to make me feel like an idiot. I like to be acting, that's true—but did I write in this part for myself? Well, look at that!'' He thrust the script before us, pointing with a stern finger. ''Read the description of the party I'm supposed to be impersonating: nice, middle-aged, good-looking, dull chap. Well, does that sound like me? Does it give you an instantaneous sort of certitude that would make you say, 'Don Stewart, or I'm blessed!' Why, it all just happened, like my getting into *Holiday*. Somebody said, 'Don—be a man, step forward, be in the play; why not, we are all friends, aren't we?' So I stepped. It's fun. It's great—,'' he paused as a slight frown crossed his otherwise appallingly cheerful countenance, ''—though it's a bit steep every night, when a fellow has a wife and kids, and wants to be sitting around the old rush light reading *The New Yorker* or tossing off another play.

''*Father William* is the name of my next, and there's a sort of hazy third back of that.'' He paused, poking his head out to listen. He drew it back. ''Not yet,'' he muttered.

''See here,'' we said darkly, ''do you realize that you and I started together, as it were? That you were tiptoeing out of Crowninshield's office about the same hour that we were creeping in? And are we on Broadway? Do you know that good-looking women, with yards of golden hair and all that, have paid, and paid, and paid, to be where you are, and are still paying, offstage? Do you know that many a Shakespeare has written oodles of dramas and has hounded Hopkins for countless eons, and has never been so much as plagiarized? Do you,'' we suddenly shouted, frenzied with blighted hopes, and maddened with years of living through the darkness before the dawn,

Actors Made Relentless with Time's Ponderous Approval

"do you ever think of those millions who have trained, and struggled, and wept, just to attain to a certain well-merited oblivion, while you, without so much as a smothered sob, roll over and find yourself famous, and not only that but appear before the public, night after night, and get a hand? Do you ever think of these things, Don Stewart, unhappy man?"

"What's the matter?" he said. "In need of money?"

We laughed in that hollow way common to the little, nonchalant match girl when she realizes that she has left her Dunhill at home. "Oh no, we interview successful people just to prevent ourselves from becoming groggy with rich port and caviar; to save ourselves from becoming blunted with idleness; to arm ourselves against doing murder to one or more of our slaves and outrunners!"

"Swell!" said Don Stewart, "that's my cue!" He was gone, only to dash back in a moment. "Any letters or telegrams come for me while I was away?" he said feverishly, sprinkling a pinch of powder on the back of his neck.

"Are you expecting some?"

"By every mail! By every wire! I hope to be remembered, if only unkindly, and you'd be surprised to know how many times it has been unkindly. The dramatic critics seem to hate their jobs, because they never seem to want to let a funny man have a serious word. If he says anything that sounds as if he had stopped laughing for one second, they are on him like a pack of wolves. Why don't they stop criticizing and write a play, or act or something," he went on in his blood-curdling way. "It's so simple. The drama of today is simple, and friendly, and just the way people live and feel. The cast of *Rebound* is just like a gathering at your house or mine. That's what life and plays should be: unprofessional. It's the only way for the playwright to come into his own. It's the only way that his play turns out something as he envisioned it. No stars get in front of him and his creation. How many dramatists of yesterday could say as I can say, 'It is eighty percent as I thought it in my own head.' The play's the thing—away with the star system! It's the day of the dramatist. And with its dawning we will see plays that are slices of life, plays that do not fall back on stage trickery and custom.

"Do you know what started the great debunking of the drama? The movies. The films carried off all the timeworn, hackneyed nonsense. They could, and did, and do produce hooey on such a vast, all-embracing scale that the legitimate stage cannot hope to compete. So the stage comes back into its own. Your life and mine will once more get a hearing, the happy ending will not be essential. You can get more of it, for less outlay, at any movie house. *We* will begin to live on the stage."

"You may begin," we said grimly, "we never shall. You are just one of the Good Luck Twins, doubling for the other twin, from where we sit. Oh, it's true enough," we went on between our teeth, "we like your play. We admit it. It's great. We don't agree with those people who get ruffled because you are wise every now and again, because you are thoughtful and show signs that you have suffered something of the vanity of life. Because we have, in our own time, said some of our most biting truths, done some of our most devastating thinking, dug up our chiefest nuggets of wisdom, leaning on the spade of wit, and have been told the same thing. The public will not realize that the funny man, the joker, the weeping buffoon, God's jester and fate's hunchback, are only philosophers turning the other cheek; that the first may heal and lose its deep purple and smart. Only those of us like you and me, Don, like Benchley and Dot Parker, know that crouching behind our smile, hidden deep in the folds of our jibes, crawls the cankering blight of knowledge. We would teach man with a joke, and man wants his wisdom heavy. We would smarten him for the great encounter with a smile on his lips. Instead, he asks to be knocked down with a club. We would have him saunter over the top with a song, and he derides us and goes down with a snarl."

"Ah sweet, sweet truth!" he said. "Professionals have always spoiled everything; it's the amateur that saves the day, even if he must be a professional amateur. The party who is willing to take any part, to be here today, gone tomorrow. Not those actors and actresses who are burdened with their glory, and made relentless with time's ponderous approval. What does it matter if we are never seen on the stage again? There are other things that a man can do. Change—diversity—is the spice of life. One can take up farming, or lightly turn to banking. The telephone is always calling. There is no work a man may not turn his hand to."

"Egotist!" we thundered. "You mean *you* can turn lightly, but can we all rebound? Answer me that!"

"I don't know," he answered, with the disarming sincerity of a child who has caught a rabbit while he is still young enough to make of the catch a great adventure. "I guess you are right, I've always had the breaks. I am just in luck. I don't think it's a drawing card to have the author on the stage, and yet here I am being paid to be there. Why I'm wanted is a mystery. A lot of people say I look uneasy and sheepish; out of place and unhappy about it. But I'm not. I haven't got stage fright, and I like being in all the excitement. I'm having the time of my life. Perhaps I show it too much, sort of too pleased about it. But shouldn't I be? It's fun to live in your own time—though naturally the thing I want to do most of all is to write, and to be amusing if I can." He frowned. "Though even about that the critics haven't been very nice. They say I swiped one of Irvin Cobb's lines, and all the time I thought it was Dot Parker's, who is a sort of sea for weary anglers, when their own front pond refuses to give up a trout. The sea is too big to mind, you know. When Dot is funny, it gets to be sort of common property, like 'Alas, Poor Yorick.' But I see I'll have to be careful.''

We crushed out our cigarette with a weary heel. ''You can use any of our brighter sayings,'' we said starkly. ''They won't get the breaks in any other way.''

We paused at the door, to take a last look at this man. The iron had entered our soul. We looked at him a long moment, standing right in the middle of the spotlight of fame, as the shadows of oblivion crept up to our chins.

We said: ''Do you want to die?''

''No,'' he answered lightly, ''do you?''

''We don't mind,'' we answered, stepping into the night.

The Green Pastures

Controversial from its premiere to the present day, Marc Connelly's theatrical retelling of biblical tales from a black perspective has been seen by many viewers as perpetuating black stereotypes and by others to be a sensitive portrayal of the imagination of black culture.

Seen either way, it cannot be denied that The Green Pastures *offered black actors of the day a chance to demonstrate their talents on Broadway. James Weldon Johnson observed of the play that "the Negro established conclusively his capacity to get the utmost subtleties across the footlights, to convey the delicate nuances of emotion. . . ."*

The Green Pastures *opened at the Mansfield Theater on February 26, 1930 to mostly rave notices such as that in the* World: *"It will move you to tears, and make you gasp with the simple beauty of Old Testament pageantry." Richard B. Harrison as the Lord, Wesley Hill as Gabriel, and Lou Vernon as Cain received special praise for their performances.*

Wesley Hill's prediction in Barnes's interview that the play was in a long run proved correct. The Green Pastures *was performed on Broadway 557 times, gaining it a permanent place in the listing of productions that have lasted for 500 or more performances. The film version of 1936 starred Rex Ingram.*

"I'M Zipporah, the woman, and the truth is in me. Don't listen to them colored men, for forgetfulness is on them, and they'll say this here play isn't the way they see the Lord. They are tryin' to be a long way from their beginnin', like white folk, so they talk great nonsense, tryin' to pretend they got a yesterday and a tomorrow. When they know Lord well, they only got today. Havin' only a today keeps the hate out.

"There ain't never been such a race for lovin' fun. That's 'cause we ain't got no time to look back, nor patience to look forward. We colored people don't dig deep, makin' a cryin' to know what we shouldn't ought to. We just let the river go rollin' along. We get born in one piece, and we die in one piece, not all in sections like your philosophers. Have you seen a darky singin', when no one is lookin', 'I lay down my heavy load'? Well, and isn't it a light little parcel he's makin' of it, singin' light and high? And when we has a wake, and goes down moanin', it ain't because we are sorrowful, it's to humor the dead, because they got a conception of themselves as laid up in grief, and we humor them. Yes, white woman, we humor them. It saves them from spendin' their last breath a-lamentin' for their case. It prevents them from undignifyin' their passin'. But we, we ain't takin' on in our natures, but just in our mouths for a ceremony, just like the play. We ain't grievous about the Lord. We takes Him happy, just like Mr. Connelly says—happy and easy. And when we are afraid of Him it's just fun goin' backward, which is terrifyin' enough, Ma'am—like a man swallowin' his cup before it's given to him. That's the way I believe, and I was born Mercedes Gilbert, out of

Florida. I ain't Louisiana born, but if I kin see this play as the truth, then to them primitives it must be standin' up before them like His heart come true!

"I got to go now, but remember this, white woman, if you wants to see the world and the heavens in panorama, and not like a room with a pisonous low ceilin', get a child's heart like our hearts, and a head full of momentary, like our heads, and you'll be wakin' up some mornin' with your grief left out!"

The Lord brushed past. "Only a moment, only a moment!" he kept repeating, like one of the characters in *Alice in Wonderland.*

"And a moment," I said, "will do."

Richard B. Harrison—at sixty-six, son of fugitive slaves, a preacher, lecturer, and dramatic reader—found himself famous overnight in the first part he has ever essayed, that of the Lord. Famous perhaps because he had no stage trick for dignity, but that strangely aloof and proud inner life that makes blasphemy impossible.

I asked him if he felt that he was portraying a type of the Deity as seen in the minds of the primitive Negro. He answered that he thought many Negroes saw the Lord as a sort of replica of their preacher, but he was doubtful if they saw Him as colored. They might see Him with a Negro's features, but as a white Negro. He would have preferred to play Him without make-up (Mr. Harrison could almost pass for white), but he was requested to put on a coat of yellow grease paint.

"The primitive Negro must have God close to him. He cannot stretch out too far. He is like a child who sees the moon and weeps bitterly until his mother puts a shining penny in his hand, which takes the place of what he cannot bear to forgo. Children have toys, and primitive people make touchable idols; it is only the civilized man who makes his God very lonely and far-off. He has been taught that glory and religion are in the reach, in the very inaccessibility. But a Louisiana Negro can see Him at a fish fry, and in a frock coat. And in so doing offers Him no disrespect, because the heart of the Negro has been an oppressed heart, and an oppressed heart is not disconcerted to have the Lord resemble someone as local as the village preacher.''

I then asked him if he did not think it would be an excellent thing to give an annual performance of *The Green Pastures*, as a Negro passion play; that it might become a tradition of his people, the title role descending from father to son. Or if in some strange shuffle of fate a Harrison should be born out of part, then to have it acted by the next most eligible, for the grave necessity that the depicting of God implies. I pointed out that the people of Oberammergau have, since 1634, enjoyed a sort of titular magnificence, and that certain persons, such as the Langs, have become a sort of religious royalty, due entirely to their participation in this yearly event.

He was very pleased with the suggestion, saying that *The Green Pastures* had undoubtedly opened up not only a new field for the Negro author and actor, but that it was also the medium through which the Negro might eventually come into his own. ''I have been asked,'' he said, ''why a Negro had never written such a play. The answer is that, even written by a white man, it came pretty close to never being produced at all. What would

I Believes Everything

have been its fate then had it been written by one of my own race?"

I looked up and saw Gabriel (Wesley Hill) standing in what seemed to be the grip of an overwhelming, sarcastic melancholy, his wings pressed against the wall. "Gabriel," I said, "how do you feel, being so fine a fellow?"

"Lugubrious, lady—and let down and tricked. I don't want to be a member of a howling success like this here portends to be. It means work, for weeks and weeks and weeks! And I ain't built for work without pausin'. It means money—but who wants money? What can you buy with money? Happiness? Then you and me parts intellectually, and pretend no further communion or understandin', because I think happiness is a wife and kids and a banjo playin'. Why don't I marry, then? Because she won't have me! Every night I have to see her standin' right there where you are standin' now, and her shakin' her head. Seven nights a week and two matinees I got to be passin' up my joy, by the sight of that obdurate woman! So what good does money do me? I'm going to give it to charity."

"It's this gal's middle name!" said Mercedes Gilbert.

"I ain't meanin' the kind of charity what spends on gauds and ruffles, Mercedes woman; I mean downright charity."

"I sure wouldn't do nothin' but just dress up and go pretty."

I heard laughter from Noah (Tutt Whitney) and Cain (Lou Vernon), and one unidentified.

"Noah, do you believe there should be another Flood?"

"Lady, I don't think another Flood is called for. We are

gettin' out of the ways of sin without a wettin'. Still, I'm none too sure!'' He turned his great, gentle eyes on Cain, who was rocking with mirth. ''It's been predicted, boy, that in nineteen hundred and thirty-two, all of the land 'ceptin' four little bits will sink into the sea, and that Atlantis will rise again.''

''Say, are you believin' all that jungle talk?''

''I believes everything,'' said Noah simply. ''It prevents injustice, and it broadens you. It makes you ready for the spirit. The spirit ain't always in a man, but it's always waitin' for a day when a man is empty of notions, and then it comes in.''

''Cain, do you believe that you will be born again?''

''Reincarnation and all that?'' He slapped on something dark from a china jar. ''Coming back again like Sir Oliver Lodge says? Well, of course not, but—''

''I believes, I believes!'' cried the unknown in a sort of sighing voice, thin and quick and fervent. ''There's lots of things nobody knows, because they can't put their hands on them, and nobody believes, because they isn't in the eye, and that is just my property. I owns lands and pastures and a mansion of other folks' doubts. I is rich in faith.''

''Bein' born again,'' said Noah, plucking at his side-whiskers that had got entangled with the glue, ''is one of the most easy acts of faith. If one can be born once, there's no knowing what we may be doin' a second time. I don't put myself up to know more than Sir Oliver Lodge, because if he's right when he says Theodore Roosevelt was a reincarnation of Queen Elizabeth—and he did say it—then there's no particular reason why I shouldn't

turn up pretty dumfoundin'. Because in this life I've lost
no time in tryin' to improve myself for a miracle when
it comes. I've been a preacher, yessir, and when I couldn't
believe every word in the Book I stopped preachin', and
that's honesty. Then I took up writin', but when my
newspaper wanted me to sit in an office all day and write
when the writin' wasn't on me, I says, 'No sir, that is
pushin' inspiration into the ways of sin, because what's
in my heart was put there by a lot of trouble, and it's
a trust, and it isn't goin' to be pulled out by glitterin'
gold, nor fawnin' words.' "

The unidentified spoke up. "I don't believe a whole
lot I'm told. I don't believe that Negroes anywhere
believe the Bible like this play makes out they believe,
'cause there ain't no halos, and if there was one thing I
saw when I was a child, it was halos. They was there
every time the preacher spoke, flying away over his head
like a flock of birds."

The small voice of a little child came out of the darkness. "I didn't like this play, at first. I thought it was
a musical comedy, because of all the singing. And when
all the people spoke of the Lord's word, it was with the
th left off, and I thought that was a sin. And the Lord
walking about in a coat, and that was wickedness, because you can read it plain, it was robes the Lord walked
in. But I like the play now, because I understand it. It
has been explained to me. My mother says there are some
people in the South who can't afford Bibles, so they have
to make them in their heads without rules and without
lessons, the best they can. So now I like it, all but a few
things—one thing . . ." The small voice of Alicia Escamilla

trailed off into silence.

"What thing, Escamilla?"

"The fish fry," she whispered. "I *know* they didn't eat fish in heaven, and anybody ought to know it without being told."

"What did they eat, little Escamilla?"

Softly, she said, "Milk and honey."

Alla Nazimova, One of the Greatest of Living Actresses, Talks of Her Art

"The great Nazimova," as she was known to her audiences, acted in some of the most notable roles of early twentieth-century theatre. As Hedda in Hedda Gabler, *Nora in* A Doll's House, *Hilda in* The Master Builder, *Mme. Ranevsky in* The Cherry Orchard, *Christine Mannon in* Mourning Becomes Electra, *and Mrs. Alving in* Ghosts, *Alla Nazimova made theatrical history and established herself as one of the most gifted leading actresses of the stage.*

As the Barnes interview indicates, Nazimova came to the United States from Russia in 1905, performing in a troupe headed by Pavel Orlenev; upon Orlenev's abandonment of the troupe, Nazimova learned English in a few months' time in order to perform in Hedda Gabler. *The play, which opened at the Princess Theater in 1906, made her an immediate celebrity and led to her playing a series of Ibsen heroines.*

A long string of mediocre dramas followed, and by 1916 she had shifted to films, making her debut in War Brides. *Over the next few years, Nazimova acted in twenty-two motion pictures, including* Camille *(1921),* A Doll's House *(1922),* Salome *(1923),* Song of Bernadette *(1943), and* The Bridge of San Luis Rey *(1944)*. *Most of her film roles, however, were of exotic and spellbinding temptresses, and the pictures—several of them produced by her and directed by her husband—were full of bizarre images which served as a backdrop to her highly stylized acting.*

In the 1930s, however, Nazimova returned to the stage, performing in A Month in the Country—*at the time Barnes interviewed her—and in revivals of* Hedda Gabbler, The Cherry Orchard, *and* Ghosts. *"Probably Ibsen wrote* Ghosts *for Nazimova," declared Brooks Atkinson of her performance in 1935. "'Great' is a word for sparing use; it paralyzes linotype machines toward midnight. But there is not other way to characterize a transcendent performance of a tragic role in a drama that is not essentially pertinent now." In addition to playing Mrs. Alving, Nazimova directed the production.*

The great actress's theories of performance were perhaps best expressed by her own words in an interview with Theatre Arts: *"The actor should not play a part. Like the Aeolian harps that used to be hung in the trees to be played only by the breeze, the actor should be an instrument* played upon *by the character he depicts. . . . The wind had but to ripple through the trees and the harp would play without conscious effort. . . . The breeze which stirs the player must sift, from the character, through the player's brain, his imagination and his body. And then, by conscious technical effort, the player must create the sound or fury, sense or sensibility, which the characterization demands."*

Nazimova died in Hollywood on July 13, 1945.

WHEN was it that I first saw Alla Nazimova? In what was she playing? Certainly in none of the Ibsen plays which she made glorious, but in one of those emotional things that leave forethought to tomorrow. She wore ten good yards of that slinky material which, when molded about the hips, spells a woman bent on the destruction of the soul. She reclined upon a hundred cushions with but one idea, toying with a pistol with but one aim—the heart of the hero. Her managers had forbidden her to display any of her other myriad abilities, in order to set in relief her equally splendid physical ability to look "dangerous" and inexact, that look that is necessary to the popular conception of a thoroughly able adventurist. And all because this woman—born in Yalta, Crimea, Russia, and brought up in the Alps—had gorgeous eyes, winged nostrils and an upper lip to match, made doubly dangerous by a lower, which for a brief inch in its middle, ran as straight as any Puritan praying for rain.

To Nazimova the memory of these plays is a neurosis, the radix of which is pain and calamity, because they obliged her to feed her great talents to a public which had appetite for nothing more than the conventional stage vampire. She took her beating without humor, because she is at heart a child pondering her adult childhood. Otherwise she would be armored with the very paradox of it, would be made inaccessible by a surmounted injustice, made a little witty at the hands of such a picturesque betrayal.

There has never been any reasonableness in her "fate"; a glance backward shows a meteoric condition that almost no one could cope with. Alla Nazimova was born in

Russia and educated at Zurich. She studied the violin at Odessa, and when she found that instrument "too difficult" entered Stanislavsky's dramatic school at Moscow. She played the provinces, she toured one-night stands, she did the showboats on all the rivers. Small parts, varied parts. She was noticed, forgotten, noticed again. She became the leading lady of a company in St. Petersburg, and presently joined Pavel Orlenev, visiting Berlin, London, and finally New York in some musty house on the East Side. Sensation! Delirious enthusiasm! New York journeyed down through the smells to the Bowery to marvel at this miraculous pair—these two Russians whose language none could understand, but whose art pierced and dazzled all! And one of them anonymous—for Nazimova's name was not even on the program!

Then, almost as soon as it had appeared, this meteor was consumed in its own heat. Between Orlenev and Nazimova there arose a raging professional jealousy, made more bitter because of their mutual regard. The company dashed on the rocks. Orlenev escaped his creditors and fled back to Russia. Nazimova was stranded in an alien land.

Had it been the authentic fire of art, or only a flash of stage lightning? New York was soon to discover. The Messrs. Shubert, through an interpreter, offered this exotic actress a contract. Within six months she had learned English and appeared on Broadway as Hedda, her newly acquired speech precise but slightly halted with the gentle reluctance of a foreign tongue.

She was no longer the extraordinary unknown. She was discussed and acclaimed. Her series of matinees gave way to regular evening performances at the Princess. One after another, Ibsen's women came to life before the eyes of astonished thousands. Hedda, Nora, and later Hilda Wangel and Rita Allmers—four utterly different persons, and each a universal, unforgettable type.

Then came the fall. Nazimova had a trace of that divine gullibility common to all who are greatly of the stage. She received, and took, bad advice. Her artistry was so extraordinarily flexible and persuasive that she could make a common vampire of melodrama seem, for the moment, as great a creation as Hedda. And the great public preferred vampires—or so it was commonly thought.

So, after toying through a dainty nothing called *Comtesse Coquette*, she began playing that series of lust-and-vengeance dramas which brought her nationwide fame—and grief. *Comet, The Passion Flower, Bella Donna, The Marionettes, That Sort*—sorry plays that besmirched, rather than dimmed, her genius. She made huge sums of money, she was the darling of every tea, she was feted and cried over, complimented and kissed! One can see her longing in her every fiber to play parts that called for overtones and underacting. (She has the intelligence to know that quietly the world was made, and quietly it turns its sterner cheek.) One can see her valuing that sort of thing, the kind of thing she had once portrayed in Ibsen. And yet, like someone walking in the slow, narcotic sleep of those banished to hell, for less than hell's requirements or reason, she moved on in an ever narrower path of distaste. Until, with a grin of malice, the devil took her by the heels and slung her into the

Palace with *War Brides*; into *'Ception Shoals*. For a brief season she caught her breath and staggered back into Ibsen. And then, like the gentleman he is, the devil leaned out and gently pulled her into Hollywood and catastrophe.

B. A. Rolfe of the Metro pictures contracted her for an enormous sum, and what he wanted her to play she played. When she signed the contract she was fearful; for once before, under contract, she had been whistled for, to play Joan of Arc. Theresa Helburn had done the whistling, and Nazimova had been unable to come. What might happen now if she signed for the pictures? Was she, by trying to live, aiding and abetting that sinister faculty she had always been stalked by? She signed.

There are stories of this Hollywood parenthesis that are too incredible to be false. Nazimova never could have played those amply elemental and passionate vampires if she had not been a very simple woman with a very guileless heart. Someone talked her money out of her— most of it. What was left she put into a production of Wilde's *Salome*, with settings designed by Natacha Rambova—and proved, though her friends said Hollywood had spoiled her, that she could get the head of her John with as authentic a conception of misdemeanor as had been seen since that act became common property.

And then there was silence.

What happened to Alla Nazimova as a woman, as an actress, as a thinking person who had felt too long and too little valued her own certitude, is matter for biography. If she is ever angry enough we shall hear of it. But in spite of her fame as a "tigress," as "passion's avenger," she is simple and quiet and small.

For a season she was with the Civic Repertory. Now she is again with her own people, with Turgenev, with the Theatre Guild.

Interviewing her, after an evening with *A Month in the Country*, I made my discovery. To me she had been entirely and rightly splendid, in one of splendor's many ways. To me my memory of her was the point where I had mounted romance—to her, where she had been thrown into the abyss.

"I wanted to do thoughtful things, things subtle and only hinted at. When anything is very great it is like that, is it not? When love is very great it is whispered, perhaps; when one wants something terribly, there is only a motion of the hand. When one is horrified beyond words, one does not shout and scream; one says, 'There,' and you can hardly hear it. So it is that I wanted to play. One fails when one is asked to give less than one has, though the public may think it is success.

"No, I do not want to do Ibsen now. I want to do some plays that America has little knowledge of, more Turgenev perhaps. What do Americans really know of him? And there are others. Anyone can play a *Red Lantern*, a *Madame Peacock*, an *Eye for Eye*, because it means something to others. To me it means nothing. I feel like the woman in the *Makropoulos Secret* who had lived a thousand lives and was still young. Wise in youth!"

She broke off. She looked down at her dressing table and at all the things on it; then, without raising her head, repeated:

"Wise in youth! I have never been weighed down with

knowledge of myself; I think it is a lack. It is called an inferiority complex, is it not?" she queried; and she laughed with her eyes, her mouth still mournful.

"Well, that is very wrong. But there is the solace, the pleasure of living by proxy. Other people's lives make me happy. I delight in their loves, I who have never known what it is to be in love." (What a gorgeous lie that was, what a brazen effort to say, "You do not see this face as you look at it!") "I have become a good mixer—ah yes, a very good mixer. I like other people's plans, I play the piano and I draw houses. I spend a lot of time drawing houses. I built some in California, you know— oh, but they were ugly to look at, and so comfortable!"

She smiled again. Suddenly I felt very tall and awkward. She is so little. I leaned down and said, "It's one of those quiet questions, Alla Nazimova. When was it you frightened yourself with what you are?"

She started; she turned halfway about.

"Oh," she said—and I swear she put her hands together like a child—"that night when I first saw my name in lights. I went up to my hotel room, way up under the roof, and I opened the window and leaned on my arms; and I was afraid, terribly afraid. Then. It was then!"

I've Always Suffered from Sirens

One of the most gifted set, lighting, and costume designers for the American stage, Raymond Sovey worked in one or more of these three capacities for over 157 Broadway productions.

Born in 1897 in Torrington, Connecticut, Sovey began his theatrical career as an actor in The Burgomaster of Belgium *in 1919. The following year, however, he turned to scenic design, doing the settings for* George Washington. *Over the next forty years Sovey designed and lit some of the most famous of twentieth-century Broadway productions, including* Gentlemen Prefer Blondes *(1926); the Alfred Lunt and Lynn Fontanne version of* The Brothers Karamazov *(1927);* The Front Page *(1928); A Month in the Country, starring* Nazimova *(1930);* Green Grow the Lilacs *(1931); the Helen Westley vehicle,* John Ferguson *(1933);* The Petrified Forest *(1935);* Our Town *(1938);* Arsenic and Old Lace *(1940);* Jackpot, *with Robert Edmond Jones (1944);* State of the Union *(1945); T.S. Eliot's* The Cocktail Party *(1950);* Witness for the Prosecution *(1954);* The Chalk Garden *(1955); and Dylan Thomas's* Under Milk Wood *(1957). In 1960, Sovey did the costumes for* All the Way Home, *his last Broadway production.*

THE light touch being somehow unforgivable in a critical survey of a man and his art (why this should be so I do not know), it becomes nothing short of formidable to write of Raymond Sovey. Add to this the fact that your outstanding emotion in regard to his stagecraft is that it is of an honesty downright and final, and you have about come to a period. If you trust a man there is an end of it; you need the rest of your wit to handle the tricky and the temperamental.

Producers trust him. Authors trust him. "If Sovey says that set will cost three thousand dollars, it will cost three thousand dollars, neither more nor less. If he promises the sketches for Monday, Monday you will have them, and when he says they will be right for the play, they will be."

This is his almost unique position, within this boundary lie his merit and his defect. If he is commissioned to do a Louis Quinze salon, he will go away, study the times of Louis, unearth his very background, and return with it to a doorknob. The ghost of the King could wander through the set without tripping over one misplaced article of furniture, without suffering consternation because of a wried design in drapery or an offending window. That "something" else—that magic reiteration of a past that makes of an old statement a new wonderment and a new reality—this will be missing. In Sovey there is an almost mid-Victorian restraint. There are still some families, probably southern, who consider it vulgar to make a splash in the world, to draw attention to themselves, to be obvious. He is not astounding, he is mannerly.

In his sets—say, *Vinegar Tree, Wings Over Europe, Strictly*

Dishonorable, Meteor—this mannerliness is always apparent. The room of the councilors is lofty, the windows long, the feeling right. It is a man's room in which there is space even for the entrance of a mad ideal. A set suitable and in keeping with the play, exactly that and no more; should the actors take it into their heads to overstep the bounds of propriety they may do so, but it will not be Sovey's fault. And so with the others, from the seducer's chambers (*Strictly Dishonorable*) to the parlor of that country house (*Meteor*) where the gentleman who thought he was God decided to keep on thinking so.

This same honesty of approach is responsible for the great diversity of plays he has been called upon to mount. Given a more personal and fanatic point of view, his adaptability might have been taxed; as it is, it merely amuses him to do *Saint Joan* one day and *The Second Little Show* the next.

A portrait of Sovey would include one very well knit and life-size body; two dark eyes under still darker brows running off at a tangent; one slightly mocking mouth set between distinctly marked cheeks; a pose at once nonchalant and weary; and the small plump hands of a woman.

He is most distinctly someone you might meet on the Riviera dressed with that careless detachment common to Englishmen who have come up from the tropics, or who have just completed plans for entirely disrupting the life in one of the colonies. You might, in fact you would, meet just this sort of chap wandering through the better buildings of the Loire with that slightly haggard and gentle smile with which such natures register approval;

standing in one of a dozen European museums, mentally fingering the stuffs in the gowns once worn by queens come to a bad end. You might meet him in London discussing saddlery with one of the guards at the outer Royal gate; yes, all these things. The one place you would *not* expect to find him would be on Broadway, one with a scrambling million that make a season.

For some unknown reason the exponents of stagecraft are expected to be somber and agonized; reticent and tormented, gnawed ragged by inspiration, about to cry aloud of the pains of creation and thoroughly damned if they can stand it another moment.

Well, I'm very sorry, but Raymond Sovey is not in the least like that. If there is work to be done he will do it; if not, there are places to go, things to be seen.

His story runs with the light plash of brook water. "Born in Torrington, Connecticut, quite long enough ago. I started my career, believe it or not, as a civil engineer—that means bridges, you know; well, there's only one Thornton Wilder, the rest of us are expected to keep the bridges up. So my father said, 'Ray, you know as well as I do that for you civil engineering is pure vanity, a feeble gesture, a laugh in the dark as it were, a mad caprice, a what-you-will. Stop it.' So seeing that he felt that way about it, I decided to go to Columbia and learn interior decorating. I went, I learned, I hung out my shingle as Consulting Interior Decorator to architects. I went to Baltimore and taught everything I could lay my hands on, all about the chiming of colors, period furnitures, and such. That was at the Maryland Institute.

"Well, somehow it began to pall on me, this matching

stuffs and shading off burgundy satins into the lighter
cherry, so I played around with the Vagabond Players,
and presto, I went mad! The stage—that was what was
calling me, that had been the trouble with me all along.
I have always suffered from sirens. Something is always
calling from far places, 'Raymond!' Something always
beckoning from a distance—'Raymond!' I hear it in the
turmoil of the city; it sits upon my pillow and breathes
down my spine—'Raymond!' It was there even when the
war broke out and I had to go away to Augusta—what
a climate!—to teach the delicate art of machine gunning.
There amid the maneuvering, the map-making it whispered . . . (ah, I shall come to a bad end!). The fact
is I had the time of my life teaching the boys what I
myself did not know. Have you ever experienced the
delicate delight of teaching that which you yourself have
only the vaguest sort of idea about? My training as an
architect came in, my passion for the stage came in.
Laying out possible strategic points was exciting. Then
when all that was over—by the by, I never saw any of
the war, but then I don't imagine I should have been
a shiner in any event—I went on the Board of Foreign
Missions of the Methodist Episcopal Church.

"Do not chide me. It was done with zeal and love. I
have never seen anything so amazing as what followed.
There was a centenary exposition pulled off in Columbus,
Ohio. It was planned to depict missionary work and just
what missionaries are up against. Forty natives of every
country which deserves a missionary were imported. We
built little villages—Chinese, Japanese, Indian. We all
dressed up to look like something exceedingly foreign. A

defunct circus was purchased and apportioned among the natives. We had a Juggernaut built of soap boxes; we had floats with dancing girls; we even had a central feature. The Wayfarer's Pageant—that's where Walter Hampden shone. I can assure you the whole thing was unique. More; it was topping, it was superb, it was priceless.

"What has all this to do with the stage? Why my dear young lady, everything has something to do with the stage if it is fantastic enough. The real way to find your niche in life is to set your brain to work on a problem about which you could not possibly find the answer. It's that way that you get visions, and I assure you, when I came back I was up to my ears in visions. I saw myself designing sets with a patina of truth upon them, *real* rooms, not stage rooms, but rooms which by some magic I would make over to the characters on the stage and in which they would seem to have lived all their lives when the curtain went up, and would die in when the curtain went down.

"However, let us go on with the story. For two years I associated myself with Walter Hampden and his company. I acted, I did sets, I designed costumes. Then Bergman said I should stop playing and come into the business seriously—and here I am.

"And now at last," he said, punching holes in the blotter with the point of a pencil, "we have come, I'm afraid, to the moment of seriousness. I will make it as brief as possible—my theories in regard to stage designs. Frankly, I have one and only one—to help the poor playwright to put over his own ideas. I have no need to express myself. I consider a designer who expresses himself essentially a barbarian. It is not the function of the designer to put himself forward in any way. There is an old saying among architects that every problem suggests its own solution. It is the same with a play: the play suggests its own treatment. The designer should work with the author and with the producer, but most certainly with the author. The author will in varying degrees know what he wants. It is his room, he has seen it in a tonal relation to all that he has written. True, he cannot build the set for himself, but what he needs is not a new vision and another mind's interpretation; what he demands is an intuitive acceptance and knowledge of what he himself has already fancied. The greatest instance of clarity of sight in the matter of stage sets is that of Mr. Shaw. His directions are so explicit, the entrances, exits, tables, chairs, and stage plan for the movements of the actors so precise, that anyone could get across his stage in a dream, and anyone could design his rooms without one spasm of anguish. In fact, his is such an exact eye for everything that the designer has little or no fun following his orders; he does, in fact, make one feel rather useless. I like to know what the author wants, but I am just vain enough to wish for at least one chair to be left to my own discretion, one window to be where I would like it to be, and with a damask of my own choosing.

"I don't mean to suggest that the designer has no right to inspiration. What I mean is that the better the designer, the nearer his inspiration will meet and join that of the author. If the play is expressionistic and calls for a Meyerhold-like framework and suggestion; if it is fantastic and calls for angels on horseback, well and good. The settings should be just as fantastic and as experimental as the author, neither more nor less. So far, few such plays have turned up in America. The American mind is not as daring as the European; and though I shall be killed for saying so, our playwrights are not nearly so highly evolved as the productions they get.

"Do you remember *The Brothers Karamazov?*" I said that I did. "My sets," he said, "but with that stunning staircase motif brought in again which was seen in Copeau's original. Did you see *A Month in the Country?*" I had. I thought it one of the most delightful of the season. Colorful, cool, and dangerous. "Taken from the original Russian," he said. "You can't beat the first outlay of emotional insight, so I did not try to. Now for some that were all my own. Did you see *Animal Crackers, Strictly Dishonorable, Gentlemen Prefer Blondes, Coquette, Icebound,* or that really frantic play, *The Ladder,* or *The Inspector General?* Yes or no, the titles will make it clear to you that the subhead of this life of mine should be diversity, variety, uncertainty. I've done a dozen kept-women's homes—as if anyone knew what they look like! I've done pink and gold French interiors until I've seen them coming at me in my sleep. I've done resurrections and pageants and garden parties and kitchen dramas. I've even done a folk drama, *Green Grow the Lilacs.* It's rather fun because it's so very simple. Just three buildings, two outsides and one interior! Then you turn them around for another act and they become two interiors and one exterior. Riggs, Biberman, and I worked it out together. I think it is amusing.

''The future of the stage? I'm not one of those chaps who can see that far, you know.'' It was the amused, slightly mocking gentleman wandering the world again: the Riviera, Paris, London. . . .

The Tireless
Rachel Crothers

Born in Bloomington, Illinois in 1878, Rachel Crothers graduated from the Illinois State Normal University and studied
drama in Boston and New York City before joining various
theatrical companies. She wrote her first play, 39 East, in
1904, but the play was not produced until many years later.
Her Broadway premiere was The Three of Us, one of the
few critical successes of 1906. For the next three decades,
Crothers's plays appeared on Broadway on the average of
one every season.

The large majority of these plays were centered on feminist
issues, cast in witty and humorous contexts. She was, from
the beginning of her career to her death in 1958, an ardent
opponent of all social injustices, which she used as thematic
material in her greatest stage successes. Among her best plays
are A Man's World (1909)—one of the first feminist statements of the American stage—Young Wisdom (1914), The
Heart of Paddy Whack (1914), A Little Journey (1918),
Nice People (1921), Mary the Third (1923), Let Us Be
Gay (1929), As Husbands Go (1931), When Ladies Meet
(1932), and Susan and God, her last Broadway play, which
opened in 1937.

During World War I, Crothers helped found the Stage
Relief Fund, which she directed until 1951. She was active
also in creating the American Theatre Wing, which operated
the Stage Door Canteens of the Second World War.

IF you are a playwright of what you consider to be the first water and yet have failed to attract your merited attention; if you are, by any chance, a woman and wish you were a producer; if you are an actor or an actress— and heaven knows an actor or an actress has at least one chance in a million, which is more than can be said of the other two professions—and you are still unable to secure a part; if indeed you are anybody who has reached the age of thirty-odd and have not as yet made your name or fortune, then dear creatures, it were better— yea, wiser and altogether more seemly—to hold your peace. And if that be something you can by no means manage, it were better far to give your chatter to God, the great silencer. For Rachel Crothers maintains that such being your single or several case, you have merited oblivion.

She does not believe that anyone is born to blush unseen. She thinks that many a bad play has been successful but never a good play a failure. As she so speaks there is an uncomfortable, hard, and unsympathetic look in her face; a look that flickers ever so slightly when you murmur: "You may be right, but *Mr. Gilhooley* died in three weeks and Herman Melville was fifty years under sod before *Moby Dick* was seen spouting, and Blake was jeered by his contemporaries, and Dostoevski sold his wife's red flannel petticoat to keep the wolf away for a night. And, getting down to our own immediate times, Joyce is thought by some to be quite good, but as his wife said when she met with an accident, 'There's not even a kimono decent enough to die in about the place!' "

Yes, the light of defiance flickers in Rachel Crothers's

face, and the mouth remains firm and hard. "Many great people have died unsung," she said, "but not playwrights. It is easier to get a play on than to sell a picture, strike gold with a novel, receive your just deserts for poetry. But show me one script going about Broadway that is not already produced, or about to be, that is worth the paper it was written on."

"Well," I said, "*The Green Pastures* was turned down by half-a-dozen producers. In fact it only got on because Marc Connelly happened to be a very good friend of a banker who was so tired of financing flops that he told Marc that he would back *The Green Pastures* just as a sort of wholesale farewell, a goodbye in the grand manner; for he would have no more money to risk after that piece—"

"Well," remarked Rachel Crothers, "that's an extreme case, a very rare, highly stylized, and fantastic thing of beauty. It may have been difficult—but it *did* get put on."

"And there was *Mr. Gilhooley*," I repeated, "one of what I believe to be a very small handful of great tragedies, and as I said it flopped—why?"

"I did not see it," parried Miss Crothers. "Then, too, there is Pirandello, never received his proper ovation."

"Ah yes, that strange fellow from Italy. There have been others—I could name a few—"

"If they are what you say they are, they will come into their own. Everyone receives the attention which he deserves, everyone gets a chance sooner or later. I do not believe there are any masterpieces in oblivion; anyway, no plays. Producers are simply yelling for good plays. They don't get them, that's all. A play may have a touch

of genius or a great idea in it, but if it is not written
with knowledge of the demands of the form, then it is
not a play, it is a badly executed plan for a play.''

But let us go back and begin at the beginning. In 1878 a
girl child was born to the Doctors Eli Kirk and M.L.
(Marie Louise Depew) Crothers, then practicing in Bloomington, Illinois. From the start the child was determined
to be an actress, in fact *the* actress of the world; the
very best, the most brilliant, the most breathtaking
actress of her day. The desire to be an actress, with the
passing years, has gone, but that desire to be the most
brilliant, the best known, still shadows her. Maturity,
that unkind but inevitable light thrown on the great,
dark splendor of first desire,has given her that flickering,
that stubborn look; a little woman with white hair, fan-
shaped over the ears, close-set misty eyes, a slightly
receding chin offset by a mouth nipped in at the corners.
A person who will listen, but who will not change her
mind.

In her teens she began writing plays; she acted and
directed for the Bloomington Dramatic Club. Upon graduation she entered the Wheatcroft School of Acting in
New York City. Soon Mrs. Wheatcroft was only too glad
to let the responsibility of instructing amateurs fall upon
such able shoulders as Miss Crothers proved to have,
for Mrs. Wheatcroft was very tired, as well she might
be, having served for many years. In this school Miss
Crothers wrote and produced many one-act plays for the
student matinees which finally led to her career as a playwright. Had she been born twenty years earlier she would,
or one feels she would, have been the head of a young

ladies' seminary.

In the past twenty-five years, Miss Crothers has seen over twenty of her dramas in production. She has in many instances chosen the cast and staged the play herself. Among the titles of her many successful pieces are: *The Three of Us, The Coming of Mrs. Patrick, Myself Bettina, A Man's World, Ourselves, Young Wisdom, Old Lady 31, Mother Cary's Chickens* (in collaboration with Kate Douglas Wiggin), *Once Upon a Time, A Little Journey, Nice People, Everyday, Mary the Third, Expressing Willie, A Lady's Virtue, Let Us Be Gay,* and now *As Husbands Go.* Of these I have seen only the last mentioned, but from its tone I gather that all were light, amusingly handled, dealing with the social problem of the moment, rather than that of the race.

I asked Miss Crothers how it was that she had succeeded in convincing the men of the theatrical world that she was capable of doing her own plays as she wished them done. (I fancy it is harder for a woman to get a footing as a producer than it is for a man.) She answered that once she had proved herself, men were very willing to let her do the work. But the first chance to convince them was given her by a woman none other than Maxine Elliott, who took the leading role in *Myself Bettina*.

"When I think back on it," said Miss Crothers, "I realize that it is to three women that I owe my freedom: Carlotta Nielson, who liked my play; Mrs. Wheatcroft, who asked me to be coach; and Maxine Elliott, who let me in on the professional work. For a woman it is best to look to women for help. Women are more daring, they are glad to take the most extraordinary chances (they do in marriage, you know, why not in life?). I think I should have been longer about my destiny if I had had to battle with men alone.

"There are a great many people who talk about what marvelous authors, actors, and producers they are, if only someone would let them do something. That is sheer nonsense. Write, act, produce, if it is only in the back parlor! If you are great you will be discovered.

"Some claim that poverty keeps them back. I believe need is the whip to great creative accomplishment. Not starvation, not fear, but the knowledge that unless you strive, that unless you put your mind on your work and keep it on, you will be in difficulties. If you know that any lagging on your part means that next month the rent will not be paid, this will be of greater help than a bank full of dollars. Learn your job, then keep at it.

"I think the American theatre would do well to revive one-act plays as a custom. I believe in the English curtain raiser because it is the one best chance for the amateur playwright and actor. One-act plays are an excellent training for authors, and I wish we had more of them in this country. If we gave them a hearing we would have to sit through fewer bad three-act dramas. I think too that it is a great mistake for really talented authors to write for the movies. The silent picture was a delightful art: it rested and quieted, it afforded many poor people a means of diversion; it opened up a new silent and wide world impossible for the stage to emulate. But the talkie is an abomination; it is the stage cheapened and made vulgar. One can make a lot of money in the talkies, but at least make it after your play has had proper presentation on a stage.

"I used to want a theater of my own, where I could design not only the sets but the ushers' costumes, and in all things do utterly as I pleased. But I know now that one cannot do everything, and that to conserve one's own talents is task enough. Therefore, I live in the country. I cannot work when there is anything amusing going on. Happily for me, I love the country, and I love to lie in bed and write from eight o'clock until noon. Then I have the rest of the day to myself, a self with which I am content because I have made it work."

Nothing Amuses Coco
Chanel After Midnight

Fashion designer Gabrielle Chanel was born the second daughter of Jeanne Devolle and Albert Chanel in 1883 in Saumur, France. Her parents remained unmarried until a year after Gabrielle's birth; and the next eleven years were brutal ones for her mother, who suffered beatings and sexual abuse from her husband until her death in 1895.

A few years later, Gabrielle was sent to an orphan's hospice where she remained until she was seventeen, when she was admitted to a convent in Moulins. At twenty she left the convent to become a shop assistant for a seller of "trousseaux and layettes," but she quickly grew impatient with the job, and in 1903 she began to perform at local cafés. Her convent-girl innocence combined with her mature-sounding, gravelly voice—somewhat reminiscent of Yvette Guilbert's—won her a year's contract at La Rotonde. Beginning her nightly show with a verse from the popular song of the day "Ko Ko Ri Ko," and ending her routine with "Who's Seen Coco in the Trocadéro," Gabrielle quickly became known by the chant her audience took up to call for an encore: "Coco! Coco!"

As the mistress of Etienne Balsan, Coco moved onto his estate at Royallieu in 1906. Balsan was a noted horseman, and Gabrielle—having loved horses from her youth—was determined to become a horsewoman. But women's fashions *of the period—long skirts, high hats, and tight shoes—proved an encumbrance for open-air activities. Chanel requested a nearby tailor to make her a pair of jodhpurs, based on those worn by an English groom. Wearing these and other clothes she designed or borrowed from her lover, Chanel caused a small sensation among Balsan's set; and such clothing and her unusual hats soon began to attract the attention of the crowds at the polo and race tracks which she and Balsan frequented. By late 1908, bored with Royallieu, Chanel had taken an apartment in Paris, from which she began to sell her hats and, soon thereafter, other clothing.*

In 1910 the small apartment could no longer contain her growing business, and with the help of her new lover, Arthur "Boy" Chapel, Chanel moved to the rue Cambon, whose name was linked with hers for more than half a century.

The style she created over the next decades—more tailored and trimmer than the clothes women had worn for centuries —helped to change the course of fashion and made the sharp-tongued Chanel the rage of French society. She became the confidante and/or lover of writers and artists such as Jean Cocteau, Paul Morand, and Salvador Dali; the Grand Duke Dmitri of Russia (a collaborator in the death of Rasputin); the Duke of Westminster; and artist Paul Iribe, who died playing tennis at her villa.

In 1931, the year of Barnes's interview, Chanel was involved with poet Pierre Reverdy and joined him regularly at fashionable meeting spots for artists such as the Dôme, and Jimmy's in Montparnesse. Recalling their 1931 meeting, Barnes revealed to Douglas Messerli in 1973 that she had been given a newly designed dress by Chanel; "however," Barnes gleefully admitted, "I gave it to some French tart."

By 1940 the House of Chanel—famous the world over for its clothes and perfume—occupied five houses in the rue Cambon. When the Germans entered Paris in June of that year, Chanel closed her offices. "I stopped working because of war," she explained to Marcel Haedrick. "Everyone in my place had someone who was in uniform. . . . The House of Chanel was empty two hours after war was declared."

After the war, Chanel reentered fashion, influencing the styles of the 1950s and 1960s. She died in Paris in 1971.

"THE figure is more important than the face, and more important than the figure is the means by which you keep it. More important than all three is the enjoyment of life on your own basis, which is secured only through good health. Find out what it is that you like to do, and do it. If you say you can't, it is simply an admission that you have not built up your body to the point where it can play the role you desire for it. You live but once, you might as well be amusing. If you are not amusing it is because you are sick, and sick people are discourteous to nature."

Gabrielle Chanel, the *plus grande couturière* of Paris, with an income of several millions, employing 2400 persons in her *ateliers*, practically owner of the rue Cambon where her creations are on display, mistress of several homes in Europe—who refused the hand of the immensely wealthy Duke of Westminster, and who numbers among her friends half the great names of the world, born of humble country folk of the Auvergne, and

bowed down to by women who would be well dressed—
likes loneliness, fresh air, country life, sport clothes, dogs,
fishing, early rising, early retiring, lolling, and hard work,
especially hard work.

She is world famous for two things, perfume and severe-
tailored suits—in other words, for the height to which
she has brought olfactory sophistication, and for the depth
out of which she evolved the almost lowly severity of
the chic, terribly chic, creations. (The peasant woman and
the Apache, washed bright and new and fashioned with
a pair of angel's scissors, such seems to be the stuff of
her offerings.) Chanel stands as the embodiment of her
own nativity, of the earth to the earth beholden.

Her philosophy is the cause of her success and her
fame. She believes in being natural, and when she uses
the word "natural" she does not use it as it is customarily
used, to denote things ugly, uncouth, untrained. To her
that thing is natural which is the most complete and coor-
dinated. If you say that your way of being natural is to
sit up until dawn, drink everything in sight, dress so that
you are conspicuous, eat so that you are gorged, she will
say, "Very well, but what a *bad* nature you have!"

Like all French women, Chanel is reasonable with that
degree of reasonableness that we of the Western world
look upon as a sort of unholy ease in the face of the
miracles of nature. Of course! Chanel is one of the
miracles just because she is natural. We are seldom
natural because we are incredulous. We are afraid of
nature and that is why, she asserts, we take our exercises
like medicine, not like play.

"In a woman I prefer charm of manner, of speech, of

carriage, of dancing, to merely classic beauty. Classic beauty can be very stupid, outside of a museum. A pretty face can be very inaccurate on the state within. I like a face that says something, that is simply and accurately informative of the personality. Of course, if you can be all these things, and beautiful as well, you have been the objective of divine dispensation.

"Observe," she says, "how the woman who attracts all eyes comes into a room. How she walks, how she seats herself, what gestures she uses when in conversation. She may be downright ugly as far as classic standards are concerned, nevertheless there is something about her figure, her posture, her gestures, that is stylish and handsome because they are not decorations, but essentials.

"Why, among twenty, fifty, a hundred is she the most attractive, be she tall or short, dark or fair, athletic or feminine? Because she knows *how* she wants to walk, *why* she wants to sit down and *to* what her gestures are related. She is herself.

"She is indebted to no 'fashion' in walking, such as the once popular debutante's slouch, which I thought most unlovely because it was what I call a 'trade walk,' one woman walking exactly like another. Think for yourself, even in the matter of fashion. A woman should not be a manikin, which she will be if she follows the mode too slavishly, and without a certain selective preference.

"If a woman wants to keep her figure, let her be employed, let her work. She will be happier, less self-conscious, and this state will be reflected in the figure. Men like capable women. There is no fear in her as there used to be when she was economically dependent, therefore there is more real beauty in her.

"Work, then play, relax, swim, fish, do a turn at golf or tennis, get out in the open, enjoy the air and the sun. Here I wish to make a distinction between exercise and sport. Exercise is a substitute for sport. Exercises are very good if you have time and love for nothing else, but in my estimation setting-up exercises as a health medium are to natural sports—such as swimming, walking, riding— what canned goods are to fresh garden products. If you can afford your body nothing better, setting-up exercises are good, but if you want to have and to keep a charming figure and a flexible carriage, you must delight in the outdoors, fresh air, sports.

"What is a bad figure? That figure that is in all its joints a timid figure. Such timidity of posture comes from knowing that you have not done by your body as you should. The shamefaced girl who has not learned her lessons has the same expression as has the body of the woman who has not learned nature.

"You cannot maintain two destinies, that of the fool or the intemperate and that of the wise and the temperate. You cannot keep up a nightlife and amount to anything in the day. You cannot indulge in those foods and liquors that destroy the physique and still hope to have a physique that functions with the minimum of destruction to itself. A candle burnt at both ends may shed a brighter light, but the darkness that follows is for a longer time.

"In the matter of what diet to follow in order to maintain the perfect figure, I can only repeat what I have said of every other function of life—be moderate, be simple, be honest. An honest appetite will be simple, and a simple appetite will be modest. Eat less than you think you want, eat with your intelligence, not your stomach. Never get up from table with an inward silent apology for being a pig; it is an insult to the table.

"Sleep well, seven to eight hours if you need it; sleep with open windows. Get up early, work hard, very hard. It won't hurt you, for it keeps the mind busy, and in turn, the mind will keep the body interested. It sounds funny, but if you think it over you will find that it isn't. Don't sit up late. After all, what is there in this so-called social life of such worth that you leave your pillow to follow it into the early morning? Bad air, bad food, bad liquor, ugly surroundings that do not gladden the heart, stupid people who repeat, night after night, the same interminable *histoires*—*histoires* of lives that have been lived that they may be recounted, and for that reason not worth the recital. Save something for yourself. Save your ears, save your eyes, save your thoughts, save your nerves. What have you heard after midnight that you count worth sitting up for? It is only what you have heard before, a hundred times, and it is what you will hear again tomorrow unless you stop the stupidity.

"Personally, nothing amuses me after twelve o'clock at night!"

Fleurs du Mal à la Mode de New York—An Interview with Djuna Barnes by Guido Bruno

Born Curt Kisch, son of a Czechoslovakian rabbi, Guido Bruno was one of the greatest charlatans and pretenders to participate in the Greenwich Village Bohemianism of 1912-1918.

From the editorial pulpit of his chapbooks and pamphlets, Bruno preached the fin de siècle *aesthetics of Oscar Wilde and Aubrey Beardsley, while promoting his own name and reputation as an impressario and dealer of experimental literature and visual art. Explaining to some friends that he was Italian, while admitting to others that he was an exiled officer of the Hapsburg army, Bruno insinuated himself into the Village artists' circles, and through his several publications—*Bruno's Review of Two Worlds; Bruno's Bohemia; Bruno's Review of Life, Love and Literature; Bruno's Weekly; *and* Bruno's Scrapbook—*gained the skeptical allegiance of Alfred Kreymborg, Hart Crane, Clara Tice, and others, including Djuna Barnes.*

Barnes's The Book of Repulsive Women *was his first chapbook; of others he claimed to sell no fewer than 32,000 copies. Bankrolled by Charles Edison, the son of Thomas*

*Alva Edison, and by unsuspecting would-be women poets,
Bruno—to give him his due—helped to introduce the works
of Wilde, Lord Alfred Douglas, and John Addington Symonds
to the American public and fought various battles with
the American censors.*

*Barnes introduced Bruno to Frank Harris in late 1916 or
early 1917, and Bruno—recognizing in Harris a fellow pre-
tender with talents greater than his own—attached himself
to him, becoming Harris's literary secretary. The results of
the association are detailed in Bruno's memoirs,* My Four
Years with Frank Harris, *which appeared in several issues
of Bruno's publications.*

Bruno interviewed Barnes in Pearson's Magazine *in 1919,
soon after the opening of her play,* Three from the Earth.

THE Provincetown Players opened the sixth season of
uncommercial theatricals in their remodeled stable in
Greenwich Village, with a new play and a new playwright.

The auditorium very Elizabethan: narrow benches, few
lights, high, white-chalked ceilings. A light behind the
curtain! The curtain parts. Shrill sounds of a bell. Quiet.
The auditorium pitch-dark. *Three from the Earth* by Djuna
Barnes is the play. The quiet deepens. What does it all
mean? The stage settings, the actors, figures, faces, movements seem a collection of Beardsley drawings. The
language is that of Oscar Wilde. Extraordinary language
that flutters the air: brilliant at times, startlingly para-
doxical, annoyingly frank, but somehow never touching
the heart. Smiles flit through the audience; everyone
intent; listening, looking, waiting.

The scene opens in the boudoir of a lady who once had a lover who left her. She is about to marry another lover. A grand lady of the world in a sweeping, fantastic tea-gown. She entertains three visitors: young boys evidently fresh from the country, made up as vaudeville rubes. Sullen boys who speak in gutteral tones, they have very little to say, but what they say carries weight with their hostess. These are the three sons of her old lover's rightful wife. Their father has cut his throat, and now they would embark for Europe. But they wish first to secure certain letters of their father still in the possession of his old sweetheart. The boys, it seems, have been systematically kept in seclusion, away from human associations: digging the soil, plowing, sowing, harvesting. Only Sundays were they permitted to visit a nearby town and to watch pious people go to church. They also seem to have been fed up on Nietzsche and Kant, de Maupassant and Voltaire. They quote these authors freely. The requested letters are delivered to them; their mission seems at an end. They rise, ready to tramp out as solemnly as they came in. The hostess urges them to take tea and tell some more about the ghastly suicide of her former lover. The youngest of the boys has aroused her interest. "Don't leave me *this way*," she calls after the departing visitors. The youngest boy embraces her brutally, like an animal. . . . The curtain is rung off, light in the auditorium. Everybody looks at everybody. What does it all mean?

I asked Djuna Barnes: "Why are you so dreadfully morbid? At first in your pictures, then in your poems. Your prose stories are overpowering even for one who has digested Russian literature for the last twenty years. Now comes your play. No one can deny that all of your efforts are picturesque, unusual, even beautiful in their ugliness. No one denies that you have talent. But why such morbidity?"

"Morbid?" was her cynical answer. "You make me laugh. This life I write and draw and portray is life as it is, and therefore you call it morbid. Look at my life. Look at the life around me. Where is this beauty that I am supposed to miss? The nice episodes that others depict? Is not everything morbid? I mean the life of people stripped of their masks. Where are the relieving features?

"Often I sit down to work at my drawing board, at my typewriter. All of a sudden my joy is gone. I feel tired of it all because, I think, 'What's the use?' Today we are, tomorrow dead. We are born and don't know why. We live and suffer and strive, envious or envied. We love, we hate, we work, we admire, we despise. . . . Why? And we die, and no one will ever know that we have been born."

"But Djuna," I interrupted, "this is one of your pessimistic moods. You cannot mean it all. You, of all the persons I have known, have had your fill of joy in this world."

"Joy! Is this what you call joy? When we are desperate, doing the first best thing, throwing ourselves at someone for whom we really do not care, and trying to forget ever after by repeating the same folly? In between times we work and talk. Laugh at intervals. . . . Joy? I have had none in my twenty-six years."

You have never met Djuna. The picture reproduced on

this page is a self-portrait. She insists that it looks like her real self. I think it contemptibly bad. Not a shadow

of likeness. There isn't a bit of that slovenly doggedness in the real Djuna.

Red cheeks. Auburn hair. Gray eyes, ever sparkling with delight and mischief. Fantastic earrings in her ears, picturesquely dressed, ever ready to live and to be merry: that's the real Djuna as she walks down Fifth Avenue, or sips her black coffee, a cigarette in hand, in the Café Lafayette.

Her morbidity is not a pose. It is as sincere as she is herself.

She is only one of many: a new school sprung up during the years of the war. Followers of the decadents of France and of England's famous 1890s, in vigorous, ambitious America.

Index